D0150534

Mysticism
& Social Transformation

Mysticism

&

Social Transformation

Edited by

JANET K. RUFFING, R.S.M.

With a Foreword by
ROBERT J. EGAN, S.J.

 SYRACUSE UNIVERSITY PRESS

Copyright © 2001 by Syracuse University Press
Syracuse, New York 13244-5160

All Rights Reserved

First edition 2001

04   05   6   5   4   3   2

The paper used in this publication meets the minimum requirements of American National Standard for Information Sciences-Permanence of Paper for Printed Library Materials, ANSI Z39.48-1984.∞™

Library of Congress Cataloging-in-Publication Data
Mysticism and social transformation / edited by Janet K. Ruffing ; with a foreword by
Robert J. Egan.—1st ed.
     p. cm.
     Includes bibliographical references and index.
     ISBN 0-8156-2876-5 (hardcover : alk. Paper)—ISBN 0-8156-2877-3 (pbk. : alk. Paper)
     1. Mysticism—Catholic Church. 2. Mysticism—Social aspects. I. Ruffing, Janet, 1945–
BV5082.2.M58 2001
248.22—dc21   00-055702

Manufactured in the United States of America

To Robert J. Egan, S.J.,
teacher, mentor, colleague, and friend

Contents

PART THREE: Emerging Contemporary Approaches

Foreword

R O B E R T   J .   E G A N ,   S . J .

> Politics begins in mysticism, and mysticism always ends in politics.
> —Charles Péguy

It is a pleasure for me to introduce this collection of essays on a subject that has been close to my heart for more than thirty years: What is the relationship between, on the one hand, the human longing for holiness, for active participation in the sacred, for what might be called the vision of God or union with God, and, on the other, the human longing for compassionate justice, for the alleviation of poverty, suffering, and oppression, for a more equitable configuration of human dwelling on this earth? What is the relationship, in other words, between the mystical and the political dimensions of religious existence?

When I first became interested in this topic, I was convinced that it was precisely in these two areas—in the struggle to appropriate in an intelligent, contemporary way the practical demands of a spirituality and in the struggle to make common cause in transforming the conditions of life for the excluded and the impoverished—that authentic religion remained a possibility in this age. It seemed to me that these great passions or transcendent longings moved the souls of the finest and most inspiring members of my generation. The question that gripped me with the force of a destiny, then and now, was how *to think* the inner relationship between these two longings.

Over the years, different aspects of this question came, for a time, to seem most urgent. Why do the mystical and the prophetic or political manifest themselves so often in tension, if not opposition? How does the organization of authorized power in a culture sometimes become the object of a religious analysis and criticism? How does the experience of an absolute claim being made on one's will to stand in solidarity with the helpless, the sorrowful, the other-than-oneself so often become the excuse for a murderous hatred of outsiders and of those who are weak? What are the factors, both social and historical, that so complicate the relationship between the categories of the prophetic and the political? How does the trivialization of mysticism contribute, perhaps inevitably, to the trivialization of politics? And how does the longing at the heart of an authentic politics continually reopen the question of how properly to conceive the relationship of the human and the divine?

If, as John Macmurray claimed, all human knowing is ultimately for the sake of action and all action ultimately for the sake of friendship, it may equally be true that all sanctification, all interior transformation, is ultimately for the sake of transformative action, *redemptive* practices and institutions, and that all such redemptive action is ultimately for the sake of friendship, of a more genuine intimacy, of a deeper communion—becoming friends with one another and with God. If spirituality entails an interior access to more abundant life, the awakening of a *surplus* or *extravagance* of life from within, could the goal of a spiritual politics be the struggle to move beyond deficiency motives in our common life together or a search for shared cultural forms of this greater abundance? Could this transformation of the self, of the heart, of *consciousness* lead to an experience of the provisional and constructed character of culture, a spontaneous understanding that social institutions are never merely *given*, but created out of the habitualization of our patterns of action, which are, in turn, rooted in creative interpretations of what we are experiencing? Is the very idea of abounding, of fullness and overflowing, a clue to this relationship about which we are inquiring?

The essays collected in this volume reflect a wide range of interests and concerns, as well as a common academic ethos, but they also show striking differences in theoretical and methodological complexity. Each is well worth reading; together they provide an impressive sample of the contemporary academic study of mysticism and of the tendency for mystical experience to awaken a fervent discontentedness with human relationships as they stand. The fine introduction by Professor Janet Ruffing surveys this constellation of queries and claims from several different angles, making some real progress in mapping the terrain. It seems to me that two points emerge from these essays that significantly illuminate the central theme of the volume. The first is that mystical experiences are liberating. By providing the direct experience of a reality that transcends and overwhelms the meaning, density, finality, and obviousness of the reality of everydayness, the mystical experience relativizes conventional judgments about plausibility and frees the person having the experience from conventional definitions of reality—that is, from all literalized metaphors and reified categories concerning *the way things are* in ordinary social life, including gender relations. Things do not have to be the way they seem to be. But the second point, less clear but no less urgent, that emerges from these investigations is that the relationship between the obvious present and the possible future is not exhausted by the category of the ethical. What the mystical experience seems to suggest is that the fully desirable future, in contrast with the misery of present circumstances, is not exclusively the object of a moral demand made on the will, not exclusively a matter of *ought,* but is always already an emergent possibility available to the imagination that requires an inner gesture more like *allowing*—or better, *welcoming.*

Other episodes of Christian history need to be placed in this context, and other traditions need to make a contribution to this conversation. In my judgment, it is not an accident that this conversation should begin from within Christianity, for it pertains ultimately to the category of *the messianic.* But for that very reason, the lived experience of Jewish and Muslim faith has crucial insights to add and to develop. But beyond these traditions, every tradition of mystical realization—Buddhist, Hindu, Taoist, and others—points to an alternative *form of culture* and *intends* an alternative way for human beings to dwell together.

I hope this volume will inspire other such volumes, but more importantly, I hope it will inspire serious efforts to think through the social implications of mystical disclosure and to put into practice spiritualities that consciously cultivate their sociological possibilities. I hope it will also inspire serious efforts to develop the spiritual roots of movements of intentional social change, which have for so long remained wishful and hortatory and ego centered. As Kabir says, "More than all else do I cherish at heart that love which makes me to live a limitless life in this world."

Acknowledgments

A volume of essays, more than any other book, is a collaborative project in which particular contributions merit recognition. I am grateful to Cynthia Maude-Gembler at Syracuse University Press, who expressed interest in this book when papers on the topic of mysticism and social transformation were presented in a session I chaired of the Mysticism Group at the American Academy of Religion Convention in Philadelphia in 1995.

Robert J. Egan, S.J., was coeditor at one stage of the project, provided the preface, and helped with conceptualizing the expanded version of essays. Throughout the project, he remained available for consultation, reading all of the essays and critiquing my introductory essay. If I had not studied with Bob at the Jesuit School of Theology in Berkeley as I did my doctoral studies, I would never have been able to integrate the bodies of knowledge required for this project. Likewise, I am indebted to two other members of the Society of Jesus: Michael J. Buckley, who introduced me to *The Spiritual Exercises of St. Ignatius* at the University of San Francisco at the beginning of my graduate theological studies, and Vincent O'Keefe, who graciously critiqued my essay on Ignatius and Arrupe.

I am grateful to all of the contributors to the volume, but especially to Joy Bostic, Carol Slade, Amy Hollywood, and Roger Gottlieb, who were on the original panel and who have waited patiently through the many delays in bringing this volume to completion.

Dr. Maria Calisi rendered extraordinary service in managing the manuscript production, editing, bringing every essay into conformity with the style sheet, communicating with authors, and endless word-processing. We are both grateful to her husband, Nicholas Palos, for his patience with the project and for his expert service and advice on all matters related to computer technology.

I am grateful to Fordham University for awarding me a faculty fellowship for 1998–99, gifting me with valuable time to write and to complete this project; for small research grants covering some of the expenses for this volume;

and for a publication grant enabling an ampler exploration of the theme than would have been possible without it.

Finally, I am grateful to the Maryknoll Contemplative Community in Ossining, New York, with whom I lived while writing my essays for the volume; to the Sisters of the Holy Name, especially Mary Garvin, Sheila McEvoy, and Frances Kendrick, who provided hospitality while I was working with Bob Egan in Spokane; and to the women in the Novitiate Community in St. Louis and the St. Louis Regional Community of Sisters of Mercy who provided hospitality and companionship as I brought this volume to completion.

April 29, 1999   Feast of Catherine of Siena

Contributors

Margaret Benefiel teaches at Andover Newton Theological School. She edited *Hidden in Plain Sight: Quaker Women's Writings, 1650–1700,* with three colleagues. She is author of "Spiritual Direction for Organizations: Toward Articulating a Model" and coauthor with Rebecca Darden Phipps of "Riding the Wind: Spiritual Nurture and the Organizational Process," in *The Hidden Spirit: Discovering the Spirituality of Institutions.* She is a consultant offering spiritual direction to organizations.

Joy R. Bostic is a Ph.D. candidate in theology at Union Theological Seminary in New York and an ordained minister in the Progressive Baptist Church. Her essay "It's a Jazz Thang: Interdisciplinarity and Critical Imagining in the Construction of a Womanist Theological Method" appears in *Women's Studies in Transition: The Pursuit of Interdisciplinarity,* edited by Kate Conway-Turner, Suzanne Cherrin, Jessica Schiffman, and Kathleen Doherty Turkel.

Roger S. Gottlieb is Paris Fletcher Distinguished Professor of the Humanities at Worcester Polytechnic Institute. His work has focused on social and political theory, Marxism, feminism, the Holocaust, contemporary spirituality, and environmental studies. His most recent books are *This Sacred Earth: Religion, Nature, Environment, The Ecological Community,* and *A Spirituality of Resistance: Finding a Peaceful Heart and Protecting the Earth.*

Amy Hollywood teaches in the Religion Department at Dartmouth College. She is the author of *The Soul as Virgin Wife: Mechtilde of Magdeburg, Marguerite Porete, and Meister Eckhart.*

Grace M. Jantzen is the John Rylands Professorial Research Fellow at the University of Manchester. She has recently published *Power, Gender and Christian Mysticism* in the Cambridge Studies in Ideology and Religion series, and *Becoming Divine: Towards a Feminist Philosophy of Religion.*

Paul Lachance, O.F.M., is the editor and translator of *The Complete Works of Angela of Foligno* in the Classics of Western Spirituality series published by Paulist Press. Author of many articles on Franciscan and Christian spirituality, he has conducted numerous retreats, conferences, and workshops in the United States and abroad. He is also adjunct professor of spirituality at the Chicago Theological Union.

Rebecca Darden Phipps is a member of the Religious Society of Friends. Her ministry to the wider Friends' community has involved leading workshops, retreats, and courses on adult religious education and spiritual formation. She is coauthor of "Riding the Wind: Spiritual Nurture and the Organizational Process."

Donald Rothberg is on the faculty of the Saybrook Graduate School and Research Center in San Francisco. A coeditor of the journal *ReVision,* he has published widely on socially engaged spirituality (particularly socially engaged Buddhism), critical social theory, transpersonal psychology, and epistemology and mysticism. He is coeditor of *Ken Wilber in Dialogue: Conversations with Leading Transpersonal Thinkers.* He serves on the board of the Buddhist Peace Fellowship and has led groups, retreats, and training programs on spirituality and social action.

Janet K. Ruffing, R.S.M., teaches spirituality in the Graduate School of Religion and Religious Education at Fordham University. She is the author of *Uncovering Stories of Faith: Narrative Aspects of Spiritual Direction, Spiritual Direction: Beyond the Beginnings,* and of numerous articles on spirituality, spiritual direction, religious life, and mysticism.

Carole Slade teaches in the Department of English and Comparative Literature at Columbia University. During 1995–97, she also participated in the project on religious experience at the Rutgers Center for Historical Analysis. She has published several articles on the medieval mystics, as well as *Approaches to Teaching Dante's Divine Comedy* and *St. Teresa of Avila: Author of a Heroic Life.*

Dorothee Sölle was the Harry Emerson Fosdick Visiting Professor at Union Theological Seminary in New York from 1978 to 1987. She is currently a freelance writer in theology and poetry in Hamburg. Recent publications include *Theology for Skeptics, Creative Disobedience,* and *The Silent Cry.*

Mysticism
& Social Transformation

Introduction

J A N E T   K .   R U F F I N G ,   R . S . M .

Mysticism is, at the present time, a topic of great interest in both the popular and scholarly worlds. The study of mysticism is now a specialized academic field either within the "field encompassing field of spirituality" (Schneiders 1986, 274) or more traditionally within the study of religion, as an element in the religious life and belief of many cultures.

Bernard McGinn divides recent scholarship into two periods beginning with the middle of the twentieth century. He characterizes the themes and issues in research and publication in the first of these periods, from 1950 to 1975, as debates and contributions from philosophical and comparativist perspectives—theological attempts to heal the split between theology and spirituality, and "the creation of a new genre—the history of Christian mysticism" (1998b, 13).

McGinn identifies three additional major concerns in the subsequent period of the last two decades: "(1) the retrieval of mystical traditions; (2) debates about the constitution of mysticism; and (3) the role of mysticism in post-modernity" (13). Explicit attention to gender is important for feminist scholars in all three of these concerns, but not generally for others in the field, who seem to remain largely indifferent to questions of both gender and power in their theories and definitions (Bruneau 1998; Jantzen 1995; Erickson 1993).

The breadth and intensity of the interest in mysticism during the last half of the twentieth century have given rise to many different interpretations of mysticism and many conflicting theories about it. These interpretations define mysticism as a subjective and mainly affective phenomenon, a particular form of discourse, an element of lived religion, a source for doing theology, the experience of a certain type of knowing, the experience of a kind of intersubjectivity, and a set of texts from a variety of traditions requiring a complex hermeneutics.

Within the field, the relationship between mysticism and social transformation has received relatively little exploration. This lacuna in the scholarship is rooted in a modern construction of mysticism in both philosophy and psychology that often fails to account for the social and religious contexts and institutions that influence historical mystics and within which mystics live and act and communicate. The increasing privatization of religion in general during the modern period has tended to separate mysticism, often referred to historically as the contemplative or inner life, from the worldly life of politics, commerce, academics, and public life. Even within religion itself, mysticism and theology have since at least the fourteenth century become increasingly alienated from one another. These splits have obscured the real relationships between contemplation and action, theory and practice, and mysticism and ethical behavior.

Conceptual categories for linking the struggle for social justice, social transformation, and various liberation movements to explicitly religious practices and convictions as well as to various mystical teachings and experiences were developed in social and political thought throughout the modern period, especially in political attitudes and philosophies supporting the ideal of democracy. Meanwhile, theologies of the "apostolic life," beginning in the late medieval period, have explicitly linked a personal love of Christ with love of one's neighbor concretized in acts of service and even in systematic efforts to alleviate the suffering of the poor and oppressed. But without sociological categories, desires for the transformation of society usually appear as prophetic proclamation in the cause of "reform" or "renewal" rather than as intentional or directed social change. Finally, Marxist social analysis began to alter the way the relation between theory and practice was conceived, promoting the ideal of a more dynamic and dialectical relationship.

These political and economic frames of reference have not figured strongly in the field of religion when religion is conceived of as a private rather than as a public sphere of action or when mysticism is defined primarily as a psychological phenomenon or as an altered state of consciousness without reference to any larger or encompassing reality or to an Ultimate Other that discloses itself through mystical experience and requires some type of action in response. When this subjective pole alone is emphasized, the concrete claims of human and nonhuman "others" for sufficiency of the conditions for life required by justice and compassion may slip from active and shared concern.

This volume represents a modest exploration of this relatively neglected theme within the larger context of the current interpretations and theories of mysticism. As such, it does not resolve any of these current debates, nor does it present a unified theoretical approach to its major theme. It does, however, bring many of the available perspectives into dialogue with one another as the contributors develop specific aspects of this topic in relation to the various traditions and periods of their specialized interests.

Within the current scholarship, the comparativist and philosophical perspectives have tended to interact with one another. The term *mysticism* was first extrapolated from Christian contexts, then defined by philosophers and scholars in comparative religious studies, and applied to broadly analogous phenomena in other religious traditions. The initial positions established by William James, W. T. Stace, and others were largely "essentialist" ones, based on a conviction that there is in mysticism an "inner unity, common core or essential sameness" across religious traditions and historical periods (McGinn 1998b, 15).

By the late 1970s and early 1980s, these views were forcefully challenged by Steven Katz and others who argued for a "contructivist" position emphasizing the relationship between particular religious contexts, the composition of mystical texts, and the mystical experiences of persons within a given religious or mystical tradition. This conceptual perspective argues that the historical, social, religious, and theological influences within religious experience are decisive, but it makes impossible the identification of any common core or set of family resemblances as a starting point for comparative studies. It makes the term *mysticism* in the titles of the books edited by Katz at best equivocal, at worst meaningless.

A more sophisticated counterreaction then ensued "in favor of a philosophical-phenomenological inner unity of mystical experience/consciousness" (McGinn 1998b, 15). Although this approach does recognize the need for dealing with a wide variety of cross-cultural expressions of mysticism, as well as for a more careful study of particular mystical texts and their historically situated character, there remain some problems with it in its usual expression.

If mysticism is reduced to a psychological experience, those elements of mystical practices and texts that by definition are not central to the experience itself remain displaced or neglected in the study. Furthermore, this approach tends to downplay such nonpsychological factors as the interpersonal bonds of loyalty and service that connect mystics with their wider religious communities or to ignore traditional criteria for determining the validity of mystical experiences, such as the religious and ethical practices required of everyone within a given tradition or the qualities and implications of action subsequent to the mystical experiences—that is, their "fruits."

The scholarly work assuming either of these positions therefore raises critical questions about whether the category of mysticism is a coherent one or whether it refers to phenomena that are so different from one another as to constitute a category mistake.

Typologies and Definitions

A second problem related to defining mysticism at the present time relates to currently available typologies of mystical teaching or experience. On what basis are these typologies developed? Even more importantly, do they credibly account for the stunning differences apparent in the great variety of mystical texts that have been retrieved and translated from different religious and esoteric traditions?

Within Christianity alone, for instance, certain mysticisms emphasize the intellect, others emphasize the heart, and still others emphasize dedicated action in the world. The mystical path to God through knowing is often largely speculative and theological in its emphasis. The encounter between the divine and the human results in insight, realization, awe, and an integration between theology and contemplation. This integration used to be known as *mystical theology* and figures strongly in Pseudo-Dionysius, Thomas Aquinas, and Meister Eckhart. It seems to correspond to the *jnana yoga* of the Hindu tradition and certain parallel spiritual attitudes and practices in Judaism, Buddhism, and Islam.

The mystical path to God through the heart is often known as *affective mysticism,* which became prominent in Christian history with Bernard of Clairvaux, Francis of Assisi, and others, and which medieval women mystics developed to a high degree. The path through love and devotion emphasized symbols and practices related to desire, eros, and intense feeling. The Sufi mystics, Rābi'ah and Jalāl al-Dīn Rūmī, exemplify this tradition in Islam. Something similar occurs in the *bhakti* traditions of Hinduism, and in some forms of Mahāyāna Buddhism, as well as in Jewish Hasidism.

A mystical path of action is exemplified in Christian tradition by Ignatius of Loyola and others whose mystical apprehension of God sent them on particular missions in the world, often entailing the corporal and spiritual works of mercy. The path to God through action in the world in the service of others seems to correspond to the tradition of *karma yoga* in Hindu traditions, to the bodhisattva ideal in Mahāyāna Buddhism, and to the strong emphasis on the mystics' specialized roles within their religious communities in Jewish and Islamic traditions. This threefold pattern is associated with bodily "centers" of head, heart, and belly in some esoteric schools of meditation (Naranjo and Ornstein 1971).

Yet typologies can obscure as much as they inform. One might be able to characterize mystical texts along these lines, but individuals may themselves employ two or all three forms at different times in their spiritual development, with one or another path tending to be dominant.

Within Christian tradition, a classic binary typology of *kataphatic* and *apophatic* mysticism also originates in Pseudo-Dionysius and was fused with distinct theological approaches. The elite theological tradition has preferred to emphasize apophatic forms characterized by negation, silence, nothingness, an absence of content, or an "unknowing" with heightened affective experiences. Many women and some men, on the other hand, have favored and even rejoiced in kataphatic forms, involving images, sensory impressions, visions, voices—a mysticism mediated through the senses, through symbols, through concrete objects, and through human relationships. Some have taught that one may begin with kataphatic practices and experiences, and then mature or develop into more apophatic ones.

However, as predictors, these categories are highly problematic. They are sometimes mixed in the life stories of individuals. My own qualitative research tentatively contradicts the succession model, at least for many women (Ruffing 1995). Jantzen (1995) has shown a gender bias at work within these particular definitions; and Bruneau (1998), drawing from the work of Michel de Certeau, shows the creative ways in which some women used "negative mysticism" as a powerful "tactic of opposition" and altered or minimized their sensory descriptions whenever they made them known to clerical authorities and made themselves vulnerable to clerical social control.

Recent linguistic studies of mysticism, moreover, suggest that categorizing mysticism in these ways often betrays a serious misreading of the intentions of mystical texts themselves. Careful textual analysis may show that the language of negation is often a corrective to or warning against valorizing any single type of practice or experience as more important than another or to be sought more than another (Turner 1995; Sells 1994; McIntosh 1998). Apophatic practices and experiences are not to be valued more than any other specific practices or experiences. Apophatic language may be understood properly, at least in some contexts, as referring more to the ineffability of God than to the experience of the human person at prayer, although in general both conception and experience are probably more often interrelated.

The sociology of religion offers yet another binary typology: "world-rejecting" and "inner worldly" forms of asceticism and mysticism, as originally developed in the work of Max Weber. Religious virtuosi of the world-rejecting type of religious orientation "sought contemplation as they sought political and economic goals 'by avoiding interruptions caused by nature and the social milieu' " (Erickson 1993, 74). In the gesture of radical renunciation can be read a negative determination about the promise and prospects of "the world." The inner worldly type of religious virtuoso participates fully in the world, but seeks changes in the self and its motives so as not to be co-opted by the world. The first orientation tends toward a conception of the divine as utterly transcendent mystery, favoring apophatic emphases and tending toward silence, whereas the second discovers the divine to be immanent within the world as perceived by a transformed self and often favors kataphatic practices and expressions, tending toward proclamation.

Erickson notes that Weber left out the erotic orientation altogether in developing this typology (1993, 75). Many mystical texts creatively employ erotic metaphors in the service of both explanation and evocation. Jantzen (1995) shows that women often employ these images and ascribe gender to God in their mystical writings in ways quite different from men.

For nearly three decades now, feminist scholars have focused simultaneously on creating a usable feminist history and on deconstructing the masculinist assumptions that characterize virtually all the fields of knowledge that impinge on the study of mysticism (Lerner 1993). Feminist women—notably Caroline Walker Bynum, Elizabeth Petroff, Grace Jantzen, and Marie-Florine Bruneau—have developed distinctive theoretical approaches, and numerous others have worked on specific figures and periods, viewing mysticism through a variety of complementary lenses. In the process, they have accumulated a sufficient body of scholarship to facilitate, with some adequacy, a deeper understanding of gender differences in this field. The cultural construction of mysticism, of the sacred, and of power have all been "gendered" through and through, affecting men and women quite differently. These themes weave through this volume explicitly in the essays by Jantzen, Hollywood, Slade, and Bostic.

Two issues emerge as especially significant in this work. The first is the creativity women mystics have demonstrated in their development—through mystical transformation—of a God-empowered "agency" when this very agency and its characteristic sense of selfhood seemed permanently threatened within patriarchal contexts. The second is the way the role of mysticism itself has been a source of resistance to woman-negating forces and a source of solidarity with others who suffer the same deprivations and conflicts.

Although gender constitutes only one concrete form of oppression, the experience of other oppressed groups often resembles the social experience of women. Most feminists embrace a perspective that seeks to include the liberation of other oppressed people and groups as an intentional part of their agendas.

Within the field of Christian mysticism, Bernard McGinn has done a great service by undertaking a multivolume history of Western Christian mysticism and by offering a preliminary heuristic definition of mysticism along with his valuable sketch of the history of the study of mysticism. According to McGinn, "the mystical element in Christianity is that part of its belief and practices that concerns the preparation for, the consciousness of, and the reaction to what can be described as the immediate or direct presence of God"

(1991, xvii). He crafts his definition in such a way that mysticism does not equal haphazard one-time experiences but an entire process within a person's life. He emphasizes that, historically, persons judged to be mystics have practiced a "religion" rather than "mysticism" and that their practices were usually guided by and interpreted through religious texts of varying kinds. Further, McGinn includes reactions to the consciousness of the presence of God in what he means by mysticism. These reactions could be the production of mystical texts or of a way of living or acting consonant with this consciousness, or the formation of a community that can sustain and enrich and pass on a mystical lifestyle.

Mark McIntosh reports that McGinn continues to refine this definition, emphasizing a vocabulary of mystical "consciousness" in preference to mystical "experience." According to McIntosh, McGinn takes this turn in order to encompass experience without eliminating or obscuring the roles that cognition and context play (1998, 31). McGinn's definition, therefore, encompasses the dialectic of contemplation and action envisioned by a number of the contributors to this volume, and includes prophetic consciousness, which is intimately related to the question of the relationship between mysticism and social transformation.

Mysticism and Prophecy

One of the most important—though often neglected—theoretical issues related to types, descriptions, or definitions of mysticism and the mystical is the relationship of mysticism to *prophecy* or *the prophetic*. The connection between these two phenomena is rarely explicitly discussed, although it may be evoked in some communities, in some authors, and in some situations.

This theme lies behind Johann Baptist Metz's frequent allusions to a "mystical-political" dimension in Christianity (1998) and behind Edward Schillebeeckx's use of this same language (1968b), followed by David Tracy's more recent transposition in his "mystical-prophetic" element and by a parallel development in the work of some of the Latin American liberation theologians, including Gustavo Gutiérrez. The notion of a relationship between the mystical and the prophetic or the political also appears in the work of Theodor Adorno, Max Horkheimer, and the other thinkers associated with "the Frankfurt school" of revisionary Marxism that influenced Metz. Metz also came upon a strong apocalyptic strain in Ernst Bloch and Walter Benjamin, discovering in them neglected resources within Judaism. It was especially this apocalyptic theme that enabled Metz to recover a mystical-political element that challenges the privatization of bourgeois religion and locates the experience of God not in peaceful tranquility but in protest to God about evil in the world, a questioning of God, and a "suffering unto God" (Metz 1998, 16).

This latter kind of mysticism, then, entails an active form of resistance to suffering in the world; it demands that human beings act courageously to create a more just social order and struggle for a more universal realization of the Enlightenment ideal "that all persons be able to be subjects" of their own histories; it becomes the inspiration and provocation of "the struggle for a universal liberation" (Metz 1998, 37). Metz dramatically describes the primary conflict facing the churches today as "a conflict between bourgeois religion that cannot get beyond just taking care of its members, and a messianic religion of discipleship" (1998, 45). And it is a particular form of relationship with God that Metz describes—a radical hope that God will bring about salvation in the form of justice and that, contrary to some postmodern conceptions of endless evolutionary time, the end of time belongs to the biblical God who comes toward humanity at the eschatological moment.

The ability to link religious commitment to social action as well as to an intimate relationship with God demands a coherently articulated connection between mysticism and prophecy. To relate these categories through yet another binary opposition, construing them as opposites in the manner of Friedrich Heiler (1997) or, more recently, of Peter Berger (1981), seems strained and artificial. Yet there is not yet anything like an adequate history of prophecy or prophetic phenomena that can be brought to bear on our understanding of the mystical traditions, even with all of their definitional difficulties.

For religious traditions rooted in the Bible, however, prophecy is everywhere. The most characteristic form of "religious experience" in the Bible, as Martin Buber has pointed out, is not realization or rapture, but vocation and mission. The prophet is the ultimate model and designation for the founder of Islam, Mohammed, who has always been understood within Islam as the last and the greatest manifestation of this type. Jesus, too, clearly functioned as a prophet in relationship to the Judaism of his time and, in fact, was called a prophet by his contemporaries.

Analysis and description of the prophetic task and role usually remains safely hidden within biblical studies and divorced from systematic theology, spirituality, or the study of mysticism unless and until believers begin to interpret these prophetic narratives and discourses in reference to contemporary contexts of suffering and injustice. Once again, then, prophecy surfaces but often in ways that lack theoretical clarification to support its relationship to mysticism. Yet prophecy remains a key category for religiously motivated social criticism and directed social change.

It is no accident that the prophetic and the mystical have been systematically separated from one another. Karl Rahner claims:

it can be said with but little exaggeration that the history of mystical theology is a history of the devaluation of the prophetic element in favor of the non-prophetic, "pure" infused contemplation. People are . . . more suspicious of prophetic mysticism, which invokes revelations and instructions from above to claim a mission and right in the Church to admonish and guide the Church and her members, than of the image-free, ineffable mysticism of pure contemplation. Certainly, the former is more dangerous and prone to come into conflict with Church authority than the latter. Nevertheless, prophecy has its foundation in Scripture, and in practice has a great history in the Church . . . yet orthodox theology has never paid any serious attention to the question whether there are prophets even in post-apostolic times, how their spirit can be recognized and discerned, what their role is in the Church, what their relationship [is] to the hierarchy, what the import of their mission [is] for the exterior and interior life of the Church. (1963, 20–21)

In this essay and in his piece on the charismatic element in the Catholic Church (1964), Rahner is carefully retrieving the role of prophecy and other manifestations of the Spirit's capacity to "do a new thing," to innovate and to reform or correct situations that are contrary to the foundational experiences of faith out of which the community originally formed.

There are at least two critical reasons for the devaluation of prophecy. From the perspective of social change within a community, if a prophet or the prophecy can be discredited, change is effectively prevented. Second, prophecy is often identified with a certain visionary mystical tradition in which the visionary seems to be predicting the future or literally interpreting these symbolic communications in ways that prove to be patently false. Karl Rahner argues in his *Visions and Prophecies* (1963) that the decisive criterion for determining the validity of prophetic utterance is its compatibility with the entire thrust of biblical faith rather than its accuracy in foreseeing concrete particular details. Later scripture scholars characterize this activity of prophets as "interpretation" rather than "prediction."

The possibility and the fact of false prophecy do not thereby invalidate the whole phenomenon of prophecy or render unimaginable a mystically grounded version of prophetic speech and action in the service of renewal, reform, and even innovation within a religious tradition. The biblical model of the prophet offers a variety of examples of men and women who enjoyed both friendship and communication with a divine revealing Other. In fact, the prophetic task requires friendship with God—an authentic intimacy with God. It is this intimacy with God that eventually overcomes the would-be prophet's resistance to both speech and action, which are born of contemplation. How else does one hear God's word spoken in the heart or in dreams and visions? How else can one be confident it is God's word and not merely one's own? The mysticism of the prophets is what frees their imaginations and desires from the defining and constraining power of the world as it is, the world as it stands.

Walter Brueggemann's brief classic book *Prophetic Imagination* (1978) describes in detail the dynamics of this prophetic task. The prophets suffer in their own hearts the discrepancy between what is and what ought to be. They are somehow unable to maintain the "false consciousness"—Brueggemann calls it "the royal consciousness" in the case of ancient Israel—that is essential for the perpetuation of unjust social structures and that benefits those most invested in maintaining the status quo. However, the prophet is more than a complainer. Denunciation is only one part of the task. The prophet's heart is broken: there is a work of grieving and mourning the prophet must initiate—lamenting the suffering wrought by injustice and numbness. What is the origin of both the perception of discrepancy and the compassion that impels the prophet to speak? It is a deep and expansive appropriation of the vision, values, and moral responses inherent in the community activated by the divine Spirit, by the summons and mission of God.

The prophet's criticism is grounded in deeply held shared convictions about the way, for instance, a Jew ought to behave and about the way the community ought to order its life. The prophet is able to convince others only from the perspective of shared memories and norms. The prophet appeals to something the community already knows and wants to value but has managed to hide from itself or keep separate from the domain of its present behavior.

To be effective, the appeal of the prophet needs to be poetic and symbolic. It needs to reenergize its listeners and help the community remember its own history and promises and possibilities in a way that will inspire conversion and fresh resolve. According to Michael Walzer, "Prophecy aims to arouse remembrance, recognition, indignation, repentance" (1987, 75). Moshe Greenburg points out that such prophecy is based on "an appeal to their audience's better nature, confronting them with the demands of God that they know (or knew) but wish to ignore or forget" (1983, 56). In the end, prophets deeply trust that their desires and their words will find advocates in the hearts of their own people.

Prophetic speech is the creation of a fresh interpretation of that part of the tradition that has slipped from view and thus is failing to make an effective claim for action in the community or in the larger society. Prophetic speech also is full of amazement and wonder. It cannot criticize without also evoking a positive vision of the people's realization of their original calling and covenant. Something better, more just, something more fully human, more full of praise and God's shalom, is possible if only the leaders and the community will change their ways. The prophet's words mediate the possibility—in spite of everything—of a truly desirable future.

Walzer claims this prophetic pattern of discourse is the standard form of social criticism involving "the identification of public pronouncements and respectable opinion as hypocritical, the attack upon actual behavior and institutional arrangements, the search for core values (to which hypocrisy is always a clue), the demand for an everyday life in accordance with the core. The critic begins with revulsion and ends with affirmation" (1987, 87).

The prophet, according to Gustavo Gutiérrez (1973, 1988), both denounces and announces, both criticizes and engenders hope. But hope emerges not only from limit situations, but also from positive experiences. Hope arises from experiences of joy and gratitude, of solidarity and festival, of love and friendship. The experience of joy is "one that opens the heart, quickens the human spirit and ultimately brings about a movement of self-transcendence" (Lane 1996, 61). Equally important are experiences of meaning, however provisional or fragmentary, and the felt sense of the positive worth of human life—the conviction that human lives are simply worth living. And finally, the experience of friendship and of passion awaken hope and engender a selfless love that in turn enables others to hope.

The prophet works with all of these sources of hope, but especially with the process of interpretation and emergence of new meaning—the process of *reimagining* meaning—which makes possible both trust in God, with all the struggle that may entail, and trust in the resources of faith, whether in times of darkness or in times of abundant life. The remembrance the prophet evokes encompasses all of those fragmentary experiences of spaciousness, harmony, bliss—the shalom that God desires and promises, and that fleetingly makes its appearance in the lives of individuals and communities.

Christian traditions have historically developed contrasting relationships to the mystical and to the prophetic, creating a false dichotomy that functions differently within the diverse traditions. Protestant scholars in the early twentieth century espoused prophecy and rejected mysticism. The assessment by Karl Rahner above aptly describes the Roman Catholic position of accepting but taming mysticism and largely rejecting prophecy. Yet social movements have often had mystical roots, and without mystical depth, it is impossible to discern between the products of one's own inflated consciousness and the impulses of the divine Spirit mediated through a prophet's personality. Without contemplative depth, it is extremely difficult to sustain ongoing resistance, which so often entails suffering at the hands of the very community the prophet serves.

Contemporary theories of mysticism that rely too heavily on William

James's analysis of religious experience uncritically accept an idea of the self that tends to be decontextualized, divorced from the resources and social support of a religious community and tradition. As Grace Jantzen pointedly observes, this reliance on James

> plays directly into the hands of modern bourgeois political and gender assumptions. It keeps God (and women) safely out of politics and the public realm; it allows mysticism to flourish as a secret inner life, while those who nurture such an inner life can generally be counted on to prop up rather than to challenge the status quo of their workplaces, their gender roles, and the political systems by which they are governed, since their anxieties and angers will be allayed in the privacy of their own hearts' search for peace and tranquillity. (1995, 346)

When connected to adequate theories of social change, an understanding of the social construction of the self, in which postmodern thinkers are particularly interested, can lead to a more contextualized understanding of the relationship of mystical consciousness and social transformation.

McGinn's account of the mystical element as an entire process, extending through a lifetime, hints at this possibility. Mysticism is a transformative process that supports self-transcendence, the overcoming of too small a sense of self. This limited self may be understood as being both self-centered and isolated, as well as being defined by the conventional—a self programmed for a socially determined form of "normality." In other words, the conventional isolated self with its anxious self-preoccupations takes for granted current social arrangements as "given" and uncritically conforms to the requirements of the dominant culture. Late-capitalist and postmodern culture tends to foster a self that is rootless in relationship to community and place, closed in on itself and essentially nomadic, uncommitted to projects beyond employment and the multiple diversions that make such rootlessness provisionally tolerable.

Mystical consciousness calls into question both of these conceptions of the self. It reveals something more to life. The self discovered in mystical consciousness is a self related to Ultimacy, a self that is more than the self can imagine itself to be and surely more than any society conventionally wants it to be.

In a distinctively postmodern approach such as Michel de Certeau's, the confrontation of scientific and theological discourse with mystical discourse, according to Bruneau,

> allows [the contemporary individual] to retrieve a space in which the heterogeneity and irreducibility of lived mystical experience can at least partially

emerge and which scientific epistemology makes impossible to conceptualize. De Certeau states that we cannot say any more than the mystics themselves what indeed the mystical experience is. We can only accept that, according to them, it opens up "a space that the mystic can no longer live without," that it is "like throwing open a window into one's dwelling," and allowing "a new sense of ease . . . a breath of fresh air to enter one's life," and that "it seems to rise up from some unfathomable dimension of existence, as from an ocean whose origins precede mankind." Mystical experience seems indeed to bring deep transformation to existence itself.

What emerges is a radicality that consists in an unrelenting resistance to and an undoing of procedures of reification. Mystical experience . . . becomes the repository of "that immense remnant" of everything in human experience that has not been tamed and symbolized by language. (1998, 6)

Hermeneutics

This place of resistance is not yet social change, but it can lead to and support such change. Theories of social change can be used to get at the approaches to mysticism that are insufficiently hermeneutical, insufficiently political, and insufficiently historical.

Hermeneutical theory is extremely helpful here as long as it does not adopt the option of a hermeneutics of mystical texts that reduces them "to nothing but a form of linguistic practice, one that is worth studying for its disruptive and gender-inclusive character" (McGinn 1998b, 16).

Questions about how to interpret mystical texts are of utmost significance, and they raise all the standard questions relevant to the distinctions and relationships among explanation, understanding, and interpretation. Paul Ricoeur (1976) painstakingly describes the unfolding dialectical relationship of explanation and understanding that results in adequate interpretation, which is always a provisional and ongoing process between a reader and a text. Ricoeur describes the process of explanation through which unfolds "the range of propositions and meanings, whereas in understanding we comprehend or grasp as a whole the chain of partial meanings in one act of synthesis" (72). These activities always overlap with one another in practice. Ricoeur associates "explanation" with the scientific method, which discerns recurring patterns of motion in material objects, and "understanding" with the human sciences, which have more to do with subjects and their distinctive intersubjective complexities.

Within the field of mysticism, the interpreter confronts an amazing array of texts that both conceal and reveal the experience of the mystic and the teaching of the mystic about living in a particular way that facilitates mystical consciousness of and response to the divine Other. For academics to generate successful theories about mysticism, they must take into account a sufficient number of instances of the mystical element expressed sometimes in poetry, at other times in narratives, and at other times in treatises, along with descriptions and analyses of likely mistakes and dangers along the way. Considerations of genres, biographies, original audiences, the cultural and historical circumstances embedded in the texts (including power structures)—all require attention in developing adequate theories that can provide "explanations" that chasten and guide and correct the process of our understanding.

Theory and text interact with one another through the reader. This process allows a validation of the theory in relationship to a particular case, or it results in a judgment of its inadequacy, in turn requiring a more sophisticated theory to encompass features of the text not engaged by the original theory.

Both Paul Ricoeur and Hans-Georg Gadamer, each in his own way, introduce the idea of *horizon* in their accounts of interpretation. Ricoeur discusses this idea from the perspective of "multiple meaning" and "meaning belonging to the margins" (1976) determined by the horizon of the text. In this sense, *horizon* refers to an assumed background for the metaphoric and symbolic language of the foreground of the text. Gadamer describes horizon as that which one sees from a given perspective (1975). For Gadamer, the reader and the text have quite different horizons. Understanding occurs when a "fusion of horizons" can take place. Readers, with their own horizons, allow the horizon of the text to affect and change them.

Thus, multiple readings of a given text are possible and desirable. It is not purely a matter of the horizon of the text being ignored when read in a significantly different contemporary horizon, but a matter of creative, interactive possibilities that emerge by keeping both horizons in tension. Historical texts question contemporary assumptions in any authentic interpretation and are, in turn, questioned by contemporary thought and experience.

Amazing things happen when texts that have become dislocated from their original temporal and cultural milieus are read by persons who live in other times and cultures but who may share some elements of hope or fear or longing with the world the text projects as possible. Biblical texts are instructive here. In the case, for example, of third-world peasants who read, say, the New Testament, originally produced in a poor and largely agrarian society, and who then reflect on their social reality and faith experience, they may recognize themselves and their own situation in these texts in ways that metropolitan middle-class people in capitalist nations do not.

Thus, Ricoeur and Gadamer, each in his own way, have taught us that reading a text is not such a straightforward event. Texts disclose their meanings to us in complex and interactive ways. They "mean" or "produce meaning" in different ways. Different kinds of texts make different kinds of claims upon their readers.

Mystical texts emerge from the matrix of an encounter between the divine and the human. The profundity of this encounter often results in incredibly nuanced, rich, and paradoxical uses of language—sometimes ornately allegorical, sometimes sparse and demanding, sometimes full of sensual and erotic metaphors, and often extravagant and yet elusive. Frequently, the internal structure of these mystical texts defies explication or systematic ordering. McIntosh observes that this complexity is "all part of their *performance* as mystical texts"; that is, they "work precisely by means of this metaphorical language which cannot simply be abstracted" (1998, 142, emphasis in original).

They work as texts by inviting the reader into the divine/human encounter. Their purpose is to bring the reader into an aliveness and a stance of receptivity toward God in which God can supply the meaning the text does not offer directly. Thus, these texts are oriented not simply to a meaning "behind" the text, back in the past, or even to an experience of God "behind" the text, back in the past, but toward the future of the reader and his or her potential encounter with God. The text, in other words, opens up the possibility of a new divine/human encounter for the reader.

These kinds of texts cannot be adequately understood without some affinity for the practices and ways of living that an enacted reading of such texts require. Gadamer is fond of using law and medicine as examples of understanding and of how the work of interpretation is related to practice. A doctor has correctly interpreted and so understood a medical text when he or she can treat a patient appropriately. It seems that a certain way of life is probably required of the student of mysticism if he or she is to understand mysticism with any adequacy.

In some sense, the truth disclosed in a mystical text can be appropriated only if the reader is willing to allow the text to evoke a response—a response that entails a changed view of reality, a willingness to try out through participation his or her own understanding of the text as a guide for his or her own living.

Gadamer's conversational model of hermeneutics includes the notion of a relationship between tradition and experience that is also very helpful in reflecting on the themes of this volume. In mystical texts, contemporary persons are not only addressed by a tradition that makes particular and stringent claims on them, but also invited to contribute in a creative fashion to the ongoing tradition itself. Later members of their community and the heirs of their tradition are shaped by what is given and disclosed in these texts, but they also contribute to their history and the expansion of their meaning.

This process occurs in at least a couple of different ways. The horizon within which one experiences some aspect of the tradition may impel a retrieval and reinterpretation of some neglected aspect of the tradition (Gadamer 1975, 245–74). The relationship between mysticism and prophecy is one example of such a possible reinterpretation and retrieval actually going on among some contemporary communities of Christians. A second possibility is what Gadamer names the capacity for "new experiences." For him, new experiences are those that resist our established mind-sets or interpretive frames of reference. They simply do not fit. They are something completely other than what we expected and already know how to name (1975, 317–21). The person who is truly experienced is particularly adept at ongoing learning because human experience is acquired only historically.

Mystical texts can certainly be explained on some level without a corresponding faith vision or mystical horizon. But these interpretations may not adequately account for the full range of meaning and possibility in such texts. These more restricted interpretations of mystical texts would most likely confound their creators, who wrote primarily for mystical purposes.

These texts may also be politically charged. The politically destabilizing potential of mystical discourse has long been recognized. Why else would Eckhart's writings, for example, have been condemned? Why were so many women who heard voices, such as Joan of Arc, and who faithfully discerned and heeded them, burned at the stake? Steven Ozment (1973) was among the first historians of mysticism to suggest that mystical consciousness is one of the primary resources for social or religious dissent. He saw in his historical examples "dissent, rebellion, or revolution" (8). But the possibility of *reform* and *reinterpretation* within a tradition is also present as well.

For instance, some of the developments within Christianity that are not represented explicitly in this volume are those that have taken place within the liberating praxis of base communities in Latin America. Built on the political-mystical theology of European post-Holocaust experience (represented by Metz and Dorothee Sölle) and on the suffering, celebration, and insight of the Latin American poor in dialogue with their pastoral workers, these liberationist communities live and articulate a politically active, communitarian mysticism, uniting the contemplative and the prophetic in their everyday lives. Segundo Galilea offers this preliminary sketch of such a mysticism:

> When Christ and all the apostles revealed the presence of God in every human being, and with it the dignity and absolute destiny of man, they not only expressed their own contemplative vision of man, but endowed this prophetic announcement with a sociopolitical content, making it incompati-

ble with the prevailing social system and with pagan attitudes toward human beings.

By giving the poor and little a privileged place and identifying himself specially with them, Christ called the poor to the Kingdom of God and mobilized them. This is not only a mystic act—"to intuit" the presence of Jesus in the dispossessed, so discovering their dignity—but leads to social commitment and to political consequences, since this incorporation of the poor in the Kingdom of God passes through history and implies a progressive liberation of the same poor and little from concrete social systems.

Jesus proclaimed the beatitudes. It is impossible to announce and live this message without living in hope, in other words, without being a contemplative. But the beatitudes themselves form the ethical attitude of the contemplatives. This radical modality of living the gospel is a prophecy which invariably questions individuals and societies.

Thus, the Biblical message from Moses to Jesus shows us the two aspects of the liberating commitment of faith. In Moses, liberation takes on a temporal, political expression, and in Christ it shows forth the full sense of liberation.

This full meaning is established in Jesus. Liberation is seen as decisive, eschatological, saving and transforming from within man and society. It implies a sociopolitical transformation, just as the liberation of Moses implied the conversion of the heart and the eschatological vocation of Israel.

We have here incarnate the mystic-prophetic dimension of faith and contemplation. Latin American Christians live out these dimensions in varying degrees in their daily lives, but they always complement each other. (1980, 539–40)

These new experiences of Spirit—a mysticism experienced within the concrete social location of love of neighbor, especially the neighbor who is poor or suffering—are retrieved from the tradition as foundational through the narratives of call and deliverance, of prophecy and courageous action.

Action is a central category here that has to be framed in narrative. John S. Dunne in *The Search for God in Time and Memory* (1969) describes one form of the story of the self as a story of "deeds," for which he uses the missionary apostle Paul as his prime exemplar. Paul is shown speaking and acting, not reflecting on his interior states of soul. Ignatius of Loyola, sixteen centuries later, on the basis of a narrative of the life of Christ and a set of stories about the lives of saints, imagines himself doing heroic deeds in the service of his God imaged as an enthroned monarch.

These kinds of Spirit-filled narratives exist in all religious traditions. They are the stories of the founder and of the founder's concrete acts of love, his or her personal calling or awakening or transformation, and finally the articulation of a teaching, of guidance on a path or "way."

Usually, in the Hebrew Bible, God calls the person to do something. Persons are commissioned to go on journeys, to talk to Pharaohs, to address their people, to write things down or rip things up—to do all kinds of things. In the experience of being called, one is also commissioned. In the process of acting, the neophyte and veteran alike complain, question, and test out if this act is what they really are supposed to do.

Narratives of such experiences inspire like kinds of responses in entirely new situations if these possibilities for action have not been eliminated from enactment by the way a given community has chosen to interpret such texts. If mystical consciousness provides "a radicality that consists in an unrelenting resistance to and an undoing of procedures of reification" (Bruneau 1998, 6), it leads naturally to the prophetic action that brings about the emergence of something genuinely new, an alternative social reality constructed by people whose minds and hearts and wills have been transformed.

Social Change and Social Transformation

Narratives of action are often stories about change. They are stories about individuals who change their minds and change their hearts and change their behaviors. They are stories about individuals who change their communities or the circumstances of their people's lives. Sometimes they are stories about the arising of new communities of people who have participated in a common experience. Stories of religious foundations are like this.

The Hebrew people were once a group of nomads whose identity and history dramatically changed as the result of God's making an appearance in their lives. The Exodus narrative recounts this process of community formation and remains a powerful story motivating liberation movements throughout history (see Walzer 1985).

When the term *social transformation* comes into play in modern contexts, it usually refers to intentional attempts to change a particular social group or some aspect of an entire society for the better according to some kind of shared norms. In situations of representative government, the "prophetic" becomes the "political" through popular education and through mobilizing coalitions.

Of course, social groups change whether or not this change is intentionally chosen or orchestrated. Anytime two societies or social groups come into contact with one another, for example, some kind of mutual influence occurs, resulting in some kind of change. Individuals and groups within those societies become more or less adept at benefitting from social change and at creatively responding to the surprising possibilities presented by such changes.

However, the process of unconscious or unintended social change is not what the phrase *social transformation* ordinarily implies in modern usage. In a modern context, it suggests the conception that social arrangements are habitualizations of behavior created and agreed to by a given social group and that these arrangements can be changed. For this kind of change to happen, the change agents must analyze the mechanisms at work in the maintenance of the existing order and share that reflection in a compelling fashion with others in order to persuade them to join in a project of intentional remaking—usually of some law, behavior, or way of imagining and acting—because of the perceived negative effects of the status quo.

Traditional or premodern societies do experience some forms of intentional social change, but the ways of bringing about this change are more limited. The combination of prophetic denunciation and annunciation is one such way. In a traditional society, the agent of change must usually persuade the people in power to change. Thus, frequently in Israel, for instance, the king or the high priest was addressed by the prophet. If such persuasion fails, another possibility is to mobilize a sufficient group of people to resist or revolt or overthrow the offending people in power.

If both of these strategies fail, subversion or some form of wider resistance may be employed. In the Hebrew scriptures, the story of the Israelite midwives is an example. The midwife in the case of Moses did not kill the boy-child as decreed by Pharaoh. Miriam developed an amazing alliance with Pharaoh's daughter instead, ensuring the boy's life despite Pharaoh's command. This kind of resistance is frequently the only option available to the group with the lesser social power, such as a conquered people, slaves, women, or anyone not granted the full status of a person in a given social situation.

Various social theories developed during the Enlightenment and postmodern periods provide heuristic tools with which to analyze present situations and to search history for examples of social change in the light of such theories. In general, social theory envisions a dialectical relationship between individuals and social institutions, including religious ones. Social institutions are created and shaped by a collectivity of persons on the basis of their current values, habits, and power arrangements. Thus, people encode or embody in their practices and institutions both positive values and negative biases. These institutions then take on a life of their own, dictating to those who participate in them what their respective roles are and what their dreams and attitudes should be. This social conditioning results in unconscious bias that prevents both those who benefit from the existing social institutions and those who maintain it by playing their accepted roles from acknowledging either their responsibilities or their moral failures. Certain biases toward injustice, the dehumanization of certain people or categories of people, destructiveness toward nonhuman life forms may simply become tolerable and taken for granted. The first steps toward conscious social change, then, require four basic assumptions about the self and society:

> (1) that the institutions we inhabit predispose us to think and act in certain ways, (2) that some of these ways are unjust and oppressive, yet mainly unconscious, since they all seem "natural" to us, (3) that sometimes we do, nevertheless, become conscious of these injustices (but how?), and (4) that in the process of trying to understand what is practically required to change these structures, we are made conscious of some of our own (cultural) "blind spots." (R. Egan 1987, 2)

How, then, do individuals and groups see through and resist such forms of structurally based injustice? The answer to this question is neither easy nor self-evident. Bernard Lonergan expressed it this way: "No problem is at once more delicate and more profound, more practical and perhaps more pressing. How, indeed, is a mind to become conscious of its own bias when that bias springs from a communal flight from understanding and is supported by the whole texture of a civilization?" (1958, xv).

Historically, the kind of conversion wrought by the mystical element—experiences of the Spirit, releasement, and abundance—open a person's heart, making possible such insight. Religious renunciation of wealth, family, or power was born historically of such insight. Such were the eremetical movements of the fourth and fifth centuries and the radical poverty movements of the Middle Ages: refusals to participate in the injustice of existing power arrangements or economic systems. So, too, were various pacifist choices maintained by followers of the radical reformers. Individuals who make these breakthroughs often attract others who join with them in creating alternative communities. The members of these new communities engage in practices that help them maintain these breakthrough realizations, which eventually, if successful in the larger scheme of things, develop a countervailing trend in the wider culture. It is this oppositional influence that helps shift the consciousness of the dominant group in the direction of insight and toward the possibility of change of heart and behavior in relationship to a particular issue.

Some religious groups do not intentionally work for social change, but instead become separatist groups. They attempt to leave the "world" as it is socially constructed and simply live apart from it, hoping it will leave them alone. The rub is that they may simply re-create elsewhere what they tried to leave behind, conforming themselves to simply another version of authoritarianism or oppression or economic exploitation.

Robert Egan suggests there are three primary ways to help individuals become conscious of their communally created bias. The first "is symbolized by 'the stranger,' the point of view of someone who is other, who is from somewhere else, and who, in a related way, reveals something of 'God's radical otherness' when the stranger breaks into one's world" (1987, 13). For an experience of such "otherness" to facilitate insight, a person has to be willing to relate to the stranger in such a way that he or she can get some sense of what life is like seen and lived from a completely different social location. It can be quite a shock to cross over the threshold, empathically, into the world of "the other."

The second way is "symbolized by the 'philosopher' or the 'saint' or perhaps in the modern period by the 'intellectual' and the 'artist,' someone . . . who is, in some positive and profound way, 'detached,' either at the level of mind or at the level of heart" (R. Egan 1987, 13). Such people have, through dedication and fidelity to an arduous spiritual practice, freed their minds and hearts from numbness and routine, creating the possibility of fresh perception, deep attentiveness, and passionate clarity. Such people have made *themselves* "strangers" and developed their capacity for seeing through to the heart of things.

The third way is symbolized by negative experiences—misery, deprivation, suffering, protest, conflict. These experiences are sometimes called *contrast experiences* by theologians such as Edward Schillebeeckx and others. In a contrast experience, some people actually *experience* the absence of what ought to be. The contrast experience violates their expectation of how things should be on the basis of espoused commitments. In addition, "this premonition of otherness, of something *more,* of justice, or of joy, of fullness of life, is linked also with the experience of *hope*" (R. Egan 1987, 14). Without hope, there is no possibility of protest or wholehearted "looking forward" or any "real possibility of a better future" (Schillebeeckx 1968a, 136).

The process of moving from the breakthrough in consciousness of some individuals to changing social structures and changing those ways of picturing reality that maintain the legitimacy of the status quo is not a matter of simply pointing out some fundamental injustice such as slavery or genocide or sexism or ecological devastation. "This consciousness . . . is something that has to be *developed* socially. It is uncovered or constructed through tracts and novels, speeches and assemblies, family arguments and . . . thousands of small acts of personal integrity, reflection, judgment, risk, and commitment, that then, somehow, become the basis for public acts. It requires, in other words, that people change their minds" (R. Egan 1987, 15).

For this to happen, an education toward justice is required—together with various types of evocation imaginatively representing fresh possibilities in which others might want to participate, even though it will also mean some kind of relinquishment.

All of this is what might be meant by social transformation. It is impossible to show the varied history of these ideas about social change in the various religious traditions both represented and not represented in this volume. These essays make small attempts to mend some of the habits of thought and action that have tended to relegate social theory and change to a secularized and decidedly nonmystical public life. Yet they remain provisional.

Overview of the Volume

The catalyst for gathering these essays was a group of papers given at the meeting of the American Academy of Religion in 1995. Five papers were presented in the session of the Mysticism Group; they evoked lively responses from the participants and the presenters. When a Syracuse University Press editor expressed some interest in publishing these papers, the idea for this volume was born. The original five papers were interesting and suggestive, but in themselves did not encompass the breadth of the questions required by the topic even at the time. Invitations to additional contributors well known in their particular fields were issued in three separate rounds in order to treat more of the major questions related to the topic.

Even so, it is with regret that we present this volume without treatments of major non-Christian religious traditions and with no treatment of the topic within third-world liberation theology or of such important contemporary figures in Roman Catholic social thought and action as Thomas Merton or Dorothy Day. Nevertheless, a fine group of essays was collected in the end.

The volume is divided into three major sections. Part one offers some current theoretical perspectives on the main theme of the volume. Grace Jantzen's work on Marguerite Porete provides a careful political reading of Marguerite's texts that highlights the destabilizing power of mystical writing, perceived in its own day to be so transgressive as to merit Marguerite's execution. Jantzen not only explicates this historical exercise of religious and royal power that effectively silenced a woman who did not fit in the authorized scheme of things, but also contests the contemporary construction of religion that persists in maintaining such a potent warning to women who might dare to speak a truth politically and religiously at odds with established authorities.

Dorothee Sölle shares with us a new pattern for describing the mystic path, which for her begins in amazement and ends in ongoing resistance. She offers an example in the figure of abolitionist Harriet Beecher Stowe of this reconstructed pattern of mystical development that assumes the unity of mysticism and resistance. This unity includes the "letting go" of false needs and wishes that impede praise and prevent responses of compassion and work for justice in the face of all that is awry.

The middle section of the volume offers a rich presentation of individual Christian mystics or traditions of Christian mysticism, organized in chronological order. Paul Lachance opens the section with a creative treatment of Clare and Francis of Assisi. He restores Clare to her place of significant leadership in the Franciscan movement and highlights major aspects of the mystical teaching of both founders and the way their subjective experiences are reflected in their texts. He traces three major themes in their social practices. The first is poverty as both an inward and outward path related to the relinquishment of wealth and power and prestige. This joyful practice of poverty, second, leads to a peaceful life, including the capacity for reconciling disputes, and creates a universal brotherhood and sisterhood. Third, Lachance characterizes their social message and action as "exemplary"; that is, they communicated their vision and purpose through who they were and how they lived rather than through the intentional creation of a social program.

Amy Hollywood's treatment of Meister Eckhart's preaching "as a social practice" relates Eckhart to the Beguine women to whom he preached and by whom he was influenced. She focuses her analysis on Sermon 86, Eckhart's famous reflection on the story of Martha and Mary in which he works out his own distinctive teaching on the relationship of contemplation and action. It is through mystical transformation that the human being "becomes capable of truly just and efficacious activity in the world." Hollywood engages linguistic theory to show that preaching, a particular use and abuse of language, is itself a way of transforming social worlds through its catalytic effects, which engender new possibilities for further social transformation that can be enacted by its audiences.

Treatments of two Spanish mystics follow. Carole Slade develops a treatment of Teresa of Avila precisely as a social reformer rather than as a purely religious reformer. She shows that Teresa's mystical experience gave her a new identity that required her to act in the world, a practical knowledge of politics that enabled her to work effectively within the established system, and a profound understanding of the principles of eternal justice. Slade's treatment of Teresa's use of the Mary Magdalen and Martha of Bethany stories exemplifies the influence of "dangerous memories" carried in a narrative tradition of saints' legends. Slade gives an extensive treatment of Teresa's innovations in relationship to women of "mixed blood" whom she fully integrated into her community.

My own essay on Ignatius of Loyola and Ignatian "service mysticism" is also situated in the Golden Age of Spain. This essay describes a type of mystical path originating in divine initiative and focused on action for the sake of others. Ignatius inspired and gathered a community around himself based on the personal transformation of each man under his spiritual guidance. This Spirit-filled community became a social embodiment of the Catholic reforming spirit that multiplied itself many times over through its members' disciplined and passionate "apostolic" activity. In this essay, Ignatius is paired with a twentieth-century Jesuit, Pedro Arrupe, who demonstrated the vitality of the Ignatian charism in leading a revitalization movement within the Society of Jesus and within a reforming church.

Margaret Benefiel and Rebecca Phipps offer a lively account of two Quakers, John Woolman and Catherine Phillips, who exemplify major themes in Quaker practice. The authors highlight the prophetic and charismatic quality of these two figures. Of particular interest is the way in which the Quakers' practical mysticism gave rise to a clear form of social criticism, which they embodied in their way of living and in their reasoned tracts. Woolman's conscience led him to radical acts of solidarity with persons he recognized to be in situations of oppression. Phillips was an abolitionist, a prophet who denounced economic injustice and poverty, analyzing the economic causes for the poverty she witnessed and offering other women the possibility of an alternative social role by her own witness.

This historical section concludes with Joy Bostic's "womanist" treatment of nineteenth-century African American women and their own distinctive religious traditions. She begins with the situation of racism and its strategies of demonarchy, then develops her analysis of the narratives of Black women's spiritual autobiographies to show their strategies of resistance and their transformation into radical subjects as a result of their spiritual experience.

The final two essays are grouped around the general theme of emerging contemporary approaches to social transformation. Donald Rothberg's essay on socially engaged Buddhism treats a number of important theoretical issues and describes a contemporary movement in Buddhism intent on supporting social change. Rothberg gives a very clear account of the way the Western philosophical tradition actually created the split that opposed mysticism and the interest in social transformation. He then shows how the emphasis in early Buddhism was primarily on personal transformation through meditation in the context of the monastic *sangha* rather than on social change through types of social action in the public world. He follows this discussion with an account of the development of an explicitly socially engaged Buddhism in both the East and the West that claims that spiritual and social transformation are not truly separate. His account highlights the development of a meditative tradition through extension of the traditional teaching into a social ethics and practice.

The volume concludes with Roger Gottlieb's thoughtful exposition of the social and mystical dimensions of *deep ecology*. The first section of the essay reprises many of the definitions and characteristic features of mysticism discussed throughout the volume. Gottlieb recognizes the potential for self-transcendence in mysticism, its presence in most major religions, and its potential for deteriorating into self-deception or escapism. He identifies the paradox of both transcendence and social construction that runs all the way through mystical traditions. He documents the neglected theme of communion with nature in several religious traditions and offers a phenomenological account of deep ecology as a kind of mysticism. With regard to the particular interests of deep ecology, Gottlieb remains critical, social, and political in his assessment of its potential for contributing to social transformation. He evokes the promise that "political solidarity blossoms into a kind of selfless love" at its best: the struggle for justice can yield a joy in service and an expansive care that extends beyond the human to the whole family of life that surrounds us.

Of course, there is much more work to be done on this topic of mysticism and social transformation. The present social constructions of religion, politics, mysticism, and philosophy have not yet managed to envision mysticism and social transformation together as two sides of one coin or as interrelated aspects of one process. The essays in this volume attempt to vindicate the claim that this interrelationship is possible. Building on the theories, histories, memories, and desires available to us, they try to steady our vision and hope and to illuminate a "way."

But there is more work to do in bringing these very different conversations and forms of discourse together into a more unified and integrated understanding. It is, surely, a *sign* of hope that scholars want to do so and that this problematic is of such passionate interest to the contributors to this volume and, we hope, to you, its readers.

PART ONE

Theoretical Perspectives

1

Disrupting the Sacred

RELIGION AND GENDER IN THE CITY

GRACE M. JANTZEN

Is it time for feminists to rethink religion rather than either to dismiss it or to defend it? After all, religion affects the lives of millions of women, whether they are adherents or not. In recent continental thought, there has been considerable impetus to reconsider what religion is and to reevaluate its effects on contemporary life. A significant example is the work of Luce Irigaray, who writes, "It seems we are unable to eliminate or suppress the phenomenon of religion. It re-emerges in different forms, some of them perverse: sectarianism, theoretical or political dogmatism, religiosity, . . . Therefore, it is crucial that we rethink religion, and especially religious structures, categories, initiations, rules, and utopias, all of which have been masculine for centuries" (1993, 75). What does it mean to rethink religion from a feminist perspective, developing a trustworthy account by thinking from women's lives? With religion as the linchpin of the Name of the Father in the male symbolic, the development of a female imaginary must surely be one of the most urgent and central questions for a feminist philosopher of religion.

Not that such rethinking of religion from the standpoint of women's lives, developing a new imaginary domain, can proceed unproblematically. How could it, given that women's lives—our hopes, dreams, and desires—have been molded in part by the very religions we need to rethink? There is every reason, especially in a feminist effort to problematize religion, to bear in mind how deeply our consciousness, even as feminists, is saturated with the Name of the Father and how our language, our concepts, and even our long-

I am glad to acknowledge the financial support of the John Rylands Institute that has made this research possible; and I am grateful to Elaine Graham for her comments on an earlier draft.

This article was first published by Sheffield Academic Press in Kathleen O'Grady et al., eds. *Bodies, Lives and Voices* (1998). I am grateful for permission to reproduce it here.

ings are shaped by the master discourse. Each "reverse discourse" of resistance will no doubt call forth new exertions of recuperative power; and both the oppressive power and the possibilities of resistance not only surround us but are also internalized in the development of our subject positions. Nevertheless, each exertion of power becomes in turn a possible point of resistance, as Foucault reminds us, and the acknowledgment of difficulty is hardly a reason not to make the attempt at all.

Indeed, it is from Foucault that I propose to begin the effort to "rethink religion," even though he himself did not pay it systematic attention. What he did do was to call into question many of the assumed universals of Western thought, showing that these so-called universals were actually historical constructions that went through various transformations: they did not refer to some unchanging essence. Foucault focused on such alleged universals as madness, illness, delinquency, and sexuality, but might not religion be treated in the same way? As he described the task,

> In the realm of knowledge, everything presented to us as having universal validity, insofar as human nature or the categories that can be applied to the subject are concerned, has to be tested and analyzed: to refuse the universals of "madness," "delinquency," or "sexuality" [or "religion"?] does not mean that these notions refer to nothing at all, nor that they are only chimeras invented in the interests of a dubious cause. Yet the refusal entails more than the simple observation that their content varies with their time and circumstances; it entails wondering about the conditions that made it possible, according to the rules of truth-telling, to recognize subjects as mentally ill or to cause subjects to recognize the most essential part of themselves in the modality of their sexual desire [or to consider themselves as "religious"—or even as "nonreligious"?]. The first methodological rule for this sort of work is thus the following: to circumvent anthropological universals to the greatest extent possible, so as to interrogate them in their historical constitution. ("Florence" 1994, 317).

Proceeding on that suggestion, then, would mean that rather than look for some unchanging "essence of religion," some sort of universal, which is what religion must always be at its core, a feminist appropriation of Foucault's method would proceed by looking at how what has counted as religion has varied according to the historical context and in terms of who was in a powerful enough position to be doing the counting. Moreover, a feminist perspective brings to that investigation an awareness that positions of power are gendered positions, so that powerful men have been able to define and redefine religion for women and other subordinate groups. What David Halperin says of Foucault's approach to sexuality offers great possibilities for a feminist critical rethinking of religion:

> The value of Foucault's non-theory, of his critical intervention in the realm of theory, lies precisely in its strategic evasion of all those questions about *what sexuality is* and in its diversion of our attention, instead, to questions about *how sexuality functions* in both knowledge and society: what role sexuality has played as a concept and an experience, in the history of European discursive and institutional practices. The effect of Foucault's inquiries into that latter set of questions about sex is to reconceptualize sexuality as a strategic device, as the linchpin of a complex socio-politico-scientific apparatus. Foucault thereby converts sex into the basis for a radical critique of and political struggle against, innumerable aspects of modern disciplinary culture. (1995, 120)

If we reread that passage, substituting *religion* for *sexuality* or *sex,* the possibilities begin to emerge. Instead of seeking (or defining) an "essence" of religion, and instead of looking for that essence in "primitive" and rural contexts, and instead of focusing almost entirely on males (all of which have been the practice of social scientists and philosophers asking, "What is religion?"), we can investigate how religion functions and the roles it has played in concept and experience in European thought and practice, where it is highly urbanized and highly gendered. We can thus begin to see religion also as a "linchpin of a complex socio-politico-scientific apparatus" of "modern disciplinary culture." Moreover, I suggest that we can also see many modern scholars of religion doing their utmost to keep that linchpin of the male symbolic firmly in place.

In the course of this essay, I can do no more than raise some questions and suggest some directions. Rather than pursue the issues abstractly, I have chosen to focus on thinking from one particular woman's life, a woman who found herself at the cusp of change for religion in the city. That woman was Marguerite Porete, in Paris, in the early fourteenth century. We can consider her life and writing as an illustration of how religion functions (paralleled to how Foucault suggested sexuality functions) and discover the convoluted triangulation of religion, gender, and the city. I show that what counted as religion was significantly different for Marguerite than it was for the royal court of the time, even though that court was powerful enough to impose its view by force.

However, my interest is more than historical. I wish to suggest not only that religion functioned as a strategic device in fourteenth-century France, but that it continues to do so today. Rather than making a general case for that claim, I use the various modern interpretations of Marguerite to show how, in the guise of scholarly exposition, assumptions about women, religion, and the city continue to underwrite aspects of a modern disciplinary culture uncomfortably parallel to Philip's inquisitorial regime in the fourteenth century, a culture that a feminist rethinking of religion and the sacred would disrupt.

In the early fourteenth century, Paris under the jurisdiction of Philip IV (Philip the Fair) was one of the foremost cities of western Europe. In the central square of that city, on June 1, 1310, Marguerite Porete was burned alive at the stake as a heretic. In the documents recording her trial, she was judged to be a *"pseudo-mulier,"* literally a "pseudo-woman." Though the documents give no explicit account of what they meant by this phrase, calling her a "pseudo-woman" immediately signals how significant gender was in her trial.

Some years before her execution, Marguerite had written a book called *The Mirror of Simple Souls,* which had been admired by Godfrey of Fontaines, one of the foremost theologians of the University of Paris. But the bishop of Cambrai condemned the book and had it publicly burned in Valenciennes sometime before 1306. Marguerite was present. She refused to submit to the bishop's injunction never to speak of the book again. In 1308, Marguerite and her friend and defender Guiard de Cressonessart were arrested at the behest of William of Paris, confessor to the king and Dominican inquisitor. Guiard did not last out: he "confessed," probably under duress, at his second consultation. But Marguerite stood firm. William gathered together lawyers and theologians, giving them a series of passages from her book: it seems that no effort was made to read them in context. They judged her writing to be heretical, and she herself to be "contumacious and rebellious" (Babinsky 1993, 21) because she refused to repent, recant, or cooperate with the inquisitors, even though she was imprisoned for nearly two years in grim conditions. So she was burned (Babinsky 1993; Dronke 1984, 217; Lerner 1972, 68–78).

What was this heresy that warranted such a dreadful end? And what, by implication, was "true religion" in fourteenth-century Paris? Why did powerful men make such a fuss over one woman and her book? The latter question is all the more pertinent in view of what happened next. Some copies of Marguerite's book had escaped destruction and began to circulate, but without the author's name attached. The book was translated into Latin and Middle English, and was taken as a book of profound spiritual teaching: Meister Eckhart, for example, drew a great deal from it (Sells 1994; Turner 1995). Its importance continued to increase throughout the modern period. In England, for example, it went from strength to strength: Evelyn Underhill praised it, and the Downside Benedictines republished it in 1927, still anonymously. It was not until the middle of the twentieth century, however, that Romana

Guarnieri, an Italian historian, definitively identified the author as none other than the heretical "pseudo-woman," Marguerite Porete. If the book contained awful heresy, that heresy had not been obvious to centuries of devout and learned scholars. Moreover, it is easy to show that the articles for which Marguerite was condemned, when put back into the context of the book from which they were extracted, give little credence to the heretical interpretation placed on them by the inquisitors (Jantzen 1995, 262). For example, in one of the extracts for which she was condemned, Marguerite says that a person who is entirely one with God need no longer concern herself with good works or even virtues. The context, however, makes clear that anyone truly one with God will do only those things that the will of God prompts; consequently, virtue has become internalized and no longer requires continuous attention.

A careful look at her book and, indeed, at the whole manner of the inquisitorial procedure in relation to Marguerite, shows that condemning the articles as heretical can have been only a pretext. So what was it that generated so much outrage among the powerful men of Paris? Why was she expendable in their scheme? How was her death necessary for their agenda of religion in the city? How was religion functioning as a strategic device in the power struggles of the time, and how did Marguerite Porete and her book constitute so disrupting a reverse discourse on what religion was that it had to be ruthlessly suppressed?

The late thirteenth and early fourteenth century is a notable turning point in France for religion in the city, marking a transition to modernity whose effects are still with us. It was during this period that the French monarchy struggled with the papacy for preeminence, a landmark in the process of secularization. As a historian of the period puts it, "the reign of Philip the Fair marked the point when the balance of loyalty definitively swung toward the secular sovereign state. From the political point of view, this shift marks the transition from the medieval to the modern period" (Strayer 1980, xiii). The shift does not mean, however, that the people suddenly became less religious. On the contrary, what was happening was that by a series of skillful (not to say devious) moves, Philip and his ministers were getting his people to identify religion with him and his monarchy, to see him, rather than the pope, as the "Vicar of God" (Strayer 1980, 13, 295). Philip's act was crucial in the modern disruption of the sacred, moving its location from the holy city of Rome to secular modern cities: the drama he generated can be seen as a dress rehearsal for the power play by Henry VIII in England a century and a half later. Philip, like Henry, needed to be seen as the one who defended the faith, suppressed heretics, and furthered the interests of the nation, taking special care to build up the growing cities.

One of the means by which Philip hoped to further all these ends simultaneously was in his actions against the Templars. The Templars were a military order that had been founded in the early twelfth century in connection with the Crusades. They grew immensely powerful and wealthy. In the thirteenth century, they became bankers for the French monarchy, a position that became even stronger when other large-scale moneylenders, the Jews and the Lombards, were expelled from France. Philip decided to move against the Templars, confiscating their property, accusing them of heresy, and showing himself more ardent for the purity of the faith than the pope. He thereby expected at a stroke both to gain great wealth that he would use to further French interests and to demonstrate his religious superiority. The charges against the Templars were preposterous, but Philip ensured that sufficient torture was used so that many of them "confessed." In May 1310, fifty-four Templars were burned at the stake near Paris—only weeks before Marguerite Porete met the same fate. By 1312, the pope had been pressured sufficiently to persuade him to suppress the Order throughout Europe (Runciman 1954, 3: 429–38; McNamara 1973, 155–69; Strayer 1980, 285–96).

Now, what connection would the destruction of the Templars have with the condemnation of Marguerite Porete? That the two events were not coincidental becomes clearer when we note that William of Paris, the inquisitor in charge of Marguerite's trial, was also in charge of Philip's proceedings against the Templars. Moreover, the bishop of Cambrai, who burned Marguerite's book and who probably sent her to Paris to be tried, was the very one who called the Council of Vienne against the Templars in 1310 (Lerner 1972, 76). So the city becomes the obvious triangulation point of power, gender, and religion. But this connection still does not answer the question of why powerful men, when they clearly had plenty on their minds already, should have been so threatened and taken so much trouble over a book by a woman who was otherwise insignificant.

Or was she? Marguerite was a Beguine. Beguines were women who lived alone or in clusters joining together for worship, mutual support, and an intensive program of work to help those who were homeless, poor, and ill, the outcasts of society. They did not live in convents, and they did not take vows as cloistered nuns did. They could be widows or single women or women whose husbands were away—perhaps in the Crusades. They could join the group for a time and then leave without blame. Beguines were a phenomenon of the growth of towns and cities: when women grouped together in beguinages, it would be in a city or at its edge, and much of their relief work was directed toward people living in cities with little in the way of social services. Many northern cities—Antwerp, Brugge, Amsterdam, Cologne, Paris, and many others—had considerable numbers of Beguines.

Beguines were a multilayered threat to the powerful in society, especially to the ecclesiastical authorities. They were strong, independent women who were under the authority of neither husband nor priest, but rather banded together for mutual help. They developed writings and liturgies, subsequently heavily suppressed, in which they spoke of God as Lady Love and used striking female imagery such as gestating and giving birth to God (Hadewijch 1980, 345). As I demonstrate later, Marguerite herself bends gender out of its normal categories in writings. Also, the way of life and relief efforts of the Beguines were an implicit rebuke to those whose activities caused such poverty and homelessness in the first place. Like Philip, they were disrupters of the sacred, but in quite a different way. Where Philip thought to bring ecclesiastical power to the monarchy, Beguines asked who the victims were of the new social order and tried to relieve their suffering.

The authorities dealt with the threat posed by the Beguines in various ways. In some areas, Beguines were treated with contempt or even as heretics, a treatment given official sanction by the Council of Vienne, 1311–1312. In other places, they were allowed to continue, provided that they grouped themselves into enclosures and accepted the oversight of a (male) confessor (Jantzen 1995, 205–7). In France, however, a different tactic was used. Beguines were under royal patronage (perhaps as another snub to the papacy?); toward the end of the thirteenth century, there were approximately four hundred Beguines in Paris alone, many of them living in the great beguinage founded by Louis IX (Babinsky 1993, 13–17). Beguine houses could also be found in many other towns and cities of northern France. Part of the price of royal protection, however, was that Beguines were required to submit to strict rules of moderate enclosure. These rules did not stipulate that they could not go out at all, but their movements were strictly regulated and supervised on pain of dismissal. However, some Beguines refused such regulation as incompatible with what they felt called to do. Marguerite was one. No doubt this refusal made her simultaneously more vulnerable and more of a threat, not only to the political authorities but even to Beguine communities, who would be under pressure to disown her.

Moreover, although the charges of heresy for which she was convicted can easily be shown to be misinterpretations of passages wrenched from their contexts, there are good reasons why her text would generate the wrath of the powerful. In the first place, it was written in the vernacular, not in scholarly Latin, and thus made itself available to those she calls the "little ones of Holy Church" (Porete 1993, 81) or "simple souls" (94), common folk without much learning, rather than only to those living in religious communities. Apparently, Marguerite had a considerable following among such "simple souls," both male and female.

Moreover, some of her text takes the form of a dialogue between Reason and Love. Throughout her book, Reason is associated with "the masters of the natural senses" and "the masters of scripture" (1993, 87), the philosophers and theologians of the intellectual and ecclesiastical establishment (Sells 1994, 130). However, Reason is shown to be quite inadequate to the requirements of spiritual progress. Marguerite mocks Reason, personifying it as hysterical at the Soul's freedom in the love of God: "O God! O God! O God! Says Reason. What is this creature saying? She is now completely beside herself! But what will my children say? I do not know what to say to them, nor how to excuse this" (1993, 161). Eventually, to the great relief of Soul, Reason dies, and Love (personified as female) takes over its functions (163). It is not surprising that the self-constituted intellectual authorities would be displeased: few male intellectuals take kindly to a woman portraying reason as hysterical and themselves as best relieved of their positions.

The disruption of their symbolic would not be alleviated by Marguerite's use of gender in her text. Marguerite's longing for and relationship with her divine lover makes use of prevalent themes in what has come to be known as "erotic mysticism." In itself, this eroticism would hardly have caused surprise, but Marguerite refuses the conventional heterosexual model in which the soul is the passive female and the divine lover is the active male. Instead, she freely speaks of God in both male and female terms (Hollywood 1994, 173–74; Sells 1994, 134). Love, who is personified female, is (the voice of) God herself, though God is also named "the Farnear," who is a male character in Marguerite's spiritual drama. She writes, for example,

> And Divine Love tells me
> that she has entered within me,
> And so she can do
> whatever she wills,
> Such strength has she given me,
> From One Lover whom I possess in love,
> To whom I am betrothed,
> Who wills what He loves,
> And for this I will love Him. (201)

There is considerable fluidity here between "Divine Love" (female) and the "One Lover" (male), as also between who is possessor and who is possessed. The same occurs in many other passages, such as this one:

> Then to me came Love, filled with goodness . . .
> And she said to me:
> Beloved, what do you wish from Me?
> I contain all things, which were,

And are, and shall be,
I am filled by all things . . .
Say, beloved, what do you wish from me?
I am Love, filled with the goodness of all things. (215)

Marguerite, however, is entirely satisfied by this fullness of Love and asks for nothing, and that nothingness has suddenly revealed to her "Him and me; that is, He the most High . . . and there was born my good" (216). Is the divine male or female in this erotically charged encounter? The only possible answer is "both." The fluidity of gender and sexuality in Marguerite's writing is characteristic of numerous medieval women's religious writings (Jantzen 1995, 290); its virtual disappearance in modern religious writing bespeaks the severe disruption of the sacred Name of the Father with which such gender bending threatened ecclesiastical authorities. Was it partly because of this threat that Marguerite was characterized as a "pseudo-woman?"

When we read her book, it clearly contains a full-scale indictment of greed and of the injustices born of ruthless pursuit of wealth—which is precisely what the king was doing, with the full complicity of his bishops, first in relation to the Jews and Lombards, and then in the case of the Templars. Marguerite never names the king, nor does she speak directly of the Templars or indeed of any current happening. Nor does she dwell much on condemnation or any form of preaching *against* corruption or injustice. Her whole focus is on building up "simple souls," guiding them in the stages of spiritual growth they will need to go through if their wills are to be united to the will of God. For anyone thinking of her book in the context of her political situation, however, it is obvious that her account of spiritual growth severely disrupts the self-perception of the Parisian court, which was touting itself as the spiritual guardian of France and defender of the faith.

Very early in her book she lays down as a ground rule that anyone hoping to make spiritual progress must begin "with the commandments of the Holy Church," foremost of which is the divine command to love God "with all our heart, all our soul, and all our strength; and ourselves as we ought, and our neighbors as ourselves." This statement she then glosses as follows:

First, that we love Him [*sic*] with all our heart: that means that our thoughts should be always truly in Him. And with all our soul: that means that until our death we do not speak but the truth. And with all our strength: that is, that we accomplish all our works purely for Him. And ourselves as we ought: that means that in doing this we do not give attention to our gain but the perfect will of God. And our neighbours as ourselves: that is, that we neither do, nor think, nor speak towards our neighbours anything we would not wish they do toward us. (1993, 81)

And she follows this immediately with the Gospel story of the rich young man who had kept the law of God to all appearances, but who fell foul when he was told by Jesus to sell his possessions and give to the poor (82). Standard spiritual teaching? Of course. But in her political context, choosing this particular emphasis and this specific story out of all the biblical possibilities was hardly without implication. The cap fit rather too snugly for comfort. The fact that modern commentators rarely ever think of Marguerite in political terms has more to do with the modern assumption that religion, especially as practiced by women, is apolitical than it has to do with how things were in the city and nation of her own time. I shall return to this point.

Moreover, Marguerite made a distinction in her book between Holy Church the Little and Holy Church the Great. Holy Church the Great is the invisible ideal community of the truly spiritual; Holy Church the Little is the empirical church on earth. The latter, though it may appear strong, Marguerite says is actually weak, often corrupt, and dependent for its spiritual sustenance on the guidance and help of those who are part of the true, divine community. "For these Souls, says Love, are properly called Holy Church, for they sustain and feed and teach the whole Holy Church. And not merely they, says Love, but the whole Trinity within them" (122). Marguerite places no positive emphasis whatever on the structures of the empirical church: confession, penance, or even the Eucharist. All these structures are part of Holy Church the Little and are all too easily taken as substitutes for direct communion with God, thus becoming the trappings of religion rather than its substance. As Caroline Bynum has pointed out, such refusal of official religious activity bespeaks "a reflection in image of women's own experience of the irrelevance of structure" (1991, 49), a structure that defined religion in ways that would further the structure's own powerful and gendered ends. Marguerite is under no illusions that her distinction between Holy Church the Little and Holy Church the Great, with its implicit rebuke to the empirical church, will find favor with its authorities, even though she was by no means the first medieval writer to use such a distinction as a way of calling for reform. Indeed, she feared that even Beguines (presumably those who accepted royal patronage and enclosure) would not understand. She writes,

> O my Lover, what will beguines say
> and religious types
> When they hear the excellence

of your divine song?
Beguines say I err,
priests, clerics, and Preachers,
Augustinians, Carmelites.
And the Friars Minor,
Because I wrote about the being
of the one purified by Love.
I do not make Reason safe for them,
who makes them say this to me. (200)

Peter Dronke is convinced that it is this challenge to the empirical church that cost Marguerite her life (1984, 217–28).

It could, of course, be objected that where there is greed, corruption, and injustice, *any* Christian teaching will sound like rebuke, whether or not that was specifically intended, so even if Marguerite had nothing political in mind, she could be interpreted (either then or now) as though she did. To some extent, that objection must be granted, but there are traces in her text that make me doubt modern interpreters who by their silence on her political context seem to suppose that because she was heavenly minded, she was far above sordid social and political realities. For instance, in a chapter in which she is discussing the fact that some folk get so heavily preoccupied with "good works" that they lose sight of who those works are intended to benefit, there is an exchange between two of her speakers, personified as Love and Soul:

Such folk are happy, says Love, but they are lost in their works, on account of the sufficiency which they have in their being.

.   .   .

Such folk, says Love, are called kings, but they are in a country where everyone is one-eyed. But without fail, those who have two eyes consider them to be servants.

.   .   .

Soul: Servants they are truly, says this Soul, but they don't understand it. They are like the owl who thinks there is no more beautiful bird in the wood than young owls. So it is, says this Soul, with those who live in perpetual desire. (1993, 132)

The writings of medieval religious women are full of striking figures of speech, and at first glance these metaphors of one-eyed servants who think themselves kings and of owls with a ludicrous estimate of their own importance might seem to be no more than such figures. They *are* more, however. In the first place, in the literature of courtly love, being one-eyed was a common (if un-fortunate) trope used to characterize someone thought to be too ugly to be capable of true love (Babinsky 1993, 225n37). This metaphor is therefore not idiosyncratic on Marguerite's part, though she presses it into her own use. But that is not all. Those who study the religious writings of women seldom study politics, and vice versa: modernity has, as I have said, split them into separate disciplines with large "no trespassing" signs over each. Because we are flouting those signs, let us consider further the court of Philip the Fair. Philip surrounded himself with powerful advisors—too powerful, many people thought—among whom was one Pierre Flote, who was deeply involved in the struggle for the ascendancy of the monarchy over the papacy. He rose rapidly in influence and in 1298 became Keeper of the Seals (chancellor). Though he had the esteem of the king, he (like many other royal officials) was hated and resented by the people, who thought that although he was officially a servant, he put on kingly airs himself. So far there is nothing particularly remarkable about this. It becomes startling only when we learn that Pierre Flote was one-eyed!—a feature for which even the pope used to ridicule him (Strayer 1980, 52, 272, 416; Lerner 1972, 77). Could Marguerite's acid comment on one-eyed servants who think themselves kings really be politically innocent?

Even more follows. One of the tactics that Pierre Flote used in his efforts to discredit the papacy was to attack a bishop, Bernard Saisset, as an enemy of the king. Though in himself he was not of major political importance, Bernard was given to rather intemperate utterances. One day he overstepped the mark, saying that Philip was just like an owl, a handsome bird who stared ineffectually while others did the work. Philip never forgave him for that remark, and when a pawn was needed in the moves against the pope, Bernard was arrested (Strayer 1980, 262).

Of the commentators I have been able to consult, only one, Robert Lerner, so much as notices the parallels between Marguerite's metaphors and the realities of Philip's court, and even he dismisses those parallels in one sentence: "it is doubtful that Marguerite intended her words to have had a political connotation, but it is not impossible that someone at Philip's court took umbrage at them" (1972, 77). On what basis does he claim she had no such intention? He offers no argument whatever. As far as I can tell, he is just repeating the modern assumption that a woman who wrote a religious book must be politically uninvolved. Yet there are plenty of medieval counterexamples: witness Hildegard of Bingen rebuking Frederick Barbarossa or Catherine of Siena negotiating the return of the papacy from Avignon to Rome. Of course, I cannot prove Marguerite's intentions any more than Lerner can, but it seems to stretch credulity to think that it was sheer coincidence that she wrote about one-eyed servants who thought they were kings and about self-important owls just when the king's one-eyed minister was arresting a bishop who compared the king to a self-important but ineffectual owl.

Marguerite never recanted, never apologized for her book, never indicated any sense of inappropriateness that a woman should write as she did. Contrary to other medieval women who struggled with the conflict between their gender identity and the authority they claimed as religious writers, Marguerite wrote with confidence and stood by her writings when they were burned in front of her face at the command of a bishop. Indeed, she used her own sexuality and erotic longing as a way to meditate on love and her longing for the divine Lover. It was all too much, and eventually she followed her book to the flames. She was burned as a heretic, but also as a *"pseudo-mulier,"* a fake woman, who was not respectful and subservient as a "real woman" should be, but was uppity, "rebellious and contumacious," a woman for whom the personal—which was religious—was the political, a woman who disrupted the masculinist symbolic with her strategies of imagination.

◆　　　◆　　　◆

So what is religion in the Paris of Philip the Fair and Marguerite Porete? If we are looking for a definition in terms of essence, the answer is unlikely to be very instructive. But if, instead of asking what religion *is,* we divert out attention to how religion functioned and how it served as a strategic device in one of the contexts that marked a transition to modern urban disciplinary culture, then a new way of thinking about the triangulation of power, gender, and religion begins to open up. Obviously, religion could serve as a discourse of repression in the contested rhetoric between the papacy and the "most Christian king of France." Obviously, it could serve as the context of enforced uniformity, where those "others" who were perceived as threats—Jews, Templars, heretics, women—could be eliminated as polluters of the city (see Moore 1987).

The story of Marguerite Porete shows that this general overview is not all there is to be said. For her, as for other medieval religious women (and some men), religion functioned as an occasion for a reverse discourse, a discourse that offered guidance toward justice, integrity, and love. The way of life of Beguines—in particular, the life and writing of Marguerite—was a refusal of the religion modeled by the court of Philip and his ecclesiastical stooges in favor of a religion they saw as patterned after the poor man of Galilee. Of course, Philip could win: he could enclose them, silence them, burn their books, and even burn them. He could impose his vision of religion. Yet her book persisted, recognized as a work of great religious insight, and in the middle of the twentieth century, Marguerite was at last recognized as its author.

Now a new story begins, in which the question of what shall count as religion is again prominent and again reveals issues of power and gender. In spite of the fact that there is now scholarly unanimity that *The Mirror of Simple Souls,* for so long a spiritual classic, was indeed written by Marguerite Porete, the result has not been—as one would have hoped—a recognition that a woman had been unjustly condemned and executed in the name of true religion. Instead (with important exceptions such as Dronke [1984] and Sells [1994]), scholars have turned to the text and trial documents to justify her burning anew. Jean Leclercq, for example, repeats (in a book generally contemptuous of women) the inquisitorial condemnation of Marguerite (Leclercq et al. 1968). He simply quotes the extract in which she says that a soul who is at one with God need no longer be preoccupied with good works. Like the inquisitors, he pays no attention to context, and it is left to appear that her conviction is understandable or even justifiable. He is more willing to listen to the inquisitors than to Marguerite.

Now, my concern is not simply with a lapse of scholarship or even with its underlying misogyny. The question I want to highlight, rather, is: What formation of the concept of religion is being endorsed when an otherwise meticulous scholar is so willing to acquiesce in a woman's execution in the name of what he sees as true religion? How is such a conception of religion, reinforced by purported "historical evidence," serving a disciplinary function in modern society, and what alternatives could be generated?

Other scholars are equally ready to condemn Marguerite. Edmund Colledge, for instance, characterizes her as a "high priestess" of the heresy of the Free Spirit (1981, 8), and Ernest McDonnell speaks of her as a "heresiarch" (1969, 490), though without offering much evidence. Yet it has been persuasively argued that the so-called heresy of the Free Spirit never existed except as an invention of heresy hunters after the Council of Vienne, 1311–1312 (that is, *after* Marguerite's execution) and that the condemned passages culled from her book were taken over by the council as the basis of *Ad nostrum,* the papal bull that defined this "heresy." Robert Lerner goes so far as to call this document "the birth certificate of the heresy of the Free Spirit" (1972, 83), a heresy that was almost entirely an invention of its persecutors (Jantzen 1995, 258–64). Once again it is necessary to ask not only about lapses of scholarship but about how such "lapses" reflect a modern symbolic and play a part in modern configurations of power. As Elizabeth Petroff points out in her study of Marguerite, her public burning must have sent a shock wave of calculated warning to other women and men who might have been tempted to challenge the religion of power of Philip's court (1986, 282). When modern scholars repeat the disparagement and condemnation of Marguerite, what message is being sent today to those who would challenge current configurations of religion, gender, and power with a new imaginary?

Not only do modern interpreters echo inquisitorial judgments of heresy, they also ring the changes on the theme of Marguerite's character as "rebellious and contumacious." In his account of the book's contents, Edmund Colledge, for instance, says, "Despite all the Soul's protestations of her wretched nothingness, the entire book is characterized by a stubborn, willful determination to persist in its opinions, by a spiritual arrogance which could surely find no place in a truly 'Simple Soul' " (1968, 114). Similarly, Ernest McDonnell writes of her "obstinacy" and "audacity" in refusing to cooperate with the inquisitors (1969, 491). What are they asking for? Is the only reliable sign of a "truly simple soul" that she submit herself obediently to the will of the masters—and if she does not, is she showing her "spiritual arrogance?" This view strikes me as an irregular conjugation, which runs: I show firm resolve; you are stubborn; she is rebellious and contumacious. The theme is all too familiar to women unwilling to accept with due meekness the authoritative pronouncements on religion of those in power.

The speculations on Marguerite's sexual morality follow with tiresome predictability. McDonnell muses that Marguerite "may very well be one of the free beguines—and her wandering life points to it—who had no permanent residence, lived by begging, *were guilty of moral laxity,* hesitated to submit to ordained spiritual officials, and were receptive to heretical ideas. She was a sectarian, far removed in spirit and practice from the real beguine movement" (1969, 492, emphasis mine). "Real" Beguines are presumably the dutiful daughters who submitted to "ordained spiritual officials." However, had Marguerite in fact been "morally lax" as McDonnell here speculates (with not a scrap of evidence offered in support), it is inconceivable that the inquisitors would not have accused her of it: accusations or innuendos of sexual misdemeanors were a well-known "favorite charge" (Bryant 1984, 207). Yet they never leveled such a charge at her. Moreover, Romana Guarnieri, who identified Marguerite as the author of *The Mirror,* shows from the text that its author must have been well educated and conversant with both theology and literature of courtly love. This knowledge and Marguerite's use of feudal-aristocratic metaphors led Gwendolyn Bryant to comment, "This aura of refinement of the patrician mystic addressing herself to a clandestine feminine following contrasts sharply with the wandering promiscuity of McDonnell's beggar maiden" (1984, 207). Quite so. But what is the disciplinary function of the modern trope that a woman whose ideas of religion are at variance with established orthodoxy can be presumed to be morally lax?

Perhaps most disturbing of all is the assumption, already hinted at, that a woman concerned with religion could not possibly be politically involved. Religion in modernity is characterized as private, belonging to the inward, personal, subjective sphere and far removed from the sordid world of power and social policy formation. It is therefore seen as eminently suitable for women, a gentle and humanizing aspect of domesticity. We have seen how this assumption is read back into an interpretation of Marguerite, so that scholars simply cannot imagine that she might have been making astute political observations. My concern, however, is not only with reclaiming *her* dangerous memory, but also with pointing out how the privatization and feminization of religion serve a sharp disciplinary function in contemporary society. On the one hand, it is widely accepted that "religion and politics don't mix," that religion is a purely personal matter: such a view is wheeled out when religious groups or individuals protest against greed and corruption, nuclear weapons, environmental degradation, or other scandals of modernity. At the same time, the rhetoric of "family values," a national curriculum in which religious education must be "broadly Christian" irrespective of the faith traditions of the children in the school, and a racist immigration policy implicitly appeal to a concept of religion that bears a striking resemblance to the one that flourished in the court of Philip the Fair.

Whether we are personally religious or not, whether we deplore it or not, all women in contemporary Western cities are affected in many areas of our lives by the disciplinary functions of what counts as religion in modernity. Feminists' ignoring this fact does not make it go away: as Irigaray insists, it is high time that we "rethink religion" instead of pretending that it is a fading relic of the past. When feminists rethink religion in our contemporary, urban context, should we just accept that it has a universal essence and that Philip's patriarchal and oppressive religion is what religion must be, a linchpin of the male symbolic? Should we not rather suspect that the assumption that religion has a universal essence is *already* a power play on behalf of that symbolic? What happens if instead we think of how it functions, think from women's lives—women such as Marguerite, who offered a reverse discourse of religion, using it as a mode of resistance rather than as a force of oppression and thus developing an alternative religious imaginary? What is to count as religion? And who will be doing the counting?

2

To Be Amazed, To Let Go, To Resist

OUTLINE FOR A MYSTICAL JOURNEY TODAY

DOROTHEE SÖLLE

Almost all mystics have struggled to distinguish as clearly as possible among the stations of the "pathless way" so as to make the "ascent to Carmel" or the "ladder to perfection" comprehensible. Here, I want to try to name the stations of the mystical way for today's travelers. My attempt has been inspired by the works of Matthew Fox, one of the earliest to portray the mystical path of a creation spirituality in a new way, above all through his new reading of Meister Eckhart (1995, 20ff.).

Fox's reading of Eckhart differs from previous interpretations on two points. The first is his chosen point of departure. In the understanding of mysticism handed down by the Neoplatonists, Proclus and Plotinus, the first step was always purification. The beginnings of mystical piety were not goodness and the beauty of the creation, but the human fall from paradise. In this Augustinian-based context, there is no mention of creation—the cosmos and its original goodness.

But, does this reading not locate the mystical tradition too late in the framework of Christian salvation history? Must we not refer first to the blessing of the beginning: not to "original sin," but to "original blessing" (one of the fundamental questions often raised by Fox)? Is it not the mystical experience that points us toward creation and the good beginning?

The second difference with the Western tradition rests in the vision of unity with God, the *via unitiva*. Here, too, I agree with Fox. He determines this goal of the journey differently, in a more worldly form, as creativity and compassion. Creativity presupposes unity with the creator; it is not understood merely as a transformation of the individual soul, but of the world in

Translated from *Mystik und Widerstand* by permission of Augsburg Fortress Press.

which we can live together. To speak of this *via transformativa* means to situate the mystical project in the postindustrial context.

For me, mysticism and resistance are inextricably and deeply bound. Without ecojustice—God's special preference for the poor and for this planet—the love of God and the longing for unity appear to be atomistic illusions. The god who is acquired as a private possession may indeed serve the quest for experience, but nothing more.

Like those of the ancient journeys, the stations of a journey today intertwine. I name these stations: amazement, letting go, and resistance.

The first step on the mystical way is amazement. To cite one experience: When my eldest son was learning to read numbers, he stood still before a house on the street and would not move. As I called to him to get moving, he said, "Mama, look at this wonderful five hundred and thirty-seven!" I, of course, had never seen it before. He spoke the number slowly, tentatively, exploratively. He was profoundly happy. I think that every discovery of the world throws us into jubilation, a radical amazement that tears the veil of triviality. Nothing is taken for granted, least of all beauty. The first step of the mystical path is a *via positiva*, which occurs in the name of the rose. The jubilation of a five year old corresponds to the experience of "radical amazement," as Abraham Heschel calls this origin of our standing-in-relation (1955, 43ff.). Without this overwhelming amazement in the face of that encountered in nature and history, without the experienced beauty that can become visible even in a blue-and-white house number on a heavily traveled street, there is no mystical path that leads to unity. We need to be touched by the spirit of life. Without reinspiration, nothing new begins.

It is as if we would hear God's statement on the sixth day, "And see, it is all very good," anew and for the very first time! It is precisely at this point—in a world in which knowledge has enabled a cosmic consciousness and, at the same time, in which it is possible to undo creation—that the Christian religion must learn from its own origins in the Jewish tradition.

This means that we do not embark on the path of our journey as seekers, but as people who have been found; we are preceded always by the goodness we have already experienced. Even before (ontologically, not necessarily chronologically) the prayer of those who feel abandoned and banished, praise exists—without which they never would have known that they were banished. This facility for *astonishment* produces agreement with our being here, being today, being now. "To be here is marvelous," as Rilke said. Like every form of ecstasy, the ability to be amazed implies a forgetting of self, which enchants us out of the normal fixation on self and its corresponding triviality.

Amazement or astonishment is one way to praise God, even when God's name is not mentioned. In amazement, with or without our knowledge, we join the heavens that "tell the glory of God" (Psalm 19:1). "We begin to be happy when we understand that life without amazement is not worth living" (Heschel 1955, 43ff.). This complete understanding of the wonder of being is independent of whether we express the origins of creation personally—as in the religion of Abraham—or nonpersonally. Radical amazement does not die with better, more explanatory, scholarly knowledge. On the contrary, it grows precisely in the best scholarly minds, which are often drawn to mysticism.

Can amazement, the radical astonishment of a child, be relearned? Whatever the often misused word *meditation* means, it contains a pause, a lingering for which individuals or communities deliberately take a different time and usually choose a different place. Listening, lingering, becoming still, observing, and praying are to make room for the miracle. "Hear this, O Job; stop and consider the wondrous works of God" (Job 37:14). The unknown name of the mystical rose reminds us of our own amazed happiness.

The practice of amazement is also a beginning of leaving oneself, of a different freedom from one's own fears. In amazement, we abandon triviality and embark on the second path of the mystical journey—that of letting go. If "praising God" is the first impulse of the journey, "missing God" is another unavoidable station. The deeper the amazed happiness (the wonder of it!), the darker the night of the soul, the *via negativa*. Tradition—which usually begins with this path to purification and always leads to new ways of asceticism, renunciation, and more modest needs—also teaches us to measure how distant we are from a true life in God.

The process of learning to let go begins with simple questions: What do I perceive? What do I avoid? What moves me? What do I choose? As Henry Suso says, we need a bit of "dis-education," or freedom, before we can be educated in Christ or transformed. In a world dominated by the media, this dis-education has an entirely different status than it would in the rural or cloistered world of the Middle Ages, which was characterized by far fewer distractions. For us, in a historical period marked by a previously unknown abundance of goods and the artificial production of new needs, this station of the journey plays a different role than it does in cultures of poverty. We usually connect the rituals of purification and fasting to those puritanically required renunciations that were necessary for the establishment of an industrial work ethic. In the postindustrial consumerist world, this ethic functions less and less; it is not work that demands *purgatio,* but the growing dependence on consumerism. Our alienation from ourselves is not rooted in our working day, but rather in the addictive and compulsive mechanisms of consuming.

The more we can open ourselves to relinquishing false wishes and needs, and give room to amazement in our daily lives, the more we approach that which the ancient mystics called "seclusion," a vibrant departure from the habits and things taken for granted in our culture. Precisely because mysticism begins with amazement and not with banishment, our outrage over destruction is just as radical. Our relation to the fundamental realities of possession, violence, and ego is altered. In this "refinement," as Thomas Müntzer (1967, 24) called it, the way becomes ever narrower; companions and friends separate, and the original amazement is dimmed. If the rose is the symbol of the first mystical path, the dark night is that of the second.

To miss God is one form of what the tradition has also termed "to suffer God." Becoming empty means not only to rid ourselves of superficial ballast, but also to enter isolation. Certain forms of withdrawal, the renewed relationship to nature, and the original amazement become increasingly difficult in view of the annihilation of nature. Presumably, a mystical spirituality of creation will fall ever more deeply into the dark night of being left at the mercy of the powers and violence that dominate us, for it is not just the poor man from Nazareth who is being tortured to death on the cross, but our Mother Earth herself.

The horizon of the ecological catastrophe is the background for the way of a mystical journey today. To praise God and to miss God as nothing else leads to a living in God, which the tradition has called the *via unitiva*. Becoming one with that which the creation intended has the form of cocreation; to live in God means to participate in the ongoing creation. The third station leads to a healing that is, at the same time, a resistance. In our situation, the two belong together. "To heal" means that human beings live cocreatively in compassion and justice. Insofar as they become healed, they experience the ability to heal. Just as the apostles experienced Jesus as the "healed healer," every way toward unity is ongoing and radiant. Oneness is not individual fulfillment; it goes beyond that in the alteration of a reality oriented toward death. It participates and is realized in forms of resistance. Perhaps the most

Table 2.1. Diagram of Mystical Journey Today

AMAZEMENT	LETTING GO	HEALING/RESISTANCE
via positiva	*via negativa*	*via transformativa*
radical amazement	seclusion	changing the world
happiness	letting go of possessions, violence and the ego	compassion and justice
the rose	the dark night	the rainbow
praising God	missing God	living in God

powerful symbol of this mystical unity is the rainbow, a sign of the creation that does not perish but lives on in sowing and reaping, day and night, summer and winter, birth and death.

The connection between radical amazement and changing the world, between "*contemplation* and *lutte*," as the brothers of Taizé live it, is discernible in many places. I illustrate it with a piece of simple natural mysticism as experienced by one nineteenth-century woman:

A Morning Song

Still, still with Thee . . .
when purple morning breaketh,
when the bird waketh,
and the shadows flee;
Fairer than morning,
lovelier than daylight
dawns the sweet consciousness,
I am with Thee.

This morning song from the Presbyterian Hymnal is a simple expression of pious nature mysticism.[1] Its author, Harriet Beecher Stowe (1811–96), wrote magazine stories that were considered sentimental and the renowned novel *Uncle Tom's Cabin* in 1851. Stowe initially wrote it as a series for a widely read magazine, *National Era,* the mouthpiece for people opposed to slavery. Her novel was received enthusiastically far beyond abolitionist circles. It became a cult book of resistance—as can be seen by the statement attributed to Abraham Lincoln, "So you're the little woman who wrote the book that made this great war" (Knowles 1999, 469). It is astonishing how highly Stowe's European contemporaries esteemed the literary and moral qualities of a book that generally is viewed today as too shrill and sentimental. In the nineteenth century, it was characterized as "the most valuable American contribution to English literature"; Tolstoy equated it with Dickens's *A Tale of Two Cities,* and Heine even compared it to the Bible!

The mystical morning song does not speak of the realities of slave trading, humiliation, and torture; it lives entirely out of the bourgeois piety of white women who sing of the Thou-God experienced in nature. God and the soul is the theme; the soul is "alone" with its God. The dawn mirrors its unity,

---

1. The original title of this hymn is "God the Father Still, Still, Still, with You God" (Presbyterian Hymnal, no. 107).

which—in an entirely traditional manner—is "fairer" and "lovelier" than the manifestations of nature.

> Alone with Thee,
> amidst the mystic shadows,
> The solemn hush of nature newly born.
> Alone with Thee,
> in breathless adoration.
> In the calm dew
> and freshness of the morn.

> Still, still with Thee!
> As to each newborn morning
> A fresh and solemn
> splendor still is given.
> So does the blessed
> consciousness awaking
> Breathe each day nearness
> unto thee and heaven.

In this song, which can be understood best when heard to the melody composed by Felix Mendelssohn-Bartholdy, the shadows are "mystic," adoration is "breathless," and the awareness of unity with God is "sweet," which was one of the favorite words of the female mystics of the Middle Ages. The word *still* plays a central role; it is connected to the ability to let go on the mystical way. To become still means to become free of worries and desires; it is more than the mere absence of noise. The New Testament relates how Jesus stands in the storm and bids the wind to be still, so that a great *Galene,* the Greek word for stillness of the seas, sets in (Mark 8:26). "You are the quiet, the mild peace," in Friedrich Rückert's words, set to music by Schubert, "the longing for you and what it stills" (Rückert n.d.). This experienced peace always signifies two things in the mystical tradition: God's invitation to enter into the stillness and at the same time the transferral of life, the giving of oneself to God.

> So shall it be
> at last in that bright morning
> when the soul waketh
> and life's shadows flee.
> Oh, in that hour
> fairer than daylight dawning
> Shall rise the glorious thought
> I am with Thee.

In the tradition, early morning is the time to regard one's own death and to understand it, in contemplation, as an awakening to true life. Earthly life is seen as night and shadow ("life's shadows"), which disappear in the "eternal dawn" (Eichendorff n.d., 1: 262). The mysticism of nature and its stillness merge with the mysticism of the hour of death.

Harriet Beecher Stowe was a woman who embodied the unity of what mysticism and resistance can mean. Borne by the abolitionist civil rights movement, she was also borne by this inner stillness, which filled her hero Uncle Tom with a humility that is difficult to bear and is criticized sharply today for good political reasons. Because he refuses to be used as a whip, he is beaten to death. Yet, his character does not diminish Stowe's historic achievement in having shaped the resistance against the criminal system of slavery, particularly because in the book itself she portrays another option for Black people: before being sold in the South, the household slave Eliza flees with her son to freedom.

For me, the word *sentimental,* used in James Baldwin's unforgettably worded debate about Black identity, has become increasingly problematic. If it means to be incapable of feeling and therefore to wallow in self-indulgent little emotions, then such sentimentality could have been found among the Nazi SS leaders who loved their Beethoven, but not in the white woman from New England who lived in outrage about state-permitted slavery precisely because she was "with Thee." The mystical becoming still, often understood as the traditional woman's role of a religious inner world, belongs together with the clear loud speech of the "No" of resistance.

PART TWO

Christian Mystics and
Social Transformation

3

Mysticism and Social Transformation According to the Franciscan Way

PAUL LACHANCE, O.F.M.

With the appearance of Francis of Assisi, as Dante put it, "a light had shone unto the world." For many, the Poverello is the most significant figure in the Christian tradition since Jesus himself. But surprisingly little scholarly effort has been directed toward presenting Francis as a mystic, and not much has been done to provide a fresh reading of the political impact of his message. At the same time, contemporary Franciscan research, prodded in part by current women's studies, is bringing into greater focus the contribution of Clare of Assisi. Not only does she provide the feminine aspect of the birth of the Franciscan movement, but she is also a leader in her own right, far less dependent on Francis than she has been depicted until now. Comprehensive studies that weld together the mystical and political dimensions of the Franciscan way are rare; even more rare are any that attempt to weave the spirituality of Francis and Clare together, noting the similarities and the differences in the paths of transformation they traced for their followers.

Francis of Assisi Revisited

"Why does all the world seem to be running after you, and everyone seems to want to see you and hear you and obey you? You are not a handsome man. You do not have great learning or wisdom. You are not a nobleman. So why is all the world running after you?" *(The Fioretti,* 10).[1] This question put to

1. The literature on Francis and Clare is enormous. In this essay I restrict myself to some of the references that are immediately useful to the topic. For the early sources on the life of Francis, I am using the following works found in Habig 1973: *The First Life of St. Francis* by Thomas of Celano; *The Second Life of St. Francis* by Thomas of Celano; *The Fioretti (The Little Flowers of St. Francis); Witness of the "Anonymous of Perugia"; Legend of the Three Companions; Legend of Peru-*

Francis by Brother Masseo, an early companion, has haunted and continues to haunt biographical efforts to capture the true image of the Poverello. Current research that attempts to determine the historical value and significance of the early Franciscan hagiographical sources—the thorny "Franciscan question"—has increasingly demonstrated not only the importance of situating Francis in the context of his times, but also how each of the subsequent *legenda* about him was a reconstruction marked by the debates among his followers about the real meaning of his message, the *intentio regulae.*

At the 1993 meeting of the International Society of Franciscan Studies, the eminent medievalist André Vauchez, in the concluding roundtable discussion, declared that the historical research of the past thirty years on the early sources had reached the end of a "process of deconstruction" and that aside from the need for more reliable critical editions and philological analysis of these sources, what was called for was a renewed interest in the religious dimension of the Poverello (Menestō 1984, 278). In the same roundtable discussion, Claudio Leonardi, another noted medievalist, reiterated that "the mystical element" would be "the key for the future image of the saint" (289).

The light of the Poverello not only illumined the medieval Umbrian countryside, but also has continued to shine, refracted differently to be sure, down through the centuries and in our own time. More so than other outstanding Christian saints, Francis makes his presence felt not only in the fields of history and spirituality, but also throughout the gamut of the arts: literature, music, the plastic arts, the cinema—as attested, for instance, by the success of Zeffereli's postcard image of the saint in the film *Brother Sun and Sister Moon,* and by the less well-known but far more profound portrayal in the film by Liliana Cavani entitled *Francesco.* A number of images have captured the popular imagination. The most familiar one, which adorns many a garden, is that of Francis as lover of animals and creation, and, more importantly, as patron saint of efforts to save the environment. In the sixties, many referred to him as the hippie saint of the counterculture. For liberation theologians, such as Leonardo Boff (1982), the Poverello incarnates the ideal of the Catholic Church's call for a preferential option for the poor.[2] For those involved in inter-

---

gia. For the writings of Francis, I am using Armstrong and Brady 1982: *The Admonitions; The Parchment to Brother Leo; Exhortation to the Praise of God; Canticle of Brother Sun; Second Version of Letter to the Faithful; Earlier Rule;* and *Later Rule.* (Citations to *Legend of the Three Companions, Earlier Rule,* and *Later Rule* refer to chapter and section numbers rather than page numbers.) For the latest effort toward a critical edition of all the sources for the lives of Francis and Clare, see Menestō et al. 1995. I would like to thank Kathryn Krug for reading my manuscript and providing indispensable assistance.

religious dialogue, he is looked upon as an important figure who bridges the East and the West, as witnessed by the gathering of the major religious leaders of all faiths in Assisi in 1986. Of the recent biographies—and new ones appear yearly—the most significant is Raoul Manselli's *St. Francis of Assisi* (1988). Making use of the best available historical scholarship, the Italian scholar bases his portrait primarily on Francis's own writings, particularly his *Testament,* and on the available documentation written by those closest to him, especially that compiled as the *Legend of the Three Companions.* Manselli also bases his portrait on his own vast knowledge of the religious, political, and social reality of Francis's time. For Manselli, Francis's encounter with the leper, where what was initially "bitter" was transformed into "sweetness," as related in his *Testament,* provided the turning point of his conversion. Thereafter, following in the footsteps of Christ, Francis was to change social class and share the condition of those at the bottom of society. Of more recent vintage and in a different genre, but now an international best-seller, is the poetic rendition by Christian Bobin entitled *Le Très-bas* (The Lowliest) (1997).[3]

Laudable as these efforts are, they do not present Francis primarily as a mystic, as someone whose life's passion was a search for and experience of the Absolute. Ewert Cousins is one of the few important scholars who has tried to capture Francis's mystical experience, but he does so through the prism of the writings of Bonaventure rather than through the prism of the written legacy of Francis, and he qualifies Francis as a "nature mystic" (1983). Attractive as this classification may be for contemporary concerns, it remains an important but subsidiary category. Two other efforts in this direction, Edward Armstrong's *St. Francis: Nature Mystic* (1973) and Roger Sorell's more insightful *St. Francis of Assisi and Nature* (1988) also fall short because they fail to situate the nature aspect within the larger scope of the Poverello's spirituality.[4]

Clare of Assisi Revisited

I have already mentioned the renewed attention being given to Clare. Contemporary Franciscan research is realizing that the power and contagion of

2. Boff's presentation is fresh and thought provoking, but suffers the constraint of preconceived theological schema. For the social and economic implications of the early Franciscan movement, see Flood 1989.

3. The title is mistranslated in English as *The Secret of Francis of Assisi.* In the same vein and a classic translated in all major languages is Leclercq 1961.

4. See Bernard McGinn's (1998a) masterful synthesis of early Franciscan mysticism as part of the third volume, *The Flowering of Mysticism,* of his monumental history of Western Christian mysticism. For an introductory essay on Francis's mysticism, see Schmucki 1989. In German, there are some helpful pages on the mysticism of Francis in Ruh 1993, 2: 380–98.

the Franciscan springtime cannot be understood without taking into account the leadership that Clare of Assisi exercised in it. The literature on Clare still pales in comparison to that devoted to Francis. Nonetheless, significant new studies are available; many of them are the result of efforts to honor the eight hundredth anniversary (1993–94) of her birth, which succeeded in bringing into sharper focus her role in the birth of the Franciscan movement.

The findings of this recent research challenge a prevailing hagiographical image of Clare as a colorless subservient woman, bereft of originality and identity, and walking—if not disappearing—in Francis's shadow, as "his little plant."[5] What emerges, rather, is a woman endowed with a powerful spiritual personality, courageous and tenacious in pursuit of her goal to follow the Christ who was poor and crucified. Clare was the first woman to write a rule for women (at a time when the Fourth Lateran Council had forbidden the writing of new rules by anyone). The so-called privilege of poverty, which she finally obtained, allowed a female community the unheard-of license to live without property—"the privilege to live without privileges," as Marco Bartoli has put it (1993, 73). As abbess, Clare struggled throughout a span of some twenty-eight years—while suffering continually from unspecified ailments—for the approval of her ideal. She fought off first the repeated attempts by her friend Cardinal Hugolino (who later became Pope Gregory IX) and then the efforts of Pope Innocent IV to impose a more mitigated form of life. Clare received approval for her rule only on her deathbed; we are told she wept and kissed the document when it reached her with Innocent IV's seal of approbation.

Perhaps equally striking as a witness to Clare's boldness and tenacity is the advice found in her *Second Letter to Agnes of Prague*. When Agnes's request to Pope Gregory IX to establish a radical way of life similar to Clare's had been refused, Clare expressly encouraged her epistolary friend not to budge from her resolve: "If anyone tells you something else or suggests something that would hinder your perfection or seem contrary to your divine vocation, even though you must respect him, do not follow his counsel" (41).[6] The counselor in question is the pope himself, Gregory IX!

Clare, then, exercised a powerful leadership in transmitting and assuring

---

5. As of this writing, only a few of the proceedings from the scholarly gatherings around the world honoring Clare's centenary have been published. The two most important published congresses are *Sainte Claire d'Assise et sa postérité* (1984) and *Chiara di Assisi* (1993). Recent literature on Clare in English includes three new studies: Bartoli (1992, 1993), Carney (1993), and Peterson (1993, 1995).

6. The English translations of Clare's writings are from R. Armstrong 1993. In this essay, I use the following works: *Letters to Agnes* (all four); *The Process of Canonization; Rule; The Legend of Saint Clare.* (Citations to *The Process of Canonization* and the *Rule* refer to chapter and section numbers rather than page numbers).

the continuity of the radical form of life that she had created in close partnership with Francis, but also in ways quite independent of him. There is a great deal more evidence of her courage and determination.

The first mention of Clare in the early Franciscan sources occurs in Thomas of Celano's *First Life of Francis*. In it, she is presented as a saint and, among other standard hagiographical virtues, as a "woman burning with love for God." It should be noted that when Celano wrote his biography, Clare was thirty-six years old and still alive. Likewise to be noted is that the subsequent early hagiographical literature on Francis, including Celano's *Second Life*, mentions Clare only on very rare occasions and always in terms that extol Francis's role rather than hers. We need to ask ourselves why Clare disappears.

To answer this question, we must begin by examining Clare's relationship with Francis. There is no doubt that the two shared a deep and amply documented bond of affection, a *"dilectio"* as Pierre Brunette concisely refers to it (1994, 39), and that Clare, at least initially, was dependent on Francis for inspiration. Perhaps there is no greater testimony of their deep intimacy than the dream reported at Clare's process for canonization, a dream censored by most biographies of Clare until recently. This process took place on November 24, 1253, two months after Clare's death. According to the testimony of Sister Filippa, a member of the community of the Poor Ladies, as they were called, Clare had recounted to some of the sisters the following dream-vision:

> It seemed to her that she brought a bowl of hot water to Saint Francis along with a towel to dry his hands. She was climbing a very high stairway, but was going very quickly, almost as though she were going on level ground. When she reached Saint Francis, the saint bared his breast and said to the Lady Clare: "Come, take and drink." After she had suckled from it, the saint admonished her to imbibe once again. She did so, what she had tasted was so sweet and delightful that she could in no way describe it. After she had imbibed, that nipple, or opening of the breast from which the milk came, remained between the lips of blessed Clare. She took into her hands what remained in her mouth; it seemed to her that it was gold, a gold so clear and bright that everything was seen in it as in a mirror. *(Process of Canonization,* 153).[7]

To interpret this dream would take us off on a tangent, but it does indicate very clearly the symbiotic bond that united Clare to Francis. The picture-perfect image of their relationship, as it has been generally portrayed,

7. For a "literal" interpretation of this dream, see Bartoli 1992.

however, needs to be complemented by one that indicates some of the tensions between the two and that demarcates Clare's autonomy.

It is not without significance that in his writings Francis never refers to Clare by name, but rather as his "Christian sister," and he refers to Clare's community as the "Poor Ladies," whereas Clare preferred the term "Poor Sisters," which she demonstrates more than sixty times. Of further significance is the fact that during the crucial formative years in which Clare and her sisters were establishing their new way of life (1215–20), Francis rarely intervened and, away on long and repeated missionary journeys, was even notably absent from the scene. It was probably during Francis's absence that Clare obtained her first (and short-lived) approval for the privilege of poverty. In other words, Clare and her sisters could not rely on the presence of their spiritual father; rather, they were on their own in taking responsibility and fighting for their destiny.

In the same vein, the available sources indicate that, as time went on, Francis's visits to San Damiano, where he had found an abode for Clare and her sisters, were less and less frequent. On one occasion, at Clare's insistence, he did make an appearance to preach. In lieu of a sermon, Francis poured ashes over his head and recited the *Miserere (Second Life,* 207). Could it be, among other reasons, that he did so because he feared the power of Clare's leadership, her capacity to bring Rome to its knees? Or was Francis's action an expression of his own uneasiness over the closeness of his relationship with her (Brunette 1995, 99)?

After Francis's death, there is more evidence that enhances Clare's stature and her leadership, for she outlived him by more than thirty years. At one point, Pope Gregory IX decided to forbid the friars access, without his express permission, to any Poor Clare monasteries, including San Damiano. Clare's response to this interdict was firm and immediate: she and her sisters went on a hunger strike. "Since he [the pope] is depriving us of those who provide food for our souls, we in turn have no need of food for our bodies." When the pope heard of her protest, he rescinded the ban *(The Legend of St. Clare,* 37). Also revelatory of Clare's political acumen is the fact that in her *Rule* and *Testament* (the basic documents that formulate and argue for her ideal), Francis's name appears thirty-seven times, but in her four letters that summarize her spiritual teachings, it appears only once and in passing. It must be remembered that when she wrote these documents, Francis was already a canonized saint. How could the pope or any ecclesiastical authority refuse to authorize a way of life that had the stamp of approval of a saint? It also must be remembered that at the same time that Clare was demonstrating how adamant she was about living a life of radical poverty, the friars were obtaining dispensation after dispensation to live a more mitigated form of life than the ideal proposed by Francis.

Recent research, then, not only makes clear the solidarity that existed between Clare and Francis in the foundation of the same form of life, but also greatly enhances our appreciation of Clare's role at the cradle of the Franciscan movement. We can even say that we are beginning to understand Francis from Clare's point of view and to understand Clare as a pillar of the Franciscan resistance, after Francis's death, even as mother of the Spirituals, the dissident wing of the early Franciscan movement. But just as is the case in studies of Francis, current studies on Clare focus, for the most part, on her historical and social matrix rather than on her role as a mystic.

Francis and Clare as Mystics

One preliminary difficulty in approaching Francis and Clare as mystics—for that matter in approaching any mystic—is defining exactly what one means by the term *mysticism*. Without entering into the ongoing debate over the issue,[8] for the present purposes I intend to subscribe to Bernard McGinn's heuristic definition: "the mystical element in Christianity is that part of its belief and practices that concerns the preparation for, the consciousness of, and the reaction to what can be described as the immediate and direct presence of God" (1991, xvii).

Within McGinn's broad and flexible definition, in what sense can Francis and Clare be considered mystics? The response is more complex than it may seem. It is indisputable that Francis was a mystic; he was stamped with the seal of the stigmata and was a fountainhead not only for the medieval but also for the entire subsequent history of Christian mysticism. Until recently, however, the picture of the Poverello's experience of God has been largely drawn from the hagiographical legends that grew up around him, rather than from his own writings, which have been surprisingly neglected. What emerges from these writings by Francis himself (aided by secretaries) is an image of Francis with a complexion quite different from the one traditionally portrayed.

Given the complexity of the material, I cannot hope to provide within a brief essay a complete and fully documented synthesis of Francis's or of Clare's discovery and penetration of God's mystery based on their writings. What follows—an attempt to obtain a more faithful picture of Francis (and of Clare, later) as mystic—focuses mainly on the primary sources and only minimally on subsequent hagiographical literature. The authentic writings of Francis are

---

8. For the state of the question on mystical theory, see McGinn 1991, 265–343.

more numerous than one would suspect: two versions of the rule spelling out the specifics of the Gospel path he and his brothers had elaborated; a rule for life in the hermitages; twenty-eight admonitions (mostly brief, pithy instructions reminiscent of the style of the desert fathers); nine letters; the *Testament;* some fourteen prayers of different types including his most memorable text, the *Praise of Creatures* or the *Canticle of Brother Sun.* It is to these writings that one must turn for a more direct access to Francis's God-centered personality, "the man made prayer" *(Second Life,* 95).

This written legacy notwithstanding (as with everything else about the saint), it is not easy to understand Francis's experience of the holy. He himself never spoke directly or subjectively of his life with God. In *Admonition* 21, he even warned against such disclosure: "Woe to that religious who does not keep in his heart the good things the Lord reveals to him" (Armstrong 1982, 34). Nor did he teach, strictly speaking, a mystical path, such as an exposition on the stages of growth or methods of prayer so common among monastic and mostly later Christian mystics. Furthermore, the vocabulary used by the spiritual writers of his time (such as *extasis, gustus, mentis excessus, mysticus, raptus, speculatio*) is absent from his writings—except for *contemplatio* (which he uses once, in *Admonition* 1). In this way, as in so many others, his piety and lifestyle are more "archaic" (Matura 1985, 64), reaching back beyond the great religious orders of his time to the age of the fathers and mothers of the Egyptian desert and the tradition of Eastern Orthodoxy, for whom autobiographical revelations are totally foreign. Thaddée Matura, in his important study on the theological vision in the writings of Francis, says the following about Francis's place in the history of Christian spirituality: "Although Francis is rightly regarded as one of the greatest of the Saints, he is never thought of as a mystic or theologian. But, as the Fathers of the Church understood the terms, a *mystic* is someone who discovers and penetrates into the mystery of God and His works, while a *theologian* discerns and contemplates the depths of visible and invisible reality. In the patristic sense, then, Francis was both a mystic and a theologian" (1997, 31).

Again, the gnawing question arises: Who is the real Francis? Recent biographical efforts to understand the Poverello usually refer to his *Testament,* in particular to the account of his conversion flowing from the encounter with the leper, as representative of what is central to his spirituality (e.g., Manselli 1988; Miccoli 1989). This document is certainly important, but following the lead set by Matura's study (1997, 33–50), I submit that two other texts from Francis's writings—namely, chapter 23 of the *Earlier Rule* and the *Second Letter to the Faithful*—are more representative of Francis's basic impulse and vision.

The *Earlier Rule,* the *Regula non bullata,* has been called the charter or the basic document (Flood 1989, 8) of the Franciscan movement, and chapter 23 of this rule has been referred to as its "creed" (Matura 1997, 34–40)—a lyrical finale to the way of life that Francis proposed to his fraternity. Pure praise and thanksgiving, its style is close to the anaphoras of Eastern Orthodoxy, such as the one attributed to St. Basil. Too lengthy to quote in its entirety, it consists, first, of a lengthy prayer addressed to the Trinity, "the all-powerful, most holy, most high and supreme God," and celebrates the whole economy of salvation, as the Trinity is perceived in its various roles as "Creator, Redeemer and Savior . . . of all things spiritual and corporal." Because men and women are the primary recipients of this "holy love" of God in salvation history, the prayer proceeds to invite everyone to join in this Eucharistic proclamation by means of faith and conversion. The lyricism of the chapter mounts with a passionate plea that all be animated by "one desire . . . to believe truly and humbly and keep in [one's] heart and love, honor, adore, serve, praise and bless, glorify and exalt, magnify and give thanks to the most high and supreme eternal God, Trinity and Unity, the Father and the Son and the Holy Spirit." The chapter ends in ecstatic incantation, singing of the One who is "without beginning and without end, unchangeable, invisible, indescribable, ineffable, incomprehensible, unfathomable, blessed, worthy of praise, glorious, exalted on high, sublime, most high, gentle, lovable, delectable and totally desirable above all else forever" *(Earlier Rule,* 130–32).

To be especially noted is that in this final chapter of his rule of life, as throughout his writings, Francis turns to enthusiastic and awe-filled praise and adoration of the three divine persons, especially of the Father, as the goal of the Christian life.[9]

The Second Version of Letter to the Faithful is another important text that demonstrates Francis's trinitarian vision of God; in this document, however, we find a greater emphasis on its Christological and ethical implications. In this representative text, Christ is perceived as the "Word of the Father," who, "though rich as he was," in a kenotic movement "chose poverty" and the frailty of the human condition. From this reference to the Incarnation, Francis passes directly to the Passion and "the Passover which Jesus celebrated with his disciples," quoting the narrative of the institution of the Eucharist in its entirety. Here, as elsewhere in his writings, what is highlighted is the

9. In this prayer alone, Francis uses forty-four different words to describe the mystery of God. In Francis's writings there are eighty-six names attributed to God and forty-eight to Christ (Matura 1997, 132–34). For the primary role of the Father in his vision of God, see Matura 1997. For the Christological dimension, see Nguyen-Van-Khanh 1994.

supreme importance that Francis attached to the Eucharist in his vision of the work of Christ and to his sacramental consciousness of the universe.[10] What follows in the text describes the appropriate response to the gracious gift of the Father in his Son. Francis enumerates the basic demands of the Christian life: love of God and neighbor, especially one's enemies; sacramental confession and reception of the Eucharist; and the need "to bear worthy fruits of penance" *(Second Letter,* 69). Then, in one of the most mystical passages in all of Francis's writings, he speaks of the benefits reaped by those who persevere in such a faithful following of Christ: "The Spirit of the Lord will rest on them and he will make his home and dwelling among them" (70). Here and elsewhere in his writings, Francis insists on the central role of the Spirit[11] as the gift that enables the Christian to recognize and to follow Christ, and that initiates and grants access to the divine indwelling so that Christians can "become children of the Heavenly Father whose works they do, and spouses, brothers, and mothers of our Lord Jesus Christ" (70). As this deep rooting and intimacy with the Trinitarian relations occurs, he continues, "We are spouses when the faithful soul is joined to Jesus Christ by the Holy Spirit. We are brothers when we do the will of his Father who is in heaven. We are mothers when we carry him in our hearts and bodies through love and a pure and sincere conscience; we give birth to him through his holy manner of working, which should shine before others as an example" (70). Succinctly alluded to here are the traditional mystical themes of being espoused to Christ, divine filiation, and the birth of Christ in the soul.

In one of the rare instances in his writings where one can detect a subjective (by the repetition of the exclamation "oh") and mystical note, Francis bursts into ecstatic praise: "Oh, how glorious it is, how holy and great, to have a Father in heaven! Oh, how holy, consoling, beautiful, and wondrous it is to have a Spouse! Oh, how holy and how loving, pleasing, humble, peaceful, sweet, lovable and desirable above all things to have such a Brother and Son, who laid down his life for his sheep" *(Second Letter,* 70). Francis concludes this letter by quoting from Jesus' sacerdotal prayer for unity (John 17) and then by developing further the positive consequences of following Christ and the negative consequences of refusing to do so.

In choosing these two texts—many others in Francis's writings could be cited—what I want to stress is how deeply Trinitarian and Christological is

---

10. For Francis's devotion to the Eucharist, see especially *Admonition* 1, 8SH22; *A Letter to the Clergy; First Letter to the Custodians,* 2–20; also, Cornet 1995; Manselli 1988, 290–97; and Matura 1997, 115–21 and 192–94.

11. For the role of the Spirit in Francis, see van Asseldonk 1991.

Francis's vision of God and how firmly he insists on the primary importance of the divine indwelling among his followers. This vision is, then, quite different from the one usually presented of him as the perfect imitator of Christ, whose piety is centered on the suffering humanity of the crucified.

It is significant to note once again that even if mystical experiences undergird Francis descriptions of his vision of God, he does not talk about them. It is to the subsequent hagiographical tradition that one must turn in order to have access to a picture of Francis as a mystical visionary, a man "drunk with divine love" *(Legend of the Three Companions,* 7: 21) and "filled with prophetic spirit" (7: 24; 10: 36). It would take us far beyond the limits of this article, however, to develop such a picture and to discern the historical value and meaning of the ecstatic moments in Francis's life as depicted in the various sources. It is more germane (and also beyond the scope of this essay) to determine the validity of the image of Francis that the *legenda* present: one who intensely and contemplatively relived the events of Christ's life and gave birth to a new form of mysticism, which Ewert Cousins has called "the mysticism of the historical event" (1983, 166). Cousins describes this type of mysticism as follows: "One recalls a significant event in the past, enters into its drama and draws from it spiritual energy, eventually moving beyond the event to union with God" (166). There is no doubt that because of the incident in which Francis is said to have reproduced the Christmas crib scene at Greccio *(First Life,* 84–87), but more particularly because of his reception of the stigmata—the physical marks of the crucified Christ in his body—Francis had a role to play in the evolution of this form of mysticism (it has also been referred to as passion mysticism). But the main impetus for this Christomimetic mysticism probably comes through the writings of Bonaventure and the pseudo-Bonaventurian *Meditations on the Life of Christ.* For present purposes, it is significant to note that immediately after the reception of the stigmata, the event in Francis's life in which he most intensely identifies with Christ,[12] he composes a prayer—*The Parchment to Brother Leo* written in his own hand—in which he makes no reference to the passion, but once again addresses himself to the Trinity, and in a long litany, he praises the wonders of the God "who is holy, great and strong . . . the Three and One, the good, all good, the highest good" (99–100).

Before I can describe more explicitly the path traced by Francis to purify and open one's heart for the indwelling of the Trinity, and before I can determine the social implications of this process, it is necessary to present Clare's vision and the variants she brings to Francis's experience of God.

12. For the recent literature on the stigmata, see Frugoni 1993 and Schmucki 1992.

Clare as Mystic

An even stronger handicap than for Francis in ascertaining Clare's spiritual identity and her mysticism is the fact that the primary sources as well as the secondary ones in her regard are much more meager. The precious little that has been preserved consists of four letters to Agnes of Prague (the Bohemian princess who sought to reproduce Clare's way of life), the *Rule,* the *Testament,* a blessing, and a letter to a certain Ermentrude of Bruges (of doubtful authenticity). Among the secondary sources, a vital one is *The Acts of the Process of Canonization,* which contains eyewitness accounts of Clare's life; the other sources include the document containing the privilege of poverty granted to her by Innocent III and the *Legend of Saint Clare,* attributed to Thomas of Celano, but perhaps written anonymously. Like the situation with Francis, the picture displayed in the early hagiographical literature that grew around her diverges from that derived from her writings (Matura 1985, 29–30).

Like the Poverello, Clare does not speak directly of her experience of God. From the process of canonization, we know that the sisters who lived with her reported (besides the account of the dream-vision of Francis mentioned previously) that she had the gift of tears, spent hours rapt in prayer, spoke profoundly of the Trinity, and while sick in bed on a Christmas day had a vision of Francis and his brothers celebrating the liturgy, for which she has been oddly named the patron saint of television. But in Clare's writings, there is no reference to such visionary experiences. It is mainly as she opened her heart in her letters to Agnes that one can perceive the basis and, indirectly, the content of her contemplative life and even some intimations of its stages.

Clare shared with Francis the vision of the way of poverty, the "following of the poor Christ," as a self-emptying process meant to provide "a dwelling place and throne for the Creator," but without Francis's Trinitarian emphasis, as is the case for this quotation from her *Third Letter to Agnes* (21). Unlike him, she gave the indwelling theme a Marian cast. As the Blessed Virgin made a home in "the enclosure of her holy womb for the Son whom heaven could not contain," likewise the faithful sister must make a spiritual home in herself "by observing holy poverty and humility" (21–24).

Clare did adopt Francis's formula of the Christian as "sister, spouse, and mother of Christ" *(First Letter,* 24), but she developed the nuptial relationship with Christ in ways markedly different from her spiritual father. Six key passages in her *Letters to Agnes* describe spiritual experience in the language of nuptial union, drawing from the Song of Songs, from the liturgical legend of Saint Agnes, and most certainly from the rich, mainly Cistercian, heritage of that mystical theme. In the *Second Letter,* for example, she exhorts Agnes as a "poor virgin to embrace the poor Christ" (18) and to "gaze upon" and "fol-low" him as her Spouse, "who became for your salvation the lowest of men, despised, struck, scourged untold times through his entire body, and then died amid the suffering of the Cross" (19–20). Note here that if Clare made extensive use of traditional nuptial mysticism, she added a new trait to it by her typically Franciscan references to the poverty and the sufferings of Christ (Peterson 1995; J. Leclercq 1996, 173). Also noteworthy in this same letter, even if very succinctly expressed, are the gradations—a threefold progression—to be observed in prayer. Agnes is invited to "gaze upon" *(intuere)*, "consider" *(considera)*, and then move on to "contemplate" *(contemplare*, a word used seven times in the letters) "the crucified Christ." The purpose of this contemplation of Christ is "to imitate him" *(desiderans imitari)* and to "possess the heavenly mansions in the splendor of the saints" *(Second Letter,* 21).

Another key motif in Clare's writings, which is not found in Francis, is the metaphor of the *speculum* or mirror (used nine times). She first used this motif in the *Third Letter to Agnes* as a description of the contents and the dynamics of spiritual development, a method of approach much more visual than that used by Francis (Johnson 1994, 202–6). She exhorts her friend, "Place your mind before the mirror of eternity; place your soul in the brilliance of glory. Place your heart in the figure of the divine substance and transform your entire being into the image of the Godhead itself through contemplation" (12–13).

The mirror imagery as a key to spiritual transformation is further developed in Clare's *Fourth Letter to Agnes*. Once again she tells her to look at the mirror who is Christ, here understood as Eternal Wisdom, and "to gaze upon this mirror each day" and to "continually study [her] face within it so that [she] may adorn [herself] within and without with beautiful robes" (15–18). And penetrating even more deeply into the mirror, Agnes as the spouse of Christ will discover "at the borders of this mirror the poverty of the one who was placed in a manger and wrapped in swaddling clothes;" then she will discover "at the surface of the mirror the holy humility, the blessed poverty, the untold labors and burdens that Christ endured for the redemption of the human race;" and finally, "in the depth of this same mirror," Agnes will be enabled to contemplate "the ineffable charity that led him to suffer on the wood of the Cross and to die there the most shameful kind of death" (19–22).

The final instance of the mirror motif is found in Clare's *Testament,* where it is used to describe what she understood to be the vocation of her sisters. They were called not only to become a Christ-mirror for one another, but also as a community to become a "mirror and example to those living in the world" (19–20).

One final observation on how Clare was both similar to and also different from Francis: if she, too, was discreet in revealing her spiritual experience, she was nonetheless more outspoken than he was in describing the rewards of contemplation—how the spouse of Christ through each of the spiritual senses (using the language of the Song of Songs) finds ecstatic enjoyment in the experience of sharing the "sacred banquet" with the poor Christ. Contemplating "the ineffable delights" of the heavenly King, the Queen (Agnes) will be drawn to smell "the fragrance of [His] perfumes," be brought "into the winecellar," be "happily embraced" and "kissed with the happiest kiss of [His] mouth" *(Fourth Letter,* 30–32).

The Path of the "Most High Poverty"

Even if the preceding argument is incompletely developed and documented, I hope I have been able to demonstrate thus far how both Francis and Clare, their different accents not withstanding, shared a common vision: the primacy of "purifying" (Francis) and "mirroring" (Clare) the heart for the divine indwelling to which, as both insist, all other activities must be subordinated *(Earlier Rule,* 5: 2; Clare's *Rule,* 7: 1–2).

Central also to the plan they formulated for living is the call "to live according to the perfection of the Gospel," as Clare quotes Francis in the heart of her *Rule* (6: 3; cf. Francis's *Later Rule,* 2: 1); more specifically, it is the call "to follow the most high poverty of our Lord Jesus Christ" (6: 7; cf. *Later Rule,* 12: 4). At the core of the Franciscan path, then, is the uncompromising manner in which both Francis and Clare were inspired to "run and . . . not tire" *(Fourth Letter,* 31), as Clare says, to embrace the self-emptying path of the Christ who was poor, had no place to lay his head, was despised, rejected, and crucified *(Second Letter,* 19–20; *Fourth Letter,* 19–23). It is in *obedience*— a word that appears forty-eight times in Francis's writings—to this kenotic movement of Christ that the path of the "most high poverty" must be situated and understood. Indeed, what distinguishes the Franciscan path from all others in the history of Christian spirituality is poverty in both its inner and outer forms, a poverty conceived as a process—that is, a therapy for the liberation of desires and their mimetic entanglement in conventional culture or "the world." The way of life Francis and Clare initiated is also the most eminent exemplification, in the Christian tradition, of the beggar archetype present in all major religions.

Francis's encounter with a leper was pivotal in triggering his conversion and a new consciousness in the early stages of his discovery of the path of the poor Christ, even if this encounter must not be separated from the time he spent alone trying to understand God's will in the mountain caves of Assisi and before the crucifix of San Damiano. He reports in his *Testament* that the encounter with the leper had transformed what was "bitter" into "sweetness." [13] As Manselli describes so well (1988, 33–36), this encounter with abject human suffering changed Francis's social condition and cast his lot with those who are considered to be of little worth and who are looked down upon: the poor and the powerless, the sick, the lepers, and the beggars who live by the wayside (*Earlier Rule, 7*).

For Clare, the new life that she and her sisters shaped together at San Damiano also entailed downward mobility and a change of social position. Generally, the sisters at San Damiano came from higher social classes than did the friars, but given the stability their life of reclusion required and the fact that they had to operate within the limits of what was possible for medieval women, their lifestyle took a form quite different from the itinerancy and mobility of the friars.

The choice to be among the "lesser ones" and "subject to all" (*Earlier Rule*, 7: 1–2) meant that both the friars and the Poor Ladies disengaged themselves from the power dynamics of their society and from the oppressive practices that were destructive to the rights and dignity of the human person, especially those most marginalized and destitute. This way of life, which they formulated in their respective rules and which evolved through time and the testing of experience, called for a total disappropriation of all forms of possession: material goods and, what is even more difficult to discern and practice, spiritual goods as well.

The goal of the Lesser Brothers and the Poor Ladies—as followers of the poor Christ—was to strive to embrace the lifestyle of the poor. In what David Flood has called "the economics of the brotherhood" (1989, 15) as spelled out in the *Rule*, the friars were to dress like the poor, not own anything, do manual labor for their sustenance, and not be afraid to beg when their labor did not suffice for their needs, as was their right according to the new order of society that had been established by Christ, his disciples, and Mary, who were "poor and transient and lived on alms" (*Earlier Rule*, 9: 5). Touching money—"a demon and a poisonous serpent," said Francis (*Second Life*, 20)— was also forbidden unless absolutely necessary.

In the renunciation of possessions, Clare echoed Francis's mandate. The most striking formulation of her refusal of property rights is found in chapter 6 of her *Rule*: "As a result of a solemn promise to the Lord God and blessed Francis," the Poor Sisters were bound to observe holy poverty "by not receiving or having possession or ownership either of themselves or through an intermediary" (6: 17). Given the condition of women in medieval society and the fact that it was impossible for Clare and her sisters to go out to beg as the

13. For a good introduction to the early conversion of Francis, see Brunette 1997.

brothers did, her choice of absolute poverty, shorn of all security and left to the mercy of her fellow citizens and of the passers-by, led to what Marco Bartoli has called the "economic paradox" of San Damiano, i.e., "working in order to give away and begging in order to live" (1989, 75).

Poverty was never conceived as an end itself but rather as a means of emancipation from what blocks and destroys true communion with others and with God; it also had its more interior, spiritual dimension: the exclusion of all means of spiritual domination and control over others. This dimension is especially evident in the concept of authority expressed by Francis and Clare in the internal structure they had formulated for their respective communities.

In chapter 7 of the *Regula non bullata,* for instance, Francis wrote that "all the brothers without exception are forbidden to wield power or authority, particularly over one another" (7: 2). In the fraternity, no one could carry the title *father, master,* or *prior,* for all were brothers—*frater* being the second most popular term (306 occurrences) in Francis's vocabulary after *dominus* (410 occurrences [Schmucki 1989, 262]). Among the great founders of religious orders, Francis is the only one to quote in his *Rule* the Gospel passage that excludes the designation of *father* and *teacher,* and he is the first one in history to give the name *fraternity* to his religious group. Furthermore, in Francis's understanding, among themselves the brothers were to be servants of one another and to "care and nourish" each other as "a mother loves and cares for her son" *(Earlier Rule,* 9: 11; *Later Rule,* 6: 8). There would also be no class distinctions in the fraternity, but rather all should universally be called "Friars Minor" and "wash each other's feet" *(Earlier Rule,* 6: 3–4).

Similar considerations are to be found in Clare's *Rule.* Her conception of authority and service was very revolutionary for her time and even more "democratic" than the rule Francis composed (Bartoli 1993, 76–97; Matura 1985, 41–47). The sisters were to be coresponsible for the direction of the community. All who held offices in the monastery were "chosen by common consent." It was only at Francis's insistence—a point of tension between the two—that Clare herself accepted the title of abbess *(Process of Canonization,* 6), preferring to name herself as "handmaid" *(ancilla,* used eleven times), "mother" *(mater,* four times), and "servant" *(famula,* three times).

Finally, with respect to the interiorization of poverty, which is articulated more fully in Francis's writings than in the available sources of Clare's work, there was also a rejection of more subtle forms of power and ownership, such as envy of the gifts of others, the inability to tolerate criticism, and, more importantly, glorification of oneself in the good that one does instead of rendering it back to "God from whom all good comes" *(Earlier Rule,* 17: 17).

Furthermore, in their dealings with people, the friars were not to judge, condemn others (especially the rich), quarrel, or affirm their rights or ecclesiastical privileges, but rather they were to be kind, self-effacing, gentle, and courteous *(Later Rule,* 3: 10–11). In short, as they went about in the world, they had to be "minors"—that is, small and least of all, or nonresistant in the face of opposition and violence *(Earlier Rule,* 14: 4–6); moreover, "whoever comes to them friend or foe, thief or brigand, must be well received" *(Earlier Rule,* 7: 14).

The Franciscan Social Message

Briefly put, what emerges from the preceding sketch of the way of life initiated by Francis and Clare is that the Franciscan political and social message consists mainly in the force of true example, an alternative way of living, and an emphasis on being rather than doing. As Manselli's biography of the Poverello so rightly points out, "If we review Francis's entire attitude from his conversion up until his death, we will find the call to good example with an insistence that could even be annoying, if it were not in its proper place with its proper value" (1988, 228). Francis wished above all that the "brothers preach by their deeds" *(Earlier Rule,* 17: 3). This wish is what Michel de Certeau, the French postmodern scholar of mysticism, refers to as "the Franciscan dream, . . .that a body might preach without speaking, and that in walking around, it might make visible what lives within" (1986, 88).

Similarly, Clare also wished that her sisters be a mirror of the poor Christ to shine for all to see *(Testament,* 20). She and her sisters created a new type of life, one that was halfway between the preceding traditional monasticism and the emerging forms of apostolic life (Beguine or Bizzoche) that were flourishing throughout Europe, but especially in northern Italy, in Brabant, and around the Rhine. San Damiano was a community open to the world and at the service of the poor (van Asseldonk 1993). As Jean-François Godet has put it, Clare's model was "a withdrawn life, but not one that was shut up behind walls" (1991, 17). The word *enclosure* is never found in her writings (Godet 1985, 278–83; Bartoli 1993, 88–97). As the recent archeological findings reveal, the initial edifice itself was no different from the other primitive Franciscan places. Even after it had been reconstructed to accommodate the sedentary and more exclusively eremetical life of the sisters, it retained its makeshift, temporary character. "Out of love of the God who was placed poor in the crib, lived poor in the world, and remained naked on the cross" *(Testament,* 45), it was a structure not very different from the huts and hovels of the Assisi peasants.

The way of life, then, that both Francis and Clare elaborated with their respective communities had to do above all with a quality of being or a manner of relating that was humble and dispossessed, that was without pretense, and that made no claims to rights or privileges for themselves. Even if both Francis and Clare played an important part in the reform of the church and in the transformation of the society in which they lived, they made absolutely no claim to be reformers. There is not a single word of criticism in their sayings or writings. In stark contrast with established mores, the radicalism of their Gospel life inevitably entailed experiencing, as Clare puts it in her *Testament,* "deprivation, poverty, hard work, trial, or the shame or contempt of the world"—all of which were considered "great delights" (27). As they went about in the world the friars were also to experience persecution, but Francis had said that they should not retaliate, should not "quarrel or fight with words, or judge others"; rather, they should "be meek, peaceful and unassuming, gentle and humble, speaking courteously to everyone, as is becoming" *(Later Rule,* 3: 11, also 14: 4–6).

Instruments of Peace

It is this nonviolent way of being among others that enabled Francis and the friars as well as, in a more invisible way, Clare and her sisters to be active and creative messengers of peace for their time. Even today, Francis's popularity rests in great part on his image as an instrument of peace, notwithstanding the fact that the well-known peace prayer attributed to him, "Lord, make me an instrument of your peace," is not among his prayers and cannot be traced back further than 1913 (Schulz 1996; van Dijk 1996).

Francis had a deep sense that he and his brothers had been entrusted by God to be peacemakers. Looking back on his life shortly before his death, he mentioned that God had revealed to him that he should greet people with the salutation "The Lord give you peace" *(Testament,* 18). The same greeting was to be used at the beginning and end of his sermons *(Three Companions,* 26), with every encounter, and with the crossing of the threshold of a house *(First Life,* 23). Two of his admonitions, the thirteenth and the fifteenth, deal with Jesus' words "Blessed are the Peacemakers" and articulate the inner dispositions of true peacemakers. Drawn into various conflicts and warring situations, Francis became a peacemaker in various cities: in Arezzo *(Second Life,* 108; *Perugia,* 81; *Witness,* 81), Perugia *(Perugia,* 35), Siena *(Fioretti,* 11), Gubbio *(Fioretti,* 21), and Bologna. His most notable success in reconciliation occurred toward the end of his life in 1225, when, although gravely ill, he made peace between the mayor and the bishop of Assisi—that is, between the political and religious authorities of the city *(Three Companions,* 26: 39; *Perugia,* 44). He had them listen to his *Canticle of Brother Sun,* to which he had added the following special strophe: "Praised be you, my Lord, through those who give pardon for your love and bear infirmity and tribulation. / Blessed are those who endure in peace for by you, Most High, they shall be crowned" (verses 10–11).

No less famous is Francis's peacemaking mission to the Sultan Melek-el-Kamel during the Crusades in 1219. Unarmed, he had managed to make his way to the Saracen camp and, probably because his shabby clothes and humble demeanor made him look like one of the Muslim Sufis present in the sultan's circles and esteemed by him, he succeeded in being introduced to the Saracen leader. Francis made such a favorable impression on him that, according to the noted medieval chronicler Jacques de Vitry, when the sultan bade Francis farewell, he said, "Pray for me so that God may deign to show me the faith that is most pleasing to him" (de Beer 1983, 34). Perhaps it is because Francis himself was also affected by his encounter with the sultan and the Muslim world that he inserted a special chapter in the *Rule* prescribing the proper behavior for those "who are going among the Saracens and other nonbelievers" (*Earlier Rule,* 16). The friars who "by divine inspiration" go to meet Muslims and people of other faiths were not "to engage in arguments or disputes" with them, but rather were to "be subject to them" and to revere and respect the presence among them of the "all-powerful God" and "Creator of all" (according to Laurent Gallant's reordering of the Latin text, 1995, 16–17). To be sure, the friars were to affirm their Christian identity and, if the situation called for it, to proclaim the full Christian revelation of God as "Father, and Son, and Holy Spirit," as well as the Son as "Redeemer and Savior and God's creating Word." But this proclamation was to be made only if, as an initial premise, the holy ground on which all religions rest were respected.

Though not as visibly active as Francis and the friars, Clare and her sisters also saw themselves as invested with public responsibility for peace. They held a common conviction that the community at San Damiano had been placed there for the safeguarding of the city. While Clare was still alive, a laud bestowed upon her the title of *Defensor civitatis* because through her prayers (and those of her community) she had repelled the invasion of Frederick II and his Saracen troops, as well as the assault of the troops of Vitale d'Aversa in the following year (Sensi 1994, 237). In *The Process of Canonization,* six sisters reported how Clare's intercession had caused the invading Saracens to withdraw from San Damiano without harming anyone (3: 18; 4: 14; 6: 10; 9: 12, 8).

Universal Brotherhood and Sisterhood

If both Francis and Clare attached such importance to following the poor Christ to the extent of rejecting all forms of ownership and sharing the condition of the poor, it was because they had discovered this road was both the royal highway that led to the riches of God and the key to brotherhood and sisterhood, communion with all creatures, true peace and joy.

The most powerful expression of Francis's mystical view of the interconnectedness of all created reality is, of course, the *Canticle of Brother Sun*.[14] It is crucial to note that this song, which marks the birth of Italian vernacular literature, was written at the end of a long salvific process in which nature indeed played a role, as witnessed by the countless stories of his love of animals and nature in the sources, but nature did not play a central role in purifying and reordering his consciousness.[15] As Leonardo Boff points out, "Whoever tries to romantically imitate Saint Francis in his love for nature without passing through asceticism, denial, penitence, and the cross falls into a deep illusion" (1982, 40). Francis composed the *Canticle* shortly after he had received the stigmata, the final seal of his identification with Christ crucified, and after his self-emptying and total surrender into the hands of the "Most High" God. As a poor and marginal man, with a heart purified and reconciled, the Poverello saw all created reality not only as useful to humanity, but above all as intrinsically worthy of admiration because it shines with God's beauty and presence. In childlike wonder, a primitive innocence regained, he called upon all to join him in singing his song of praise and thanksgiving to the Creator for all His creatures and to establish a brotherly-sisterly relation with each one of them:

> Most High, all-powerful, good Lord,
> Yours are the praises, the glory, the honor, and all blessing.
> To you alone, Most High, do they belong,
> and no man is worthy to mention your name.
> Praised be you, my Lord, with all your creatures,
> especially Sir Brother Sun,
> who is the day and through whom you give us light.
> And he is beautiful and radiant with great splendor;
> and bears a likeness of you, Most High One.
> Praised be you, my Lord, through Sister Moon and the stars,
> in heaven you formed them clear and precious and beautiful.
> Praised be you, my Lord, through Brother Wind,
> and through the air, cloudy and serene, and every kind of weather
> through which you give sustenance to your creatures.
> Praised be you, my Lord, through Sister Water,

14. For a recent study of the *Canticle,* see Pozzi 1990. For an analysis of its archetypical content, see E. Leclercq 1977.

15. Nature stories appear through the hagiographical literature about Francis, but are collected in Celano's *Second Life,* 165–71. See also E. Armstrong 1973 and Sorell 1988.

who is very useful and humble and precious and chaste.
Praised be you, my Lord, through Brother Fire,
through whom you light the night
and he is beautiful and playful and robust and strong.
Praised be you, my Lord, through our Sister Mother Earth,
who sustains and governs us,
and who produces varied fruits with colored flowers and herbs.
Praised be you, my Lord, through those who give pardon for your love
and bear infirmity and tribulation.
Blessed are those who endure in peace
for by you, Most High, they shall be crowned.
Praised be you, my Lord, through our Sister Bodily Death,
from whom no living man can escape.
Woe to those who die in mortal sin.
Blessed are those whom death will find in your most holy will,
for the second death shall do them no harm.
Praise and bless my Lord and give him thanks
and serve him with great humility.

It is significant that Francis composed a good part of the *Canticle of Brother Sun* during his final illness and staying with some of his companions near San Damiano where Clare and her sisters resided *(Perugia, 43)*. It is highly likely, although there is no recorded evidence for it, that she and her sisters learned to sing it, undoubtedly with melodic variations of their own, as was their wont.

Chesterton has written that "Francis walked the world like the Pardon of God" (1924, 224). He could have said the same of Clare. The legacy that both left continues to speak in an amazing way to the depths of the human psyche and its aspiration for total reconciliation and for universal brotherhood and sisterhood.

4

Preaching as Social Practice in Meister Eckhart

AMY HOLLYWOOD

In his writings of the 1960s and early 1970s, the philosopher Jacques Derrida uses the term *writing* in an expanded sense to designate the conditions and structures of language. For Derrida, the opposition between speech and writing relies on an opposition between presence and absence. Plato and Plotinus, for example, argue that writing is a secondary and degenerate form of language eschewed by the philosopher, who always seeks to transform his or her interlocuters through the presence of speech. Derrida, in his reading of Plato and in his comments on the traditions of negative theology from Plotinus to Meister Eckhart, demonstrates that this privileging of speech depends on an effacement of the structures of writing—temporal deferral and spatial differentiation—that lie within speech itself. Speech, then, is itself a form of writing, insofar as writing denotes the use of signs, which in their presence substitute for an absent presence. Because speech itself is composed of signs, it always already participates in the structures of writing. In undermining the opposition between speech and writing, Derrida does not deny that ancient philosophies privileged speech over writing, but rather demonstrates that this privileging always occurs within texts and that the nature of the philosopher's speech is always already marked by the temporal and spatial displacements of writing itself (Derrida 1967a, 1967b, 1972a, 1972b).

It is in this expanded sense that I wish to discuss writing as a form of social practice in the work of Meister Eckhart. The documents that survive under the name of Eckhart include written texts—such as treatises, scholastic questions, and biblical commentaries—and also sermons or oral presentations most likely transcribed by Eckhart's audiences. Yet preaching is also writing in that it participates in the deferral and differentiation that structure language. Moreover, Eckhart himself demonstrates this economy of language in ways that foreshadow Derrida's work. His language stages a recognition of its own always deferred and differentiated movement, and this staging is itself, for Eckhart, a form of social action. Derrida attempts to demonstrate the materiality of language, both as spoken and inscribed, in order to deconstruct the oppositions between form and matter, presence and absence, and speech and writing that, he argues, ground metaphysical speculation in the West (see especially 1972a, 1–29). In the process, the opposition between theory and practice is shaken. Eckhart begins with an attempt to deconstruct the opposition between theory and practice; in the process, he comes to many of the same insights about language, its materiality, and its force as those enunciated by Derrida in the late twentieth century.

Despite my claim here for the close ties between Eckhart and Derrida, I sound two notes of caution. The first Derrida himself articulates early in his career. Recognizing the proximity between the movements of *"différance"*[1] and the movement of negative theology, Derrida hastens to distinguish the two.

> And yet that which thus marks itself by *différance* is not theological, not even in the order of the most negative of negative theologies, the latter always busily working to disengage, as we know, a super-essentiality beyond the finite categories of essence and existence, that is to say of presence, and always bustling about to remember that if the predicate of existence is refused to God, it is in order to recognize in God a superior, inconceivable, and ineffable mode of being. (1982a, 6)

Différance, on the other hand, cannot be inscribed within any ontological or theological project, but rather marks the possibilities and the limits of ontology and theology themselves. It is, as Derrida constantly reminds the reader, neither a word nor a concept, and if it were to become a name or master concept, *différance* would lose its deconstructive force. To say that there is no word for the movements of *différance,* he argues, should be read "as a platitude. This unnameable is not an ineffable being which no name can approach: God, for example" (1982a, 28). It is, rather, that which "puts into question the name of the name" (29).[2]

The question of the proximity and difference between Derrida's deconstructive project and the writing of negative or apophatic theology has fol-

---

1. Derrida's essay *"Différance"* is an extended reflection on his neologism and its use in his writing. The term brings together the two meanings of the French verb *différer,* "differ" and "defer," the latter of which has been lost in *différence.* The silent *a* of *différance* is an attempt to restore this lost meaning. Moreover, the ending *-ance* remains undecided between the active and passive voices; the nontransitivity of the middle voice is intentional. See Derrida 1982a, 3–9. Derrida's translator, Alan Bass, decided not to translate this term. Others have used an English neologism, *differance.*

2. In French, *le nom* is also a euphemism for God, so that the antitheological point is implicitly reiterated here.

lowed Derrida, and he has taken up the issue on a number of subsequent occasions (for example, 1986, 1987). The suspicion that apophatic theologies harbor a metaphysics of presence, however, remains a central point of differentiation. Any comparison of Eckhart and Derrida, then, has to deal with the question of whether Eckhart's attempt to free God from God is subject to the deconstructive critique made by Derrida in *"la différance."*

A second problem concerns Derrida's conception of writing. Pierre Hadot, one of the most important commentators on the relationship between theory and practice within ancient and modern philosophies of the West, upholds the distinction between them, even as he attempts to articulate the importance of practice and spiritual exercise to ancient philosophy (1995). This distinction comes together with a renewed insistence on the opposition between speech and writing in the work of Plato, Plotinus, and the major schools of ancient philosophy. Without naming Derrida, Hadot insists on the necessity of differentiating the oral transmission of philosophy among Neoplatonists, Stoics, and Epicureans from written texts. The latter, according to Hadot, always presuppose the presence of living teachers and the spoken word (1995, 61–63). Yet, at the same time, he acknowledges that within these schools and especially within the early Christian community, writing itself has a therapeutic value and is capable of being deployed in ways that are transformative of the self (135).

Hadot implies that the emphasis on writing in contemporary philosophy reduces philosophy to a kind of discourse and as such opposes it to practice. Yet Derrida's conception of writing demonstrates that language itself is a form of practice, not reducible to other modes of material practice but also not in opposition to them. By reinstating the oppositions between speech and writing and between theory and practice, Hadot may more accurately describe the thought of the ancient philosophical schools (his goal as an historian of thought), yet he also implicitly accepts the validity of their philosophical judgments. Derrida's intervention in the texts of Plato attempts to read against the grain in order to demonstrate another logic operating within those texts (1982b). My argument here is that Derrida's broader conception of writing as constitutive of language better encapsulates the practice of Meister Eckhart. It does so because Eckhart deconstructs the oppositions between theory and practice, contemplation and action, and ultimately between creator and creature so crucial to Western metaphysical traditions.

The relationship between theory and practice is a central issue in the spiritual or mystical writings emanating from northern Europe in the late medieval period, taking the form of extended discussions of the relationship between the lives of action and contemplation. These discussions come the closest to probing issues relating to mysticism and social transformation in this period. Medieval commentaries often center around a key biblical text, the story of Mary and Martha (Luke 10:38–42). The story, however, with its clear privileging of Mary (the woman who becomes a disciple by listening to the words of Christ) over Martha (the woman who continues to serve Christ in the ways traditionally taken by women—namely, feeding) only opens the debate within medieval Christian texts. This opening position can be seen most clearly in the work of Bernard of Clairvaux, for whom contemplation is the "the better part," yet contemplation must be combined with life in this world and with the duties to one's neighbors this life demands (see Bernard of Clairvaux 1979, Sermons 57–58, which focus on the text "Arise, make hast, my love, my dove, my beautiful one, and come" [Song of Songs 2:10]).

The Beguine and mendicant movements of the twelfth and thirteenth century were practical attempts to combine the two modes of existence. The Beguines, women who chose to devote themselves fully to religious practice while in the world, deconstructed traditional opposition between action and contemplation by their very mode of life. Church authorities were not always comfortable with the Beguines' blurring of categories and of oppositions central to the philosophical and theological traditions of Christianity. Yet despite this distrust—which led ultimately to persecution, condemnation, and forced enclosure—the unsettling of the borders between action and contemplation, inside and outside, life in the world and the cloistered existence of more traditional religious women runs throughout the lives of the early Beguines. Their hagiographies continually suggest the unity of action and contemplation in the lives of those women who chose to embrace religious practice in the world (Hollywood 1995, 26–56).

This tradition runs through the writings of the Beguines themselves. In his startling reading of Luke in German Sermon 86, Meister Eckhart demonstrates his indebtedness to the Beguines and his concern with problems generated in and by their texts. For the Beguines, the relationship between action and contemplation was still a problem—one that they sought to resolve in ways compatible with their choice of life in the world. Mechthild of Magdeburg, for example, moves from an experience of ecstatic union with God and the desire to remain in that rapture, to a recognition that the suffering of God's absence is part of the movement toward God, and finally to a demand that the soul become one with Christ in His work and His suffering in order to be one with God without mediation (Mechthild of Magdeburg 1990–93; Hadewijch 1980). Marguerite Porete, intent on downplaying the role of suffering in the religious life and practice of women, also mitigates the importance of work and action, arguing that the soul who is simple and free is above the virtues. Clearly implied in Porete's arguments, however, is the claim that the absolutely free soul is the place in which God works, a position borrowed by Eckhart (Porete 1993).

In a sermon possibly preached to the Beguines and other religious women, Eckhart boldly reverses traditional readings of the Lucan story and with it the claimed supremacy of Mary and contemplation over Martha and the life of action. This interpretation is also suggested by German Sermon 2, in which Eckhart translates Martha's name (Luke 10:38) as "a virgin who is also a wife." There Martha is described as the wifely virgin soul, one who is fully detached and unified with the divine ground without distinction and is necessarily active in that she shares in the divine work of the self-generation of the Son. The soul as virgin and wife shares in the one work of the divine, which is the birth of justice (Eckhart 1981, 177–81). As in Sermon 86, this description leads to the claim that the soul should not imitate Christ, but rather *become* Christ.

I begin my analysis of Sermon 86 with the relevant passage from Luke in order to remind you of the story and to highlight the difficulties the text throws in the path of Eckhart's interpretation:

> Now as they went on their way, he entered a certain village, where a woman named Martha welcomed him into her home. She had a sister named Mary, who sat at the Lord's feet and listened to what he was saying. But Martha was distracted by her many tasks; so she came to him and asked, "Lord, do you not care that my sister has left me to do all the work by myself? Tell her then to help me." But the Lord answered her, "Martha, Martha, you are worried and distracted by many things; there is need of only one thing. Mary has chosen the better part, which will not be taken away from her."

The text presents three major obstacles for Eckhart: its assertion that Martha "was distracted by many tasks," the seeming asperity of Martha's words, and the clarity of Jesus' approbation of Mary.

Eckhart deals with the second problem first. After describing that which compels Mary and Martha, Eckhart makes a crucial distinction between satisfaction of the intellect and that of the senses, marking the importance he places on the nonaffective aspect of the contemplative life and his distance from the affective traditions associated with Bernard of Clairvaux (and often with women). Even the apostle Paul, in "his first rapture," lacks that knowledge of self, God, and the virtues given over time and "in actions" (Eckhart 1986, 339). Throughout the sermon, then, Eckhart—like Mechthild of Magdeburg, Hadewijch, and Marguerite Porete—insists that the first rapturous and ecstatic experiences of God are only the beginning of the life of religious practice.

The distinction between intellectual and sensual satisfaction underlies this account and grounds Eckhart's teaching on the unity of contemplation and action:

> God satisfies our senses and feelings by granting us comfort, pleasure, and fulfillment; but to be pampered in this with regard to the lower senses is not something that happens to God's dear friends. But intellectual satisfaction is a matter of the spirit. I call that intellectual satisfaction when the highest part of the soul is not drawn down by any pleasure, so that she does not drown in pleasures, but stands sovereign above them. A person is only then intellectually fulfilled when the joys and sorrows of creatures cannot pull the highest part [of the soul] down. I call "creatures" everything that one feels and sees lower than God. (Eckhart 1986, 338)[3]

Regarding the point at which the wise and mature Martha calls lovingly on Christ to bid Mary to get up, Eckhart—having given this peaceful interpretation of the altercation between Mary and Martha—voices the suspicion that Mary was sitting more in enjoyment of the senses than to gain true spiritual profit. According to Eckhart, Martha acts out of "endearment" in asking Christ to make Mary get up. Martha does not want Mary to become stuck in a life that demands pleasure rather than spiritual progress. Rather than a rebuke, her words are an affectionate and playful chiding.

This explanation sets the stage for Eckhart's reading of Christ's response (which seems in the biblical story to be a reproach to Martha) as a promise that Mary will receive the fullness of her desire and then will embark on a life of activity in the world. Eckhart goes on to admonish those who hope to escape action, perhaps thinking here of misreadings of Porete's text that had already been committed in the condemnation of her in 1309 (Lerner 1972). "Now some people want to go so far as to achieve freedom from works. I say this cannot be done. It was not until after the time when the disciples received the Holy Spirit that they began to perform virtuous deeds" (Eckhart 1986,

---

3. Translation modified. "Genuoc sîn nâch sinnelicheit, daz ist, daz uns god gibet trôst, lust und genüegede; und hie inne verwenet sîn, daz gât abe den lieben vriunden gotes nâch den nidern sinnen. Aber redelîchiu genûegede, daz ist nâch dem geiste. Ich spriche dem redelîche genüegede, daz von allem luste daz oberste wipfelîn der sêle nigt enwirt geneiget her abe, daz az nigt ertrinke in dem luste, ez enstande gewalticlîche ûf im. Danne ist er in redelîcher genüegede, sô liep und leit der crêatûre daz oberste wipfelîn nigt geneigen enmac her abe. 'Crêatûre' heize ich allez, daz man enpfindet und sihet under got" (Sermon 86, *Deutschen Werke,* Eckhart 1936, 3: 482).

344).[4] In the same way, Eckhart continues, not until after Mary has been taught by Christ does she go out into the world to serve—preaching, teaching, and being a servant to the disciples. Martha is already at this place, marked for Eckhart by the fact that the Lord names her *twice;* she possesses perfection both in eternal happiness and temporal works.

Temporal works are all bodily activities, pointing to the existence in Eckhart's thought of a new relationship toward corporeality established when one has become detached from all created things both corporeal and incorporeal. This idea leads to Eckhart's resolution of the first problem posed by the text— its assertion that Martha was "distracted by her many tasks." Eckhart makes clear that his understanding of detachment cannot be taken too literally as signifying insensibility to the surrounding world. Rather, detachment concerns the disposition of the will.

> Now our dear people imagine they can bring things to a point where their senses are utterly unaffected by the presence of sensible objects. They cannot achieve this. That a painfully loud racket be as pleasant to my ears as the charming tones of a stringed instrument—that I shall never achieve. This, however, one should attain, that one's will, formed to God in understanding, is free of all natural pleasure, and, whenever insight on the alert commands the will to turn away, that the will say: "I do it gladly." (344)[5]

The body and its sensations cannot be destroyed; rather the attitude of the soul toward these created things must be transformed through loss of self-will and detachment.

In the sermon, Eckhart describes three possible paths to God, showing that the goal is a relationship without any mediation between the human being and the divine. Although the language of the sermon is difficult, Eckhart privileges the third path, in which all mediators between the human being and God, even the humanity of Christ, is overcome. Eckhart argues that in the first path to the divine, "[o]ne is to seek God in all creatures through all

---

4. "Nû wellent etelîche liute dar zuo komen, daz sie werke ledic sîn. Ich spriche: ez enmac nigt gesîn. Nâch der zît, dô die jünger enpfiengen den heiligen geist, dô viengen sie êrste ane, tugende zu würkenne" (Sermon 86, Eckhart 1936, 3: 492).

5. "Nû waenent unser guoten liute erkriegen, daz gegenwürticheit sinnelîcher dinge den sinnen niht ensî. Des engât in niht zuo. Daz ein pînlich gedoene mînen ôren als lustic sî als ein süezez seitenspil, daz erkriege ich niemer. Aber daz sol man haben, daz ein redelich gotgeformeter wille blôz stande alles natûrlîchen lustes, swenne ez bescheidenheit aneschouwet, daz si dem willen gebiete, sich abe ze kêrenne, und der wille spreche: ich tuon ez gerne" (Sermon 86, Eckhart 1936, 3: 491–92).

kinds of activity and with flaming love" (341).[6] Although this path bears the sanction of Solomon and of Eckhart himself, he implies that it still represents a mediated relationship, for creatures play a role in the relationship between God and the human being. It is the way of actions and virtuous deeds. The second path, according to Eckhart, is "a pathless path, free yet bound, raised aloft and wafted off almost beyond self and all things, beyond will and images. However, it does not stand firmly on its own" (341).[7] This path is the one taken by the apostle Peter, the one on which he confronts the Godman, the Son in his incarnate form and the Father through the Son. Eckhart insists that there is a higher way, for mediation still occurs on this path, which is clearly associated with the life of contemplation and mystical ravishment. Following Marguerite Porete, then, Eckhart places the lives of action and of contemplation together as lives marked by mediation between God and human beings. Only in this way is work—both that of the body and the soul, action and contemplation—transformed into activity.

Only the third path is without mediation. Paul followed this way when he was lifted up into the third heaven. Eckhart argues that it is a "path and yet is a being-at-home" where God is seen "immediately in his ownness" (341).[8] Eckhart places Martha here, for despite the occasional perturbation of spirit by created things, she shares an unmediated relationship with God that allows her to be "in the midst of things, but not *in* things" (340, emphasis in original).[9] In the vocabulary of the sermon, she has risen above "works," or external deeds of virtue, and has attained to a pure "activity" in which true justice lies. Although Eckhart emphasizes the necessity of becoming like Christ, he goes further and claims that one should *be* Christ. He insists that the highest path is to share the same relationship with the Godhead as the Son does, rather than to have a relationship mediated by the Son. The Incarnation is the model for the human being, but in a different way than for many of Eckhart's contemporaries. The soul should strive to be united with the Father as the Son is united to Him. Through such a union, Eckhart says in uncharacteristically explicit language, each part of the body will "practice its own proper virtue,"

6. "Der eine ist: mit manicvaltigem gewerbe, mit brinnender minne in allen crêatûren got suochen" (Sermon 86, Eckhart 1936, 3: 486).

7. "Wec âne wec, vrî und doch gebunden, erhaben und gezucket vil nâch über sich und alliu dinc âne willen und âne bilde, swie aleine ez doch weselîche niht enstâ" (Sermon 86, Eckhart 1936, 3: 486).

8. "Der dritte wex heizet wec und ist doch heime, daz ist: got sehen âne mittel in sînesheit" (Sermon 86, Eckhart 1936, 3: 487).

9. "Bî den dingen und niht in den dingen" (Sermon 86, Eckhart 1936, 3: 485). And also, "dû stâst bî den dingen, und diu dinc enstânt niht in dir." Ibid.

just as it did in Christ (344).[10] Not only is the soul reunited with that spark of herself that exists in the Godhead, but, it is also implied, the body shares in this virtual existence in the divine.

The sermon clearly evokes what Dietmar Mieth calls Eckhart's mysticism of everyday life (Mieth 1969, 173–85; Mieth 1986, 63; see also McGinn 1981a, 18). Against those spiritual writers who emphasize special, individual experiences and inactive contemplation, Eckhart claims that the highest contemplation is compatible with and in fact brings about a state of heightened activity. The sermon also serves as clear evidence that when Eckhart discusses the birth of the Son in the soul as a *work,* he does not use the term only metaphorically. Rather, in reaching a point of identification with the Son, the Father, and the ground of the Godhead, the human being becomes capable of truly just and efficacious activity in the world. Or, put in another way, achieving detachment and union with the divine ground effects justice, equality, and the birth of the Son in the soul. The implication of the final lines of the sermon, furthermore, is that through this "work," the entire human being—body and soul—is sanctified. This position is best understood in terms of Eckhart's dialectic of the transcendence and immanence of God, for insofar as one recognizes God's absolute immanence to the world, one truly sees his transcendence or indistinction. Eckhart proclaims the sanctity of the whole created world, while he simultaneously maintains divine transcendence and the nothingness of creation in itself.

Yet to say that the work is meaningful does not mean that the Son provides a purpose, goal, or end to human and divine activity in the normal understanding of these terms. A central theme of Eckhart's mysticism—borrowed from Beatrice of Nazareth and Marguerite Porete—is the idea that the soul must live "without a why," as God does.[11] He argues that all creaturely things are possessed by a why; the divine is that which exists and acts without a why, merely for its own sake.[12] In a similar way, Eckhart insists that God not be understood as useful. The truly just human being performs works without intention or hope for reward.

> The just person seeks nothing in his works, for those that seek something in their works or those who work because of a "why" are servants and

10. "Kein glit was an sînem lîbe, ez enüebete sunderlîche tugent" (Sermon 86, Eckhart 1936, 3: 492).

11. See Sermon 5b, Eckhart 1936, 1: 90 (Eckhart 1981, 183); Sermon 29, Eckhart 1936, 2: 77, 80 (Eckhart 1986, 288–89); Sermon 39, Eckhart 1936, 2: 253–54, 266 (Eckhart 1986, 296, 298); Sermon 41, Eckhart 1936, 2: 289; and Sermon 59, Eckhart 1936, 2: 625–26 (Eckhart 1986, 307).

12. Sermon 59, Eckhart 1936, 2: 625–26 (Eckhart 1986, 307).

traders. And so, if you want to be in—or trans-figured into justice, then intend nothing in your works and in-figure no "why" in yourself, neither in time nor in eternity, neither reward nor blessedness, neither this nor that; for these works are all truly dead. Yes, and if you image God in yourself, whatever works you perform therefore, these works are all dead, and you ruin good works. (296)[13]

In a sense, the divine and its manifestation in the world are meaningless, in the same way that God is nothing, for they are without purpose and cannot be explained within referential language and normal logical categories. The birth of the Son in the soul does not give meaning, but rather opens access to the divine in the created world. Any attempt to capture the work within the matrix of purpose and intention kills, regardless of the worthiness of the goal, for according to Eckhart all that is sought for a specific purpose belongs to the realm of accidents and thus of the inessential and unequal.[14] One receives the all that is God by "living without a why," recognizing the nothingness of all things insofar as they are created and other than God, and their equality insofar as they are divine.

In a similar way, Eckhart's understanding of the relationship between the interior and the exterior work underlines both the unity of action and contemplation and his denial of a "utilitarian" understanding of the work of the soul and of the divine. Dietmar Mieth clarifies these points in his reading of a sermon in which Eckhart cites Aquinas only to put Aquinas's teachings to much different use than those intended (Mieth 1969, 219–22). Aquinas argues for the superiority of the contemplative life to the active life, yet claims that acts of love further the final goal of heavenly contemplation that will occur after death. He offers the possibility of a union between action and contemplation while on earth, based on the superiority of the latter (Aquinas 1964b, 66–83). Eckhart uses this Thomistic claim to make his own quite different point about the unity of the two types of life for the detached person. For Eckhart, the works of the active life are one with the birth of the Son in

13. Translation modified. "Der gerehte ensouchet niht in sînen werken; wan die iht suochent in irn werken, die sint knehte und mietlinge, oder die umbe einic warumbe würkent. Dar umbe, wilt du în-und übergebildet werden in die gerehticheit, sô enmeine niht in dînen werken und enbilde kein warumbe in dich, noch in zît noch in êwicheit, noch lôn noch saelicheit, noch diz noch daz; wan disiu werk sint alliu waerlîche tôt. Jâ, und bildest dû got in dich, swaz dû werke dar umbe würkest, diu sint alliu tôt, und dû verderbest guotiu werk" (Sermon 39, Eckhart 1936, 2: 253–55; also see Schürmann 1978, 63–65).

14. See Sermon 39, Eckhart 1936, 2: 271 (Eckhart 1986, 298). What Eckhart says here might be seen as a response to Nietzsche's critique of Christian ethics. Insofar as we are willing, we are not doing works of justice.

the soul, which is both the fruit and the cause of divine contemplation.[15] Action does not simply aid in the final goal of heavenly contemplation, but is intrinsic to contemplation itself.

Eckhart goes so far as to insist that the interior intention, sparked by the union of grounds and the birth of the Son in the soul, is alone important, thereby further altering the traditional conception of the active life.[16] This claim was cited in four of the articles condemned in the bull *In agro dominico*, which pointed to the suspicion any such assertions were under at the time due to the so-called heresy of the Free Spirit and its apparent support of Eckhart's teaching. Yet his reference to Aquinas is based on a serious subversion or misreading of the text.[17] Although, according to Aquinas, the will's lack of completion in an external action is not subject to punishment if it is involuntary, the perfection of the will demands such completion, for that is the end or goal of the will. Eckhart, on the other hand, uses the language of interior intention paradoxically to argue that one should strive to have *no will, no end,* and *no goal.*

Despite appearances, then, the appeal to interior intention is not incompatible with Eckhart's attempt to unify the active and contemplative lives, but rather reinforces the mystical themes on which this identification is based. He argues that there are four reasons why the interior act alone is important: the exterior act can be hindered; only the interior act is properly commanded by God; the interior act is never oppressive; and the interior act praises God directly as its author.[18] The unity of the interior act with the free movement of the birth of the Son in the soul guarantees its primacy over the exterior act, which is subject to outside constraint and hindrance. Through the interior movement that is the birth of the Son in the soul, true justice is brought into being; the interior intention is not the created soul's, but God's. To admit that the absence of an exterior work can diminish or alter the goodness or justice of this movement would be to admit the limitations of the created world

15. For the sermon in question, see Pfeiffer 1962, Sermon III, 18–19. Also see the *Counsels on Discernment,* n. 23, Eckhart 1936, 5: 290–309 (Eckhart 1981, 280–85).

16. See *Book of the Parables of Genesis,* n. 165, *Latin Works* 1: 634–36 (Eckhart 1981, 121); *Commentaries on John* n. 646, *Latin Works,* 3: 561; *Commentaries on Wisdom,* n. 226, *Latin Works,* 2: 561. These are the sources for articles 16–19 condemned in the bull *In agro.* See Eckhart 1981, 79. See also, Sermon 4, Eckhart 1936, 1: 71 (Eckhart 1986, 250); and Sermon 25, Eckhart 1936, 2: 17.

17. At Cologne he cites Aquinas, *Summa theologica* (Aquinas 1964a, 94–97). See Théry 1926, 195.

18. *Parables of Genesis,* n. 165, *Latin Works,* 1: 634–36 (Eckhart 1981, 121). See McGinn 1981b, 58.

into the conception of the divine and its work, for the soul shares in this work of self-creation.

Thus, just as Eckhart downplays the historical Incarnation and the particularity of the person of Christ in favor of the cosmic dimensions of the event,[19] he also deemphasizes the exterior act in favor of the interior to show that the divine work is not subject to the particularities and constraints of the created world. The first move allows him to show how the divine is radically immanent in the eternal now rather than only in one historical moment; the second speaks directly to the scrupulousness endemic to Eckhart's culture. Both must be seen within this climate. On the one hand, Eckhart insists that the soul must become detached from good works, for as particular acts they are involved in the world of intentions and goals—in sum, they are part of the created realm.[20] At the same time, he extols the interior act insofar as it is done without attachment and in absolute purity of intention: "To give a hundred marks of gold for God is a noble deed . . . yet . . . if I have the will that I should give a hundred marks if I had them—if the will is perfect, then in fact I have paid God and he must give account to me as if I had really given him a hundred marks."[21] Although interior and exterior are one in the movement of the divine,[22] Eckhart insists that creatureliness and its limitations have no power to effect the detached soul's divine intention, despite the possibility that the exterior act might be deterred. The body—experienced as present primarily in its pain and limitation—does not limit transcendence, although it shares in it.[23] Before God, all createdness is nothing and equal—not just the will and intellect, but the body as well. The equality of the divine ground is founded on this recognition. The justice that ensues subverts the very dualisms between creator and creature, and also between body and soul, whose radicalization gives rise to new consciousness.

19. See Théry 1926, 202, 233–34; and McGinn 1981b, 46.

20. See, for example, *Counsels on Discernment*, 19, and 21, and Eckhart 1936, 5: 260–62, 274–76 (Eckhart 1981, 270, 274).

21. "Der hundert mark goldes durch got gaebe, daz waere ein grôzes werk . . . aber . . . hân ich einen willen, haete ich hundert mark ze gebenne, ist eht der wille ganz, in der wârheit, sô hân ich gote bezalt, und er muoz mir antwürten, als ob ich im hundert mark bezalt haete" (Sermon 25, Eckhart 1936, 2: 17, author's translation).

22. On the ideal state, in which the exterior and the interior acts would coincide, see *Counsels on Discernment*, n. 23, Eckhart 1936, 5: 290–309 (Eckhart 1981, 280–85).

23. This is where Eckhart's thought is still distant from twentieth-century assumptions in which the body is increasingly seen as the source and ground for our transcending activity. Perhaps the differing *experience* of the body in the medieval period, particularly among Eckhart's beguinal audiences, is in part responsible for this gap. For Mechthild, the body is the source of transcendence only through pain; it is this move that Eckhart seeks to avoid. See Scarry 1985.

Eckhart's teaching applied to the possibility of social transformations grounded in mystical consciousness have certain ramifications. For Eckhart, detachment is justice, and justice is detachment. The two moments of virginity and fruitfulness are one; the paradox of "willing nothing" as social and ethical action lies at the center of Eckhart's writing. Moreover, Eckhart preached these words to women, addressing problems posed by them and borrowing freely from their solutions (see Hollywood 1995). Yet despite the radicalism of his words and preaching practice, Eckhart's apparent conservatism in his dealings with the institutional church seems to curtail any extravagant claims for the social significance of his thought. I would like to contest this interpretation, however, by suggesting that Eckhart's preaching and writing are themselves instruments of social transformation engendered by the birth of the Son/Justice in the soul. His radical reading of the Lucan passage is one such work. (I would also suggest that his overturning of Aquinas is another.) This claim rests on an understanding of language as a social force, like the understanding Derrida articulates. Derrida argues that language is itself a material system whose deployment is part of the formation and maintenance of the social world; the transformation of language effected by Eckhart (and also by Derrida in ways strikingly similar to Eckhart) is itself a form of social transformation.

To return to Derrida's objections to the comparison between his deconstructive project and negative theology, perhaps the similarities between Eckhart and Derrida are vitiated by the language of interiority, unmediatedness, and identification that runs throughout Eckhart's sermon. This language, with its emphasis on the freedom from external constraint that marks the relationship of the ground of the soul and of the divine, suggests that Derrida is right to see a continuation of the metaphysics of presence in the work of apophatic theologians such as Eckhart. I have no desire to conflate Eckhart and Derrida—the differences between them are real and historically inevitable—yet it is important to recognize that for Eckhart, the divine is always both radically transcendent and radically immanent. God's radical presence within creation is the basis for God's radical transcendence to all creation, thereby foreshadowing the interplay of presence and absence marked by the Derridean movement of *différance*. Eckhart's "mysticism of everyday life" might be seen, then, as an attempt to think religious life and practice as platitudes, like Derridean *différance;* Eckhart's writing demands that we think religion in the absence of another realm that confers meaning and in the always deferred presence of this world and its constant movement of meanings and justice.

The study of Eckhart in relationship to Derrida, moreover, might offer an important corrective to certain tendencies in the reading of Derrida. Derrida is often criticized as an idealist for whom change at the level of language is sufficient to alter social worlds (see in particular the implicit critiques of Derrida by Pierre Bourdieu [1991]). Study of Eckhart's life and work demonstrates—and Eckhart himself seemed to realize—that language is a realm of relative freedom and creativity for human individuals (as compared to other social and political structures). This point is why I give so much attention to the relationship between the interior and exterior act in Eckhart, for here Eckhart seems to distinguish between what is possible in thought and language, and what is possible in an "external" world of constraint and limitation. Writing, preaching, and other linguistic practices occupy a median place, a space in which interior acts can be immediately made present in the exterior world, despite the constraints of social, political, and ecclesial structures. Language is one social force among others and the one, Eckhart suggests, in which radical transformation most easily and unconstrainedly occurs.

Eckhart's use and abuse of the sermon and medieval exegetical traditions become particularly interesting when seen from this perspective, for they are *formalized* uses of language and hence occupy a position of great social power, yet with some of the freedom of language remaining. As Maurice Bloch argues, in formalized uses of language, creativity is at a minimum, and propositional content is downplayed as illocutionary force is strengthened, power legitimated, and hierarchies created and maintained. Sermons and other formalized uses of language mark the place in which language is most reified by the social world and hence least susceptible to change and most constitutive of hierarchalizing authority (Bloch 1989, 19–45).

Bloch points to some of the key restrictions placed on ritualized language that result in its authorizing and hierarchalizing power: restrictions on the range of possible intonations, vocabulary, and illustrations, and restrictions on "the body of knowledge from which suitable illustrations can be drawn" (1989, 34). In each instance, we see that Eckhart takes on the authority of the preacher only in order to subvert it. We have little access to Eckhart's intonations, yet his untraditional reading of the *tone* of Martha's comments and his claim that the recognition of this tone is essential to ascertaining the meaning of the text suggest he was sensitive to issues of tonality and may himself have diverged from the accepted range for preaching. There is an enormous literature on Eckhart's innovative vocabulary. What is most evident in Sermon 86, however, is the way Eckhart uses traditional authorities in profoundly untraditional ways. In other words, he takes a traditional form, one designed to maintain hierarchies and relations of domination, and systematically subverts it, thereby unleashing an egalitarian and "purposeless" experience of the divine in the everyday world.

Eckhart's condemnation by ecclesial authority and the subsequent suppression of the most radical aspects of his work suggest the limitations of social transformation in and through language. Yet analysis of his writing, of his preaching practice, and of the subsequent effects of that practice demonstrates the power contained within these linguistic strategies. To put the matter in Eckhart's own terms, insofar as his writing is an instance of justice and of the birth of the Son in the soul, it transforms social worlds. Insofar as it engenders detachment, justice, equality, and the birth of the Son in the soul of the reader, his writing becomes the catalyst for further social transformation.

5

St. Teresa of Avila as a Social Reformer

CAROLE SLADE

St. Teresa of Avila, widely known as a mystic, is not generally thought of as a social reformer. Far from picturing her in action, many see her through the gaze of Bernini, who immobilized her outside time and space. When reform *is* considered part of her legacy, it is religious reform, the creation of a new monastic order, the Discalced Carmelites. Teresa's religious reforms had a rippling of social consequences (Bilinkoff 1988), as any rearrangement of people and resources would, but I argue here that Teresa also intended and indeed effected social reforms—specifically, increasing autonomy for women and integrating *conversos* (Jews who had converted to Christianity) into Spanish society. Because she belonged to both these groups and because she articulated for her contemporaries those aspects of her mystical experience that instigated and justified her activism, Teresa's life serves well to illustrate the theory, advanced recently by Richard Woods (1996), that the entire trajectory of individual mystical experience evolves in dialectical relation to society.

Pursuing Woods's idea that the "mystic's calling, development, and subsequent activity constitute structurally integral phases of a social process" (1996, 158), I begin by isolating those circumstances that seem related to Teresa's agenda for social change. Teresa was born March 28, 1515, in Gotarrendura, a tiny Castilian village near Avila, to Alonso de Cepeda and Beatriz de Ahumada. She was the third child and first daughter born to the couple, who were married when Beatriz, age fourteen, was more than six months pregnant. The marriage was Alonso's second, and because Beatriz was a third cousin to his deceased wife, it required Alonso to buy a costly papal dispensation. Even in these degrading circumstances, both families needed the marriage: the Cepedas, who were *conversos,* gained an alliance with the Old Christian Ahumada family; the Ahumadas, who were Old Christian nobility *(hidalgos)* but impoverished, received the large dowry that *conversos* were forced to pay, even for a daughter who had lost her value with her virginity.

Teresa's father and uncles had moved to Avila from Toledo following their father's condemnation by the Inquisition for Judaizing, or secretly practicing Jewish customs. Reported to the Inquisition by his wife's brother, an Old Christian, Juan Sánchez (1440–1507) avoided a protracted and expensive investigation by accepting an edict of grace, a temporary provision offering absolution to those who denounced themselves. His confession to heresy and apostasy against the Christian faith did not necessarily indicate guilt. In *The Origins of the Inquisition in Fifteenth Century Spain,* Benzion Netanyahu argues that most charges of Judaizing were fabricated (1995, 447–49 *et passim*). Nonetheless, in 1484, Juan participated in the ritual for absolution, which required walking, on seven consecutive Fridays, through the streets of Toledo wearing a *sambenito,* a bright yellow knee-length tunic embroidered with black crosses and flames identifying him as a heretic. Teresa's father, six years old at the time, accompanied him on these walks, which Anne J. Cruz and Mary Elizabeth Perry describe as "visually and ideologically similar to the public executions described by Michel Foucault" (1992a, xiii).

Although Teresa's grandfather avoided the bankruptcy that usually resulted from this humiliation, his previously thriving textile business went into decline. As a result, he moved the family to nearby Avila and added his wife's Old Christian name to his own, becoming Juan Sánchez de Cepeda. Implausible as it now seems, the family lived there as nobility, engaging in occupations and social activities that were closed to *conversos.* This lifestyle required various kinds of maneuvering: purchasing papers of nobility, petitioning the king, and volunteering to participate in small-scale military campaigns. In 1519, the Cepeda brothers provoked litigation over their right to tax exemptions with the hope of winning not simply the financial advantage of the nobility but legal certification of their status as Old Christians. Documents from the trial suggest that they bribed witnesses to win the case in 1522 (Bilinkoff 1989, 64–67). The favorable verdict belied the continuing instability of their position. Old Christians of all classes, anxious about the constant shuffling of the social deck that often displaced them, pressed for laws requiring purity of blood *(limpieza de la sangre).* Initially relatively benign, these laws were extended in scope until by the mid–sixteenth century they excluded *conversos* from virtually every avenue of participation in society. In the words of Juan Ignacio Gutiérrez Nieto, they effected the "sociopolitical death" of *conversos* (1983, 104).

Despite the enduring trauma of her ethnic heritage, Teresa seems to have identified as much with Old Christian women as with New Christian men. Mariló Vigil argues that women were categorized by their marital status— maidens, spinsters, married women, widows, or nuns—more definitively than by their father's status: "the power relations to which all women were submitted derived primarily from their positions in the family. Being prisoners of the domestic is what unites all of them" (1986, 17). All decisions about Teresa's future belonged to her father. His options for her were limited: he might keep her at home as a spinster-servant, a situation she rejected after her mother's death to escape the emotional burdens of being a surrogate wife; he might give her in marriage to a man who would enhance the family's social and financial standing, though that option was rarely available to *conversas,* and in any case Teresa tells us that she feared marriage; or he might send her to a convent. Of these options, Teresa requested the convent, but her father said, in effect, "over my dead body"; that is, he granted permission for her to enter the convent, but only after his death. As much to reject other avenues as to embrace the religious life, at age twenty Teresa enlisted a brother to help her make a clandestine early-morning escape from home to the Carmelite convent of the Encarnación, just outside the walls of Avila. She expresses her ambivalence in terms of excruciating physical pain: "When I left my father's house I felt that separation so keenly that the feeling will not be greater, I think, when I die. For it seemed that every bone in my body was being sundered" *(Book of Her Life,* 4.1).[1] Even after taking vows a year later, she continued to vacillate between worldly and spiritual attachments for twenty years, until in 1556 she received a divine locution that functioned to secure her commitment to spiritual marriage with Christ: "No longer do I want you to converse with men but with angels" *(Life,* 24.5).

Theorists of mysticism have given various reasons for mystics' engagement in worldly action: charity motivated by an awareness of the divinity shared by all creatures; an increase in vitality; healthier psychological adjustment; and for Christian mystics, conscious or unconscious imitation of Christ. Woods finds all of these explanations incomplete because they neglect the idea, which he traces to the work of William Ernest Hocking (1873–1966), that both mystical withdrawal and the subsequent return are socially as well as religiously motivated. In Woods's estimate, mystical experience provides a new assessment of society: "Morally, the negative path sensitizes the mystic's conscience; she is better able to perceive both justice and injustice" (1996, 166). Even though Woods uses the feminine pronoun here (as an occasional alternative to the universal "he"), his theory seems less applicable to women than to men, certainly less relevant in the case of a woman doubly marginal-

---

1. For quotations from Teresa's writings, I use Teresa of Avila 1976–85, the translation by Kieran Kavanaugh and Otilio Rodríguez, *The Collected Works of St. Teresa of Avila,* 3 vols. I cite individual works by the titles and section numbers in Kavanaugh and Rodríguez. In two instances noted parenthetically, I use the translation by E. Allison Peers (1944–46), *The Complete Works of Teresa of Avila,* 3 vols.

ized by overwhelming prejudices. Teresa understood social injustice quite clearly when she ran away from home; what she lacked was the power to resist it. She describes her mystical experience as providing not primarily analysis of the world's defects, but the resources to correct them.

Teresa's mystical experience gave her a new identity—successor to Mary Magdalene—which she interpreted as authorization to action on Christ's behalf in the world beyond the convent. On the Magdalene's feast day, July 22, Teresa often received divine confirmation of this new status. A locution from Christ reported by Diego de Yepes, one of her confessors, in his 1587 biography suggests that she identified quite literally with this idealized self: " 'While I was on earth, I took her [Mary Magdalene] for my friend; but now that I am in heaven, I have chosen you' " (1570? quoted in *Spiritual Testimony* 28, no. 1, Peers 1944–46, 1: 494).

Teresa's allusions to Mary Magdalene are relatively infrequent and apparently random, but the isolated references can be fitted together into a coherent construction of her life. In keeping with medieval tradition, which Teresa knew principally through Jacobus de Voragine's *Golden Legend (Legenda aurea*, ca. 1260), she conflates the fisherwoman who bathed Christ's feet in the home of Simon the Pharisee (Luke 7:36–50); Mary of Bethany, sister of Martha and Lazarus (John 11); and Mary Magdalene.[2] Mary Magdalene— represented in all four Gospels as one of the women who followed Christ to the Cross and the one who went to embalm the body, and, in Mark and John, as the first to whom the resurrected Christ appeared—had been reduced by early Christian interpreters to a "repentant whore" (Haskins 1993, 15). In the kind of move that Alicia Ostriker calls "mythic revisionism" (1985, 317–18), Teresa alters the significance of the medieval Mary Magdalene. By adding Martha of Bethany, the virtuous and industrious sister of Mary of Bethany, to the cluster of scriptural Marys that comprised the medieval Mary Magdalene, Teresa discards Mary Magdalene's identification as a prostitute, and she sets her in motion. Referring to the patristic tradition that Origen (c. 185–254) began with his allegorical interpretation of Martha and Mary of Bethany as, respectively, action and contemplation (Constable 1997, 15), Teresa's Magdalene figure combines the active and contemplative lives: "Martha and Mary never fail to work almost together when the soul is in this state [mystical marriage]. For in the active—and seemingly exterior—work the soul is working interiorly. And when the active works rise from this interior root, they become lovely and very fragrant flowers" *(Meditations on the Song of Songs*, 7.3). To befit the Bride of Christ the King, these works must be suitably regal: "If a

2. I develop Teresa's interpretation of and identification with Mary Magdalene at greater length in Slade 1995, 57–64 *et passim*.

peasant girl should marry the king and have children, don't the children have royal blood? Well, if our Lord grants so much favor to our soul that He joins Himself to it in this inseparable way, what desire, what effects, what heroic deeds will be born from it as offspring, if the soul be not at fault!" *(Meditations on the Song of Songs,* 3.9). The "heroic deeds" born of Teresa's mystical marriage were religious and social reforms.

Teresa's Mary Magdalene is as much a Martha as a Mary. Teresa reassures those nuns following a regime of mental prayer that Christ's response to Martha's complaint about doing all the chores while Mary sat listening to Christ ("The part that Mary has chosen is best," Luke 10:42) constitutes a defense of contemplative women: "Observe how the Lord answered for the Magdalene in the house of the Pharisee and when her sister accused her" *(Way of Perfection,* 15.7). Yet because Teresa does not have in mind housework or any of the helping activities usually assigned to women in the active life, such as nursing the sick, sewing, or weaving, Teresa's Martha also requires Christ's advocacy. The work to which Teresa aspired was that of an apostle, which, according to the Gospel of John, Christ gave to Mary Magdalene when He dispatched her to spread the news of His Resurrection (20:10–18). Teresa describes the work of her apostolic Martha-Mary as "bringing Him souls": "Martha and Mary must work together when they offer the Lord lodging, and they must not entertain Him badly and give Him nothing to eat. And how can Mary give Him anything, seated as she is at His feet, unless her sister helps her? His food consists in our bringing Him souls, in every possible way, so that they may be saved and may praise Him forever" *(Interior Castle,* 7.4.12). Addressing those nuns who might be frightened by their own aspirations to do this forbidden work, Teresa names the role of apostle, ostensibly to disavow it but actually to insert it into the discourse: "The other objection you will make is that you are unable to bring souls to God, that you do not have the means; that you would do it willingly but that not being teachers or preachers, as were the apostles, you do not know how" *(Interior Castle,* 7.4.14). This passage, like much of Teresa's prose, is a complex piece of rhetoric. While counseling contentment with contemplation, she sows dissatisfaction by elevating the actions of teaching and preaching above contemplation.

Teresa's mystical experience provided her with knowledge of human affairs. William James designates a noetic quality, defined as "states of insight into depths of truth unplumbed by the discursive intellect," as one of the four marks of authentic mystical experience (1961, 300). Teresa's mystical experience is noetic in this Jamesian intuitive mode. At the same time, like many other mystics, Teresa testifies to acquiring cognitive knowledge of various domains, including eschatology, cosmology, theology, and anthropology. Hildegard of Bingen, for example, witnessed the configuration of the cosmos, and Julian of Norwich gleaned a theology with a feminine dimension.

Unlike Hildegard of Bingen, however, Teresa makes no eschatological projections, rarely mentioning the afterlife except to describe visions of others ascending from purgatory to paradise or to express her fear of hell. By comparison with Julian of Norwich's theology, Teresa's is relatively undeveloped. Neither does Teresa's mysticism orient her to the cosmos. She seems rarely to have even looked at the natural world, and when she did, it was mainly to find analogies for her mystical experience; the appreciation of natural beauty that John of Cross expresses does not appear in Teresa's works. Teresa does have a theology and an anthropology, but she seems to have derived them by commonsensical speculation rather than by visionary experience.

When Teresa refers to the noetic harvest of her mysticism, she describes it as political knowledge, knowledge proper to kings: the knowledge she needed to maneuver safely and effectively in her society.

> Blessed is the soul the Lord brings to the understanding of the truth! Oh, how fit a state this is for kings! How much more worthwhile it would be for them to strive for this stage of prayer rather than for great dominion! What righteousness there would be in the kingdom! What evils they would avoid and have avoided! . . . You know well that I would very willingly dispossess myself of the favors You have granted me and give them to the kings, . . .because I know that it would then be impossible for them to consent to the things that are now consented to. (*Life*, 21.1–2)

Efficient with her rhetoric here as elsewhere, Teresa presses several points. She equates her newly acquired perspective with God's view, which a king ruling by divine sanction, in this case Philip II, should also have but seems to lack. She also begins a campaign to influence Philip. As he became increasingly concerned about external threats to the Spanish Empire, he grew more paranoid about internal dissent, even difference, and eventually equated religious heterodoxy with political dissidence (Contreras 1992, 93). Those groups most frequently suspected of heresy were women and *conversos,* and because she belonged to both, Teresa knew that she needed his protection. Philip considered the monasteries sufficiently related to national security to become directly involved in their affairs; furthermore, as king he had the power to confer noble status by royal decree.[3] For many purposes, then, Teresa plants a suggestion of the affinity between her empowerment by God and royal power.

---

3. Because the king had the power to confer noble status by decree, New Christians had frequently appealed successfully to Philip's father, Charles V. As Philip diminished such opportuni-

A few chapters later in the *Life* she speculates about ways to get a letter past the layers of bureaucrats that surrounded him:

> I'm not surprised that one doesn't dare speak to the king or to his represen-
> tatives, for there is reason for caution. . . . If you could learn the rules once
> and for all, you could let the matter pass. But just for the titles of address on
> a letter there's a need for a university chair, so to speak, to lecture on how it's
> to be done. For sometimes you have to leave a margin on this side of the
> page, sometimes on the other; and someone who's not usually addressed as
> magnifico must be then addressed as illustrious. (37.8–9)

Teresa's capacity to ridicule court etiquette is only one sign that she protests too much; she had immense talent for verbal communication, particularly with authority figures. In Alison Weber's words, she operated by "dismantling monolithic authority into lesser competing authorities [and by] seeking out an authority whose will coincided with her own" (1990, 133).

Teresa probably never met Philip II in person. Many biographers have tried to arrange a rendezvous by plotting possible intersections of their movements, but there is no credible evidence that they came face to face. She did write four letters to him in which she wields the political acumen she attributes to her mystical experience (dated June 11, 1573; July 19, 1575; September 18, 1577; and December 4, 1577). In all of them, she attempts to secure his protection of her new order against the increasingly brutal and effective moves by the parent order to suppress it. It is not known whether any of these letters reached Philip's eyes. Yet whether responding to her requests or not, Philip did take some of the actions Teresa recommended, if not always immediately. In 1579, six years after Teresa wrote the 1573 letter, he separated the warring factions of Carmelites by declaring the Discalced a separate province *(Foundations,* 29.30). Teresa explains that he awarded this favor and others because she convinced him that the rigorous devotional practices in her monasteries reinforced his political aims, and she advises future Discalced to nurture the relationship she initiated *(Foundations,* 27.6).

For her orientation to politics, Teresa is reminiscent of Dante, who though not a mystic by virtue of a personal relationship with God, describes mystical visions. With his *Divina commedia,* Dante intended to effect change in the worldly order, specifically to promote the creation of a secular government with power equal to that of the Roman Catholic Church. At the exact center of the poem, Marco Lombardo explains the failures of the consolida-

---

ties and in addition began letting the nation slip into decline, he became the focus of rescue fantasies (Kagan 1990, 2), which Teresa may also be expressing here.

tion of "sword" and "crook": "Tell henceforth that the Church of Rome, by confounding in itself two governments, falls in the mire and befouls both itself and its burden" (1973, *Purgatorio,* 16.127–29). Dante received a mandate to *tell,* but Teresa, as we have seen, received orders to *do.*

Like Dante, Teresa measures human reality against the divine order she has perceived in mystical visions. With deed rather than word, Teresa undertakes to reform that human reality. Her foundations, she argues, will make the eternal order visible in this world. Here she invokes the specter of eternal damnation for the sin of misogyny: "How differently will we understand these ignorances on the day when the truth about all things shall be understood. And how many fathers and mothers will be seen going to hell because they had sons and also how many will be seen in heaven because of their daughters" *(Foundations,* 20.3). With respect to *conversos,* she also took the divine perspective, including them in her monasteries and accepting their financial support. A divine locution resolved her doubts about letting two wealthy brothers, Martín and Alonso Alvarez Ramírez, raise money for the Toledo foundation, "since that family was not from the nobility, although the family was very good, regardless of its social status" (in other words, they were *conversos*): "He [Christ] told me that lineage and social status mattered not at all in the judgment of God" *(Foundations,* 15.15–16). Because He also told her that "estates, inheritances, riches" have no significance in eternity, Teresa did not require dowries.

The root of Teresa's impulse to reform probably derives in part from her *converso* heritage. As the name *converso* indicates, these Jews had converted to Christianity, often by force or out of fear, but still they had converted. According to Netanyahu, those Jews who had chosen to emigrate rather than convert regarded the *conversos* in Spain not as Jews, Judaizers, or crypto-Jews, but as Gentiles (1995, 928 *et passim*). On this evidence and more, he concludes that by the end of the fifteenth century the *conversos* were "overwhelmingly Christian and bent upon a course of complete assimilation" (1995, xix). He attributes persecution of *conversos* in part to resentment of their success, in part to racism. One way *conversos* maintained their self-respect, according to Gutiérrez Nieto, was by redefining honor, which officially derived from lineage and land, to include "social utility" or public service, thus with the proverbial fervor of the convert achieving an ethical standard higher than that of Old Christians (1983, 115).

Teresa also found the exclusion of women from most church offices and significant functions antithetical to Christianity. The Spanish church had countered the Reformation by restricting women's religious life to the recitation of vocal prayers, and Teresa chafed under the restrictions on women's active participation in the evangelical mission of the church. Most often she expresses her grievances indirectly, but in a section of *Way of Perfection* that, not surprisingly, was blotted out by censors, she accuses "the sons of Adam" of preventing women from doing "anything worthwhile" for God:

> Is it not enough, Lord, that the world has intimidated us [women] . . . so that we may not do anything worthwhile for You in public or dare speak some truths that we lament over in secret, without Your also failing to hear so just a petition? I do not believe, Lord, that this could be true of Your goodness and justice, for You are a just judge and not like those of the world. Since the world's judges are sons of Adam and all of them men, there is no virtue in women that they do not hold suspect. (*Way of Perfection*, 3.7)

The inversion of values she diagnoses, in which virtues are considered faults and truth must be spoken in secret, illustrates the deterioration of worldly society. She continues by warning God that men's responsibility for this disrepair makes them unreliable and by advising Him to rely on women instead: "these are times in which it would be wrong to undervalue virtuous and strong souls, even though they are women." With a new identity as Mary Magdalene, Teresa believed she had both the mandate and the implements for corrective action.

Woods speculates that the active lives of mystics are not well known because most of them stopped writing when they began their work. He names Teresa as an example, but in fact she chronicled her work toward the founding of the Discalced Carmelite Order in her book known as *Foundations*. Begun in late 1573, *Foundations* comprehends a retrospective narrative of her activities back to 1562 and a memoir extending to mid-April 1582, a few months before her death on October 4. The order in which she took vows, the Carmelites, had developed from a group of twelfth-century European hermits living on Mt. Carmel, Palestine. In the thirteenth century, they moved to Europe, where they founded monasteries under a 1229 rule of poverty and mendicancy. Relaxed by Pope Eugenius IV in 1432, these rules no longer required strict asceticism and poverty. In sixteenth-century Spain, these rules slackened still further to the point of enabling wealthy women to live luxuriously and even to have slaves in the convent. Beside them, women without financial support from their families often went hungry. Teresa's work consisted in the founding of sixteen monasteries, twelve for women and four for men, under a primitive rule enforcing strict enclosure and discipline. For their austere dress, a coarse wool habit and straw sandals, they became known as the Discalced (Barefoot) Carmelites. Teresa's *Foundations, Constitutions* (her rules for governance), and *Guidelines for Visitation* (advice to the priests who did something like accreditation visits) provide a window into her intentions for social as well as religious reform.

How did Teresa's foundations advance the social goals of increasing women's autonomy and assimilating *conversos?* With respect to *conversos,* for whom the mark of her success would be their disappearance into the crowd, the question is difficult to answer. The force with which Spain repressed its collective Jewish heritage becomes evident on considering that although Teresa and her contemporaries knew about her familial heritage, she does not mention it in her writings, except in the occasional ironic aside: "it could not be because I am from the nobility [literally, illustrious blood *(sangre ilustre)*] that He has given me such honor" *(Foundations, 27.12).* Her Jewish heritage was not publicly discussed until 1946, when Narciso Alonso Cortés presented records of her grandfather's reconciliation with the Inquisition in the *Bulletin of the Spanish Royal Academy.* Even afterward, some critics and biographers deliberately omitted or distorted the facts of her birth and lineage.

The circumspection and evasion with which Teresa and other historians of the Discalced Carmelites treated the subject of ethnic background have effaced evidence, apart from the circumstantial, that would indicate how many of the original Discalced Carmelites were *conversos.* Although the Discalced convents and monasteries also attracted Old Christians, Teresa's choice of locations, mainly urban and commercial, suggests that she drew from the large *converso* populations there (Bilinkoff 1989, 146–47). After 1566, when the parent Carmelites joined most other orders in requiring purity of blood, *conversos* would have found the Discalced monasteries among very few open to them. Teresa judged applicants on the basis of their piety and suitability for the religious life, criteria that would have permitted *conversos* to compete successfully. The controversy over the foundation in Toledo, where she encountered opposition because *conversos* contributed a large percentage of her financial and logistical support, reveals that Teresa's order served *conversos* not only by giving havens and occupations to individuals, but also by affording their families the social prestige and religious consolation that derived from endowing religious institutions (Bilinkoff 1989, 147). The fact that soon after Teresa's death the Discalced Carmelites amended their constitution to require purity of blood suggests the perils of sheltering *conversos* and thus the magnitude of Teresa's achievement, even if the numbers she sheltered were relatively small.

It is much easier to discern the ways in which Teresa's foundations challenged the social and economic order of patriarchy. Teresa's feminist analyses of society and means of resistance emerge most clearly in the six biographical sketches she intercalates in her chronicle in *Foundations.* As Weber points out, all of these stories resonate with Teresa's own life, and they also contain details that seem purely novelistic (1990, 148–50). I have argued elsewhere (Slade 1995, 120–25) that these biographies comprise a primitive "city of ladies" constructed not with the classical heroines that Christine of Pisan used, but with Spanish women Teresa actually knew: Casilda de Padilla, Beatriz de la Encarnación, Teresa de Layz, Catalina Godínez, Catalina de Cardona, and Beatriz de Chávez.

All these women learned early that their families considered them inferior to boys and sometimes unworthy of nurture or love. Teresa de Layz disappointed her parents at birth by becoming their fifth daughter. When she was three days old, they neglected her for an entire day, "as though she mattered little to them" *(Foundations,* 20.4). Suspecting that she might have died, a neighbor woman hurried to her room and found her miraculously empowered with precocious speech: "Weeping, the woman took the baby into her arms and complaining of the cruelty said: 'How is it, my daughter, are you not a Christian?' The baby girl lifted her head and answered, 'Yes, I am,' and spoke no more until reaching that age at which all children begin to speak" *(Foundations,* 20.4). Perhaps because she reminded her parents of the Christian ideal of human value, Teresa de Layz won a place in the family: "her mother began to love and cherish her from then on." Beatriz de Chávez, who entered the convent at Seville, took last place in her parents' affections while her brothers were alive: "Although she had had older brothers, they had all died, and she, the less loved by her parents, was left" *(Foundations,* 26.7).

Having reluctantly raised these girls, parents wished to exploit their exchange value in marriage. They arranged early marriages with the men they thought best able to enhance the family fortune, severely punishing any refusal or attempt to escape. When the family inheritance passed from an older sister to Casilda, she was engaged to an uncle as a means of keeping the wealth in the family. She ran away to a convent, but her parents obtained a court order to remove her. Beatriz de Chávez's parents made her marriage contract when she was eleven: "When she reached the marriageable age, though she was still but a girl, her parents came to an agreement on whom she should marry" *(Foundations,* 26.7). For her resistance, Beatriz nearly died: "Since they had already given their word and their not following through on it would have been taken as an affront by the other party, they gave her so many whippings, inflicted on her so many punishments, even to the point of wanting to hang her, for they were choking her, that it was fortunate they didn't kill her" *(Foundations,* 26.8). If some women were nearly killed, others tried to kill themselves. Catalina Godínez disfigured herself with severe facial sunburns to thwart her parents' attempts to marry her. When that tactic failed, she developed an array of illnesses—breast cancer, consumption, tuberculosis, dropsy, inflammation of the liver, gout, and sciatica. After eight years in bed, she proposed that if God gave her complete health within a month, she should be allowed to petition for a license to found a convent rather than be forced to marry. When she was cured at the appointed time, her family released her from the obligation to marry. Her appeal to Philip II produced the license for the foundation at Beas.

In addition to refuge, Teresa's convents replaced the patriarchal system of exchange with a network of female kinship. Catalina Godínez's conversion gave her a new definition of lineage: "The Lord worked a complete change in her: She had been thinking of a marriage that was being sought for her, which was better than she could have hoped for, and saying to herself: 'With what little my father is content, that I become connected with an entailed estate; I am thinking of becoming the origin of a new line of descendants' " *(Foundations,* 22.5). Teresa's alternative social organization provided for spiritual and material inheritance. Teresa planned that her nuns would endow their descendants with the wealth of their suffering, and ultimately those with sufficient courage would "inherit His kingdom." A savvy financier, she also shows in *Foundations* that these women effected a transfer of wealth to the convents. Teresa de Layz, who received a sign that she should marry a man who would help support the order rather than join it herself, chose not to have children so that she could leave their estate to the convent at Alba de Tormes. Catalina de Godínez and her sister left their inheritance to the order "without any conditions, so that even if they were not admitted to profession, the money would still belong to the order" *(Foundations,* 22.24). Previously vehicles for their fathers' accumulation of wealth, they now enriched other women, who shared equally in whatever money came to the convents. Because most of this money was probably Old Christian, Teresa's social reforms on behalf of women reinforced her empowerment of *conversos* at the economic crux.

Not everyone agrees that Teresa's project of foundations should be considered protofeminist. Claire Guilhem judges her exclusion of *beatas*—women who wished to live in female communities but not to enter an order—an indication of her collusion with patriarchy (1979, 215). It is true that Teresa did not accept *beatas,* and although she does not explain why, the reason might have to do with her seriousness about religious practices; she did defend women hermits—a group scorned and tormented by society—praising them for the intensity of their dedication (Saint-Säens 1996, 56–57). Weber argues that Teresa's emphasis on obedience betrayed her own revolt, denying liberty and autonomy to other women (1990, 156–57). Teresa certainly was imperious, and I doubt that she tolerated challenges to her leadership. Yet her requirements for obedience should not be judged by contemporary or secular standards of freedom. Teresa understood Scripture to mean that salvation required obedience to God. And, far from being coerced, women came voluntarily to Teresa's foundations, presumably because they preferred the life there to any alternative.

Despite the authoritarian governance, Teresa's convents did empower other women. The *Constitutions* required prioresses to teach illiterate women to read and stipulated that each convent have a library, in which the nuns are known to have concealed books that had appeared on the 1559 Index.[4] Even though the cubicles in which they lived were usually minuscule and dilapidated, the convent was the only place a woman was likely to have a room of her own. Many women, particularly in the next generation, used the privacy of these rooms for writing, calling on Teresa as both subject and inspiration. For example, María de San Alberto extolled Teresa in a poem written about 1622, the year of her canonization, as "learned doctor in her deeds and works, / in her writings and her counsel" (quoted in Arenal and Schlau 1989, 139). Other women developed talents in other arenas, such as painting, sewing, teaching, and playing musical instruments (Arenal and Schlau 1989, 138). In the next generation, prioresses trained by Teresa, such as Ana de San Bartolomé and Ana de San José, and their successors extended the Discalced Carmelites throughout Europe and the New World, invoking Teresa's authority. Even if her ambitions did not extend to radical reform, Teresa did make some progress toward attaining social justice for women and *conversos*.

I would not go so far, however, as to put social reform uppermost on Teresa's agenda: I consider Teresa to have acted from entirely Christian motives and, benighted as it sounds today, to have believed that the female and *converso* souls she nurtured would compensate for those of northern European Protestants and natives in the New World. Teresa's social reforms issued from her religious belief that all Catholic Christians, including women and *conversos*, should have equal status in church and state. But I like to think that her strong sense of justice has inspired others in more enlightened times to extend equality to all of humanity.

---

4. This index, the Inquisition's list of prohibited reading, included devotional and mystical texts, many of which had been important to Teresa's spiritual development, and Spanish translations of Scripture, whether a few lines or entire books.

6

Ignatian Mysticism of Service

IGNATIUS OF LOYOLA AND PEDRO ARRUPE

JANET K. RUFFING, R.S.M.

The innovative "service mysticism" of Ignatius of Loyola (1491–1556), the founder of the Company of Jesus, later known as the Society of Jesus,[1] exemplifies with extraordinary clarity the link between mysticism and action for the good of others—the transformation of society as well as of the hearts and minds of individuals. I demonstrate this link by examining the life of Ignatius with the original founding group and later historical embodiments of Ignatian service mysticism in this century's charismatic general of the order, Pedro Arrupe (1907–91), and in the consensual decrees of the Thirty-first to Thirty-fourth General Congregations of the Society of Jesus.[2]

Before the relationship between mysticism and action in the Ignatian experience can be demonstrated, it is necessary to situate this reflection in the context of the possible meanings of both mysticism and social transformation. This problematic results from a long philosophical and cultural history. In the modern and contemporary periods, definitions of both mysticism and social life artificially separated these two domains of human experience from one another. The Enlightenment and later Marxist criticisms of religion demonstrated only too clearly the potential of a dominant religious institution to oppress large segments of a society through the manipulation of religious meanings and through the coercive uses of political as well as sacral power. Hence, as Steven Ozment so persuasively argues in *Mysticism and Dissent,* mysticism carries the roots of dissent, reform, or revolution (1973). In the six-

1. The Company of Jesus refers to the apostolically oriented religious community of priests known later as the Society of Jesus and, more popularly, as Jesuits.

2. A general congregation is an assembly of Jesuits representing every province in the world, which meets to elect new leadership, to legislate on behalf of the entire society and to authoritatively interpret their charism in the light of present circumstances and challenges.

teenth century, for instance, Ignatius's historical context and the historical period Ozment studied, religious ideology shaped history and directly contributed to the social grievances and oppression of large numbers of people. In this cultural context, mysticism became a powerful source of resistance, renewal, and reform.

> Both in terms of its objective orientation and its subjective power the mystical enterprise is peculiar, departing the ordinary way to religious truth and salvation for a more direct and intimate communion with God. It reaches further than the normal psychological functions of the soul can grasp and demands more than the normal institutional structures of the church can give. In the most literal sense of the words, the mystical enterprise is transrational and transinstitutional. And because it is such, it bears a potential *anti*-intellectual and *anti*-institutional stance, which can be adopted for the critical purposes of dissent, reform, and even revolution. (Ozment 1973, 8)

Taken to its logical conclusion, the conscious cultivation of the mystical relationship with ultimate reality may lead the subject of such experiences to a radical repudiation of all other means of mediated experiences of God in favor of a form of mystical salvation as the "final power and authority of the Self within one's own self" (Ozment 1973, 12). Ozment continues, "With the collapse of the normal activities of the soul follows as surely as the night the day the irrelevance of everything the visible world has to offer, whether it be of good or of ill. One is above popes and kings, beyond sacraments and laws, immune to worldly praise and condemnation. Even if the experience (or the theory) does not issue in dissent, reform or revolutionary activity, it uniquely drives home the ideological prerequisite for such, viz. an understanding of the penultimate character of all worldly power and authority" (12).

Because the radical freedom of persons mystically transformed in their perspective vis-à-vis worldly (social) power and its particular forms of coercion and corruption, especially should they gather followers, has such potential for challenging existing religious power relations and their social and institutional embodiments, religious institutions develop effective means of controlling, suppressing, or taming such challenges to their hegemony. When reform movements fail in their attempts to bring about incremental social change within religious or political-religious institutions through appeals to the ideals available to all within a common ideological frame, they may be ruthlessly extinguished or turn revolutionary. Hence, in the sixteenth century and even earlier, mystical reform movements were frequently suppressed by the

Catholic Church through judicial processes and violent crusades that defined many challengers as "heretical" and thereby meriting execution.

As political systems began to change in the sixteenth century, some "heretics" succeeded in establishing radical reform groups that evolved into Protestant sects or churches in opposition to the Catholic Church. The inability of the Catholic Church to respond adequately to the criticism of the reformers led to revolution in many instances. These Protestant reformers felt compelled to form alternative religious sects by developing alliances with secular authorities who also resented the control of the church in their affairs.

Reform Within Roman Catholicism

Within the Roman Catholic Church, attempts at religious reform represented a version of social transformation focused on the institution itself and on its relation to the larger society. Sociologists sometimes characterize these reform movements as "renewal" or "revitalization" movements. In order to create positive change and successfully avoid suppression, reformers aligned themselves with institutional and spiritual interests that made their contribution appear desirable to the church. These "interests" were often a shared vision rooted in the Gospel, regarding which there were real agreements about desirable actions and values. If successful, reformers were able to establish a set of conditions under which they could creatively work that would serve both their own deepest goals of personal and social renewal, and yet not appear to threaten the current power arrangements and interests of the institution. The phenomenon of mystical reformers who managed to initiate and sustain social transformation within a church has been of less interest to contemporary scholars than an ahistorical, privatized account of religious or mystical experience devoid of such social implications.

Further, both phenomenological studies of mysticism as well as the typologies developed by sociological studies define the closely related concepts of social action, prophecy, charism, and mysticism in ways that obscure their relationship to one another. For instance, is not prophecy a form of mysticism, as Woods recently argues against Smart (1996, 169–70)? Regarding the biblical religions, it is very difficult to argue that the experience of the prophet is not also mystical. It does, after all, become a matter of definition to what extent a charism, a gift of the Holy Spirit for the sake of the community, is not also received and acted on through an ongoing process of mystical transformation in the person so empowered to act for and in a particular community. This split between mysticism and prophecy impedes scholars' efforts to recognize the historical embodiments of mystically grounded social action within religious contexts.[3] Grace Jantzen (1995) has clearly shown that the power to define mysticism and who counts as a mystic is often both political and gender biased. Her study reveals that motives of institutional and political control may be operative under the guise of concerns about religious truth or doctrinal development. The power exercised by certain educated elites—usually male, celibate, and clerical—may threaten the nonordained, especially women when they claim any mystical or doctrinal authority.

Counter-Reformation mystical reformers, such as Ignatius of Loyola, were successful in creating a new social embodiment of their reforming ideals, usually a new religious community; in mobilizing resources; and in creating or adapting frame alliances (Wittberg 1996) that enabled them to participate effectively within the larger social phenomenon of the Catholic reform movements leading up to and resulting from the Council of Trent (1546–63). Thus, they successfully innovated on the basis of their mystical experience, yet presented their innovation as harmonious to the reform sponsored by the institution. They succeeded precisely because they found ways of carving out a new niche of activity within the larger institution. This adaptation of frame alliances may appear to twentieth-century interpreters as a compromise with the political reality of an institution and some of the corrupt officeholders who wielded power in its system. Contemporary scholars in the field of mysticism often fail to take sufficiently into account the actual historical record, however, which might demonstrate that reforming mystics were engaged within their ecclesial bodies in a form of social transformation when they were concerned about mediating religious salvation to those who were marginalized within society, even when they did not address all of the other economic or social needs of the group they served. Sociologists, on the other hand, often fail to recognize the range of complex social processes related to the religion mystics practiced that contributed to and supported innovating or reforming movements (Coleman 1997).

Ignatius of Loyola

In the case of Ignatius of Loyola, his project of social transformation was directly related to the broad reform movement in the Catholic Church of his day, but he gradually evolved a unique response to that movement through his personal experience and that of the founding group of companions who

3. For instance, see McGinn (1994), who defines Elisabeth of Schonau as a prophet rather than a mystic because her writing calls for church reform rather than describing the mystical process.

became the Society of Jesus. Thus, he founded a renewal movement within the church while never entertaining the option of becoming a dissenter. This movement included not only the Society of Jesus but also an entire series of institutions that became social carriers of his reforming ideals.

Ignatius's initial conversion experience in 1521 occurred only a year after Luther was officially condemned by the Catholic Church. In Spain, Ignatius was isolated from the continental Protestant reformers and took another twenty years to discern his call in a dialectical process of action and contemplation. His self-understanding always remained within the framework of the Catholicism of his day, when the church was anxious about potentially heretical movements. Ignatius saw himself as trying to live a deeply authentic Catholic Christian way of life, exceeding the ordinary expectations of his times. Such an exemplary way of life often has transformative social effects in a situation in which many others are living conventionally or superficially.

There are several aspects to Ignatius's specifically social intentions. Ignatius remained part of the church, fully embracing its theology, sacramental worship, and institutional embodiments from his mystical initiatory experiences until his death. He was inspired by the Gospel ideal of service, love of one's neighbors, and concern for their personal salvation. He cared for the spiritual and corporal needs of the poor. Eventually, he gathered to share his vision like-minded men or men capable of being converted to a similarly committed love of God and neighbor through guided spiritual exercises. Each of these men was initiated in a mystically transforming process. As they gravitated toward one another through similar personal religious experiences and fruitful ministries, the seminal company of priests pledged themselves to one another and to the church, thus initiating the Society of Jesus (1539–40). They linked this new social body to the papacy in such a way that they were seen to serve both the evangelizing interests of Pope Paul III as well as their own dream of a world mission. Finally, as these original members of the company and those who joined them responded charismatically and spontaneously to the immediate needs of the people, they usually created institutions such as schools and houses for women at risk of becoming prostitutes, as well as other means of addressing some of the causes of social and spiritual distress. At other times, they simply followed the accepted practices of the times related to their ministries.

In what sense, then, was Ignatius a mystic and not simply following an already established calling within the church not predicated on mystical experience or illumination? This rather bald statement of the question contests some of the contemporary definitions of mysticism, such as William James's, which identify abstract features from the accounts of some mystics and detach the experience and definition from the religion that functioned as the mystics' context. No account is taken of the social process inherent in the mystical transformation of the subject (Woods 1996, 158), and the social contexts (just or unjust) that the mystic may feel called to reform, transform, or cooperate with are also obscured. In other words, a purely psychological description of the phenomena associated with mysticism reduces mysticism to a purely interior and privatized experience without taking into account both the social construction (Jantzen 1995) of the definition of mysticism or the social effects of such experiences.

Ignatius's Mystical Experience

Because Ignatius was so thoroughly shaped by his Catholic Christian religious tradition, and because his most significant (from his own point of view) mystical experiences had to do not only with experiencing the presence of God in an altered state of consciousness, but also with understanding the mysteries of Christian faith and of the Scriptures in an entirely new way so that the rest of his life and action flowed from these content-filled appropriations of Christian faith, Bernard McGinn's recent definition of mysticism within a Christian context best fits Ignatius's case. "The mystical element in Christianity is that part of its belief and practices that concerns the preparation for, the consciousness of, and the reaction to what can be described as the immediate or direct presence of God" (1991, xvii). This definition of the mystical element of Christianity is, for McGinn, part of a process or way of life rather than an isolated experience: "Although . . . the goal . . . of mysticism may be conceived of as a particular kind of encounter between God and the human, between Infinite Spirit and the finite human spirit, everything that leads up to and prepares for this encounter, as well as all that flows from or is supposed to flow from it for the life of the individual in the belief community, is also mystical, even if in a secondary sense"(xvi).

Beginning with his conversion experience at Loyola when he was recovering from his battle-inflicted leg wound (1521), Ignatius began to notice the occurrence of various interior movements. They continued in ever greater intensity during his withdrawal to the cave at Manresa (1522–23) for a series of meditations, fasts, and other spiritual exercises that consolidated his religious conversion and reorganized his personality in response to them. He all the while noted and identified some of his spiritual movements and mystical experiences, which culminated with his illuminating vision along the banks of the Cardoner River. Ignatius reported in his *Autobiography* that after the experience at Cardoner, he was never the same again, but saw and felt everything differently. However, this experience was not the end of his mystical itinerary. From that time on, Ignatius appeared to his companions to be guided and confirmed throughout the rest of his life as he attempted to discern the direction his life and actions were to take in relationship to the unfolding sense of call or election he had experienced. His confirming vision at La Storta on the way to Rome convinced him that he was "being sent" on a mission, just as Jesus had been.

Recent interpreters of Ignatius and his historical project, the founding and governance of an apostolic community, assert an inherent unity between Ignatius the mystic and Ignatius the man of action (H. Egan 1984; Conwell 1997; Idigoras 1994; R. Egan 1990; Arrupe 1985b). Ignatius's entire spiritual or mystical itinerary was never characterized by purely inward mystical experiences that had no relationship to the actions toward which that interior experience was directed. Like the apostle Paul and countless other figures in the Hebrew and Christian Scriptures, Ignatius's mystical experience was a theophany that conveyed a mission and that continued to instruct him through a series of profound spiritual and affective experiences. This series of ongoing interior movements or "spirits" required him to develop a method of discerning them so that he might interpret them confidently as a guide to action and response to the divine initiative.

Ignatius, a Basque soldier and nobleman from the upper-middle-class family of Loyola in the Golden Age of Spain, was shaped by the experience and imagery of chivalry as a guiding framework for his religious experience. He "pictured"

> the relationship with God . . . therefore . . . not as a nuptial relationship, not in a mode of consciousness which is primarily receptive and impassioned, but primarily as service in a Royal Household, in a mode of consciousness which foregrounds agency and intentionality. Thus the vision of Ignatius puts its strongest emphasis on doing things, on great enterprises. "Love," he says laconically, "manifests itself in deeds." . . . [T]his priority of action, and so the need to be good at what one does . . . is the most characteristic feature of Ignatian spirituality. It is a mysticism of effective and transformative action in a world, undertaken as a mission from a beloved sovereign. (R. Egan 1991b, 34)

Thus, Ignatius experienced himself as summoned by this Lord and entrusted with an urgent mission, a specifically Gospel-inspired mission, placed in service with God's Beloved Son, entirely focused on helping to bring about the Kingdom of God. He dreamed of missionary pilgrimage, a conflation of Paul's missionary journeys and the crusading ideal of Christian chivalry.

It is important to note that Ignatius's most profound early mystical experience, which occurred to him as he sat on the bank of the Cardoner River, where he stopped on his way to a church for services, was not a critique of or an innovative departure from Christianity. Nor was it a new prophetic revelation, a new truth, or a new religious inspiration. It was, instead, an experience of Christian enlightenment in which he "received a mystically infused sense of the unity of the Christian mysteries. Mystically seeing how all things fit together, his outlook was 'architechtonic,' grasping the root unity of all the truths of the faith. He saw everything from then on in its proper universal perspective, how all things flow from and to the God of love" (H. Egan 1984, 36). In *The Autobiography* dictated to Luis Goncalves daCâmara many years later, it was put this way: "The eyes of his understanding began to be opened; not that he saw any vision, but he understood many things, both spiritual matters and matters of faith and scholarship, and this with so great an enlightenment that everything seemed new to him." In a marginal note, daCâmara added, "This left his understanding so very enlightened that he felt as if he were another man with another mind" (par. 30).[4]

Ignatius thus wanted others to experience something similar. He wanted them to appropriate a more interiorly coherent Christianity than many had previously encountered. He wanted others to understand and respond to the Christian mysteries—creation, the Trinity, incarnation, redemption, and salvation—through an intimate experience of the Persons of the Trinity and of the intentions and desires of this Triune God toward the world. Such a personal appropriation of Christianity could be described as a revitalization movement that began with personal self-transcendence. "It was this deep renewal of life and reform of customs, of mores, of ordinary ways of doing things, that was the constant apostolic goal of the society. . . . This is already in principle, what we mean by changing 'social structures' " (R. Egan 1991b, 39).

Implications for Influence and Action

As Ignatius underwent this personal pedagogy under the Holy Spirit's guidance, he was led to make notes about the process of his experiences. Thus, from August to September 1522, he began to write his book, which came to be known as *The Spiritual Exercises of St. Ignatius*.[5] Unlike the writing of other

4. Quotations from *The Autobiography* (Ignatius of Loyola 1991) are translated by Parmananda Divarkar and cited by paragraph number.

5. *The Spiritual Exercises* is the book written by Ignatius of Loyola as a guide for a spiritual director who initiates a retreatant into an intimate spiritual experience, the goal of which is both interior conversion and freedom for religious commitment to an apostolic way of life based on the Gospels. The book contains a series of notes and a specified sequence of content for meditation and spiritual practices. The "Exercises," when not italicized, refers to the experience of making or directing the exercises rather than to the book.

mystics, this book was not a record of mystical visions, but a series of notes about the processes involved in Ignatius's transformation, about how to interpret interior movements, and about the contents and techniques of a set of exercises arranged in a particular order that would enable him to guide others. The notes assume individual differences in retreatants and encourage the guide to respect their unique personalities. Through this retreat process, Ignatius expected the retreatant to experience a mystical transformation issuing in a call to apostolic action as a member of the group that would gradually gather around Ignatius or to some other equally appropriate form of action for that particular person. Ignatius understood that only God could effect human transformation. He merely tried to organize a set of exercises using all of the available spiritual resources he knew to facilitate another's receiving a similar illumination and call: a sequence of meditations focused on the central mysteries of Christian faith and the ministry and teaching of Jesus, which would evoke memory, imagination, desire, and reflection, and dispose the person to God's action.

Dialectic of Action and Reflection

After his unique experience of illumination, Ignatius still had no master plan for his activity, but he was so changed by that experience that he began to engage in any ministry formed to respond to the actual needs of other people, including listening and speaking about the things of God, giving sermons, and leading others through some version of spiritual exercises. He worked and reworked both his notes and the meditations, which became *The Spiritual Exercises*. These spiritual conversations apparently with anyone who would listen to him were the primary way he attracted followers, friends, and companions who wanted to be with him and to learn from him. He did not intend to create a community, but a community—"a company" as they eventually called themselves—grew up around him in Paris, where he took a master's degree in theology so that he could engage in the care of souls without continual harassment as a layman.[6] These original companions proceeded in the same

6. Ignatius's activities were questioned or curtailed in several locations before he and his first companions were ordained. In 1526 in Alcala, Ignatius was investigated by the Inquisition and agreed to the resultant directives regarding dress and behavior. In 1527, while studying in Salamanca, he was investigated and imprisoned; he was investigated again in 1529 in Paris and again in 1535. In 1537, another investigation was underway in Venice, and in 1538, Ignatius insisted on a judicial process in Rome. See Conwell (1997, 184–99) for an account of all these investigations and their outcomes. According to Conwell, Ignatius was insistent on collecting testimony and documents that cleared him or his companions of any sign of heresy so that even a rumor about having been investigated elsewhere might not endanger their reputations and hinder their

manner as Ignatius—experiencing a sense of call or mission and gradually discovering where it was leading them until they took vows of celibacy together and committed themselves to poverty in Paris in 1534. In 1537, prior to their projected pilgrimage to the Holy Land, they decided to apply to the pope for ordination of the five among them not already ordained. They dispersed on various missions when unable to go to Jerusalem, and in 1539, they gathered again in Venice to deliberate about their future: Were they to form some formal community, or were they to minister as individuals? Joseph Conwell movingly narrates the process and events that led to the mutual discovery made by the first fathers—who came together finally in an intensive and ongoing discernment process in the midst of their apostolic work from late March to August 1539—that they had been impelled by the Holy Spirit to join together freely in one body with the one shared desire to dedicate themselves in companionship to the service of Christ and His church (1997, 90).

In the lengthy and intense spiritual conversations with the companions whom he attracted, through the Exercises, and in their deliberations, Ignatius revealed some of the particular content or guidance he received in mystical visionary, ecstatic, or illuminative experiences that led to the formation of the Society of Jesus and that guided this "renewal movement" within the larger social context of the Counter-Reformation of the Catholic Church. Some of these companions pressed him in 1553–55 to dictate his autobiography before his death to one of their group, daCâmara.[7]

Only after founding the Society of Jesus did Ignatius keep a spiritual diary, recording his daily experiences of consolation and other mystical graces from February 2 to March 12, 1544, and from March 13, 1544, to February 27, 1545. The reason for doing so was his deliberation about income and poverty, which he would legislate for the society in *The Constitutions,* currently being drafted. In contrast to other examples of such autobiographical writings, such as *The Life of St. Teresa of Avila,* Ignatius concealed most of the content of the visions, *loquelae,*[8] and inspirations he received in prayer. He simply indicated

---

work. In such a climate, it is not surprising that Ignatius protected himself by earning degrees in theology, seeking ordination, and maintaining documentation so that they could work unhindered.

7. *The Autobiography* covers only 1521–38, beginning with his conversion and ending eighteen years prior to his death. This document was not published in Latin until 1731 or in Italian until 1943. *The Spiritual Diary* was published in its entirety only in 1934. For several centuries, these documents were not well known in the Society of Jesus, which relied primarily on *The Constitutions* and *The Spiritual Exercises* as sources for their shared life. The recovery of these documents offered fresh insight into the founder's spirit in the last half century.

8. *Loquelae* is a term used for mystically received words, usually a sentence, heard or sensed in mystical prayer.

the direction or nature of the consolations he received, which he interpreted in relationship to the particular decision he was making. Continental mystics of the same historical era described in great detail the content of their mystical experiences and frequently placed great store in them. Ignatius traced the pattern of consolation, following his own "Rules for Discernment of Spirits" noted in *The Spiritual Exercises* as a guide to action or to organizational development. According to Antonio De Nicholas (1986), this behavior emphasized his action/decision orientation. It became—as Jerónimo Nadal reported,[9] ascribing the term to Ignatius—"Our Way of Proceeding," a characteristic pattern either for making decisions in concrete circumstances for the society as a whole or related to apostolic decisions for individual men.

Contemplation in Action

Some further elaboration on the particular relationship between mystical experience and social action can now be undertaken. First of all, although Richard Woods argues persuasively for a dialectical relationship between mysticism and social action by an analysis of mystical development as a social process of periods of withdrawal, transformation, and return to society (1996), that analysis does not entirely fit Ignatius's contemplation in action. Frequently, the period of mystical withdrawal and transformation comprises a very lengthy time, preceding the return phase of the process. Such an analysis would fit Teresa of Avila well. She began the reform of Carmel and her foundations of reformed convents only in the later stages of her mystical development.

Ignatius was somewhat different. His initial withdrawal constituted convalescence at home, where he was cared for by family and servants after his serious war injuries. For him, this period was one of forced inactivity that resulted in a spiritual process. He remained part of his familiar social milieu. Only after he resolved to dedicate himself in vigil and pilgrimage at Montserrat did he express his commitment to a spiritual way of life and undergo a more complete spiritual transformation in the cave at Manresa. During this time, however, he continued to participate in the regular round of religious practice common in the church at the time, and he engaged in spiritual conversations with others and cared for the sick. He spent several hours a day in

9. Jerónimo Nadal, a Spaniard, was appointed vicar of the society by Ignatius prior to his death. Nadal, although not one of the original founding fathers, was sent on numerous missions throughout the world to explain the purpose, structure, and internal spirit of the *Constitutions* and of Ignatius's thinking. He continued in this role under Ignatius's successor Diego Laynez. He has long been considered the best interpreter of Ignatius's thinking and intentions, and did much to unify the society.

spiritual practices, but he was also involved with local people, performing either corporal or spiritual works of mercy. He participated in the sacramental life of the church and sought spiritual guidance from monastics in the area.

Likewise, while the first fathers of the Society of Jesus were involved with their deliberations about their future together, they chose not to disengage from their many ministries in Venice, but to continue them, while at the same time performing such spiritual exercises as they could and sharing the results of that prayer related to their common intention. Ignatius pioneered a service mysticism in which God is found in all things, in which the intimate love relationship with God was expressed in action, in colaboring with Christ in God's vineyard. These themes all coalesce in the final "Contemplation to Attain Love," which concludes *The Spiritual Exercises* (nos. 230–37) and that was meant to continue on a daily basis.

Ignatius expected the "withdrawal" phase to last about thirty days if a person had sufficient leisure (no. 20). Otherwise, he devised an alternate form (no. 19) spread over many more weeks of focused prayer and attention while the person continued normal activity. This intense spiritual activity of directing the Exercises is itself a form of action when it becomes focused on one's neighbor. Then it becomes a ministry—a way of animating others toward the realities of faith, of facilitating spiritual awakening and conversion of life. It is a reform of the heart, illumined by the mysteries of faith and exemplified in the story of Jesus and the saints. This action had no fixed form. "The forms were always to be discerned anew in specific contexts" (R. Egan 1991a, 10).

The corporal and spiritual works of mercy complemented all of the ministries of word and sacrament in which the first companions participated as priests. In the later history of the society, these ministries often became separated from one another, creating too large a gap between the sacred, cultic service of the clergy and active works of charity. Purely charitable responses to the marginalized or oppressed often enabled situations of injustice to continue because of a lack of analysis about the causes of this suffering when it was economically or socially based.

Apostolic Innovation and Social Concerns

With his companions, Ignatius innovated a new way of being missionary priests throughout the world. The "Formula of the Institute" [10] clearly integrated the works of mercy with preaching and spiritual ministry. Not only did

10. "The Formula of the Institute" is a summary of the way of life proposed by the first fathers for papal approval first in a series of five paragraphs in *Cum ex plurium,* which was then approved by Paul III in *Regimini militatis ecclesia* (1540) and revised again by Julius III in *Exposcit debitum*

the members of the society physically care for the sick, hear their confessions, and prepare them for death, but they also set up confraternities to continue the activity once the priests left or moved into another sphere of activity (O'Malley 1993, 165ff.). Although the first Jesuits did not have the tools of social analysis, they "consistently worked to improve the physical circumstances of the needy" (O'Malley 1993, 167). Their care for those in need was both motivated by the Gospel and rooted in their philosophy, which obligated them to work for "the common good." In many circumstances, Jesuits collected funds to provide financial assistance to individuals suffering from disasters such as famine, flood, or plague. Where adequate social institutions existed, such as the Italian hospitals, they volunteered their service within them. At other times, they founded entirely new ones. In both cases, they supported or established lay confraternities that would continue the work (O'Malley 1993, 166–67). Thus, the society created new institutional embodiments of an already established type to extend their influence in bettering some aspects of social conditions beyond themselves and their own ministries.

O'Malley's account of the early ministries of these first Jesuits shows that they are remarkable both for their pluriformity and for the breadth of their social concerns. His careful historical analysis differentiates areas in which the society innovated from those groups following conventional lines.

Although O'Malley could not establish an innovative quality to early Jesuits' ministries of reconciliation and peacemaking between feuding parties in Italy, he does show that they responded to this apostolic need and were often quite successful with it during their first ten years. It was not one of the works of charity specified in the initial "Formula of the Institute," making its first appearance later, in 1550 (1993,169).

The ministry with prostitutes in Rome and elsewhere was among the Jesuits' most innovative works. By 1543, Ignatius himself took an active role in developing Casa Santa Marta, a halfway house for prostitutes who desired to change their lives. In addition to preaching to prostitutes, Ignatius raised funds to support the house and to supply dowries for women who wished to marry. He recognized that women became prostitutes because of economic and social conditions. They were often fleeing abusive marriages or were without dowries required for marriage or the religious life. Ignatius offered the women he served a wider range of choices than other charities permitted.

(1550). To this day, Jesuits consider these formulae as encoding the original inspiration of their way of life and include them in their *Constitutions*.

These women could marry, embrace religious life as *conversae*,[11] or enter domestic service. Ignatius also recognized the intergenerational character of prostitution and provided education and dowries for the daughters of prostitutes between the ages of ten and twelve to provide them with better options than their mothers had. Ignatius was insistent that the prostitutes who came to Casa Santa Marta freely choose from the available options they had open to them (O'Malley 1993, 182–85).

Ignatius also repudiated the "blood purity" standards of the Spaniards and accepted into the society new Christians who converted either from Judaism or Islam. O'Malley comments that Ignatius's policies and decisions reflected resistance to Spanish prejudices on these matters, but did not secure universal endorsement from members of the society (1993, 188–92). Ignatius sufficiently understood the intensity of bigotry against these men and educated them outside of Spain. However, O'Malley also notes that the interest of the early Jesuits in winning converts from the Jewish community actually contributed to some of the persecution Jesuits experienced in Rome and on papal lands (1993, 188–92).

The history of educational institutions established and operated by the Jesuits is too vast and complex to treat in this essay except to acknowledge that the society responded at first to the educational needs of the poor, and its schools proliferated so rapidly that they began to absorb much of the manpower of the society and to eclipse for a long time the initial diversity of the other ministries. These schools were, however, important social institutions with far-reaching and diverse effects both on the Society of Jesus as well as on those whom they educated (O'Malley 1993, 200–242).

Ignatius and his fledgling society were welcomed in many of the contexts in which they established themselves because their manner of living and of conducting their ministries offered the witness of lives dedicated to the welfare of others and to the reforming ideals of the church. They were not self-serving, ecclesiastical careerists. They required no fees for either their sacramental services or their charitable works. They raised funds by begging for their modest needs and for those they served. They offered themselves for the universal mission of the church through their fourth vow, which grew out of their personal relationship to the pope, who, they felt, knew where the most pressing needs were. This apostolic and social action for the common good emerged out of their deep interior experience of being united with the poor Christ and of colaboring with him in the ongoing work of redemption in their church and its worldwide ex-

---

11. *Conversae* were women who became penitential religious after a life of prostitution. They were required to form communities separate from those composed of virgins.

tension. Although they lacked the tools of the social sciences, which would not develop for several hundred years, nonetheless they contributed to the revitalization of Christian life within Catholicism and created numerous institutional carriers of these reforms in their ministries, in the Society of Jesus itself, and in other organizations, which effected considerable social change of various kinds.

Pedro Arrupe, S. J.: Revitalization of the Founding Charism

Pedro Arrupe (1907–91) was elected general of the Society of Jesus by the Thirty-first General Congregation in 1965, while the Vatican Council II was still in session. He served in this capacity for eighteen years while both the Society of Jesus and the Roman Catholic Church implemented and resisted the reforms and renewal mandated by this council and by the synods that followed it. Arrupe, like Ignatius before him, lived at a turning point in history and responded to the unique challenges he faced.

A Basque like Ignatius, Arrupe grew up in Spain, attended medical school from 1922 to 1926, and entered the Society of Jesus at Loyola in 1927 after witnessing three medical miracles at Lourdes. This experience he identified as the birth of his vocation (Arrupe 1986, 18, 30–31). While he was still involved in his studies, he and the entire membership of the society were expelled from Spain in 1932, so he completed his philosophical and theological studies in Belgium and then in Holland. Ordained a priest in 1936, he did further theological studies in Kansas, where he concentrated on moral theology. He completed tertianship in Cleveland and in New York City. In 1938, he was assigned to the mission to Japan, fulfilling a "vision" he had during a much earlier retreat "that my vocation was to be a missionary and that it would lead me to Japan"(1986, 13).

Mystical Experience Interpreted Through the Ignatian Charism

Arrupe's experiences in Japan were challenging and profound, and his mystical experience was often eucharistic. He celebrated one of his first masses in Japan on Mount Fujiyama.

> Arriving at the summit, the sunrise was magnificent; it raised our spirits and disposed us for the celebration of the Holy Sacrifice. . . . Above us the blue sky stretched out pure and majestic like the dome of an immense temple; below one saw all the people of Japan, then about eighty million people who did not know the Savior. Piercing the lofty dome of the material sky, my spirit rose to the throne of the Divine Majesty, to the throne of the Holy Trinity,

and I seemed to see the heavenly Jerusalem, the Holy City; I seemed to see Jesus Christ accompanied by St. Francis Xavier, the first apostle to Japan, whose hair turned white in a few months because of the sufferings he had to endure. I too was faced with the same Japan as St. Francis Xavier, faced with a totally unknown future; if I had known then how much I would suffer, my hands would have trembled as I raised the Host. (1986, 32–33)

Different kinds of suffering came soon. He experienced a "feeling of great loneliness" as he adjusted to yet another new culture. Suspected of espionage because of his time in the United States, he was imprisoned for one month in Yamaguchi, where he served as a parish priest. He claimed he learned during this time "the science of silence, of solitude, of severe and austere poverty, of inner dialogue with the 'guest of my soul' " (1986, 21). He was appointed master of novices in 1942, outside of Hiroshima, where he and his men saved nearly two hundred lives after the atomic bomb exploded in the city on August 6, 1945.

Living through the aftermath of the bombing altered his life forever. Again, he described both intense suffering and profound consolation when he celebrated mass in the ruined chapel, overflowing with wounded victims who had no understanding of the ritual that so strengthened him. "I stayed there as if I were paralyzed, my arms outstretched, contemplating this human tragedy—human science and technological progress used to destroy the human race. They were all looking at me, eyes full of agony and despair as if they were waiting for some consolation from the altar" (1986, 33). Arrupe spontaneously prayed for those who had dropped the bomb and for the victims.

Arrupe had deeply appropriated the charism and spirit of Ignatius of Loyola. His mystical experience occurred in moments of ritual and in moments of ordinary experience. He described experiences in prayer in which he felt destined for a particular mission—in his case, Japan. He was thoroughly shaped by the kinds of intimate experiences of the three Persons of the Trinity that the Spiritual Exercises seek to facilitate. His priestly ministry and his care of the sick were completely integrated. He sensed himself in continuity with the first Jesuits in Japan and recognized that he was living through momentous historical times. Eventually he was appointed vice-provincial of Japan in 1954 and then provincial in 1959.

Arrupe assimilated the Ignatian tradition to an extraordinary degree. When he was expelled from Spain, instead of visiting his family, he studied the *Monumenta historica Societatis Iesu,* absorbing a great deal of the spirit of the founder from the narratives and documents about the founding group (Arrupe 1986, 46). These texts were not widely known among ordinary members of the society. While novice master in Japan, he wrote five books on the Exercises because he recognized they needed to be reinterpreted for entirely new situations. He spoke seven languages and studied many historical layers of the Ignatian experience. He could cite by memory from Ignatius's voluminous correspondence, the early narratives, and the founding documents. Moreover, he simply lived from the mystical level in all of his activities.

He acted on spiritual experience. As general of the society, he was uniquely able to offer an authentic interpretation to various groups in the society and governed the society entirely according to these principles. After a plan of action had been developed, he reported, "Above all I followed the Spirit. All the points which supported me did not come from me, but from the Spirit who has animated the life of the Church, during and after the Vatican Council II" (1986, 26–27). His decision to convene a general congregation in 1974 was one such Spirit-guided action. "I have never doubted, even for a moment, that God wanted the convocation of that Congregation. I had already understood this clearly beforehand in such a manner that all doubt, all possibility of doubt, had vanished from my soul *(Spiritual Exercises* #118). And, with time, this certitude became stronger. When subsequently I wanted to 'consider through reflection' *(Spiritual Exercises* #181) the reasons for God's will, several appeared to me, which St. Ignatius enumerates in our *Constitutions* (#680)" (1986, 27). Part of following the Spirit was involving all other appropriate persons in the process. He consulted with the Congregation of Procurators [12] in 1970 about convoking this historic meeting, and they voted to support it, giving him the authority to determine when it was to be held.

Arrupe Revitalizes Governance in the Spirit of Ignatius

Arrupe brought unique gifts to his governance of the society. In the language of contemporary leadership theory, he exemplified the characteristics of transformational leadership. He embodied the mission of the organization and exemplified the spiritual, apostolic, and relational qualities that the Society of Jesus was attempting to retrieve and renew.

Arrupe was keenly aware of the complexity of personal and communal conversion. He constantly appealed to the common ideals of the group, recognized the generosity of disposition in his men, and named the conflicts and resistance irrupting from those individuals not yet converted. Above all, he

12. The Congregation of Procurators is a meeting held every four years to conduct necessary business of the society in concert with the general. It is an elected body with one person sent from every province worldwide, approximately eighty delegates.

trusted in the activity of God in their midst and placed their work within an entirely new interpretive horizon.

Arrupe, like Pope John XXIII, who convoked Vatican Council II, had personally experienced many aspects of the challenges the church faced in the modern world. He had experienced unjust political actions, first in Spain and subsequently in Japan. He witnessed the technological destruction of human life by that creation of modern science, the atomic bomb. He was a man of science, trained in medicine, and a man of the social sciences, trained in psychology. He ministered in diverse cultures and recognized the need for careful inculturation. As provincial in Japan, he led a community of men from nearly thirty different countries. He recognized from personal experience the limitations of a social structure that did not entirely fit his apostolic situation. He also recognized the limitation of all human means that were not animated by God's Spirit.

His election as general in 1965 enabled him to participate in the fourth session of Vatican Council II. At that time, the council was deliberating on *Gaudium et spes,* the role of the Catholic Church in the modern world, which included all aspects of culture—in particular, the challenge of atheism. The new context for mission was a world in which unbelief and injustice were facts. Arrupe made an important intervention in the council related to inculturation (October 12, 1965). Likewise, after his election, he presented his own vision of the global reality of the Jesuit community and a vision of church and society that had gradually been emerging throughout his own lifetime and that culminated in Vatican Council II and in the Thirty-first General Congregation. With tools from the social sciences, they could address questions of justice and faith in an entirely new way.

Church Reform as the Context for Transformation

Everything Arrupe advocated was based on deep fidelity to the church—a relationship of personal loyalty to the popes under whom he served and of fidelity to the implementation of the agenda of Vatican II, which included an entirely new relationship of the church to the world, a renewal of religious life based on an adaptation to the changed social contexts of modern life, and an authentic renewal of the original charisms of religious communities. These initiatives were mandated in the conciliar documents. The documents of the Thirty-first General Congregation cite the relevant papal encyclicals related to matters of social justice as well as the consensual documents produced by Vatican II. Arrupe unconditionally accepted these new directions.

Decree 32 of the Thirty-first General Congregation, "The Social Apostolate," gave increased priority to this apostolate for Jesuits. It identified the goal of the apostolate: "to build a fuller expression of justice and charity into the structures of human life in common . . . [so] that every man may be able to exercise a personal sense of participation, skill, and responsibility in all areas of community life" *(Documents* 1977, Decree 32, par. 569). The decree acknowledged that "social structures, above all today, exert an influence on the life of man, even on his moral and religious life" (par. 570). The document described an awareness of global social and economic inequalities. It placed a universal love for the peoples of the world at the heart of this apostolate so that it could not be reduced to ideology or temporal activity alone. Further, it attempted to integrate this mission more fully into the society—giving it priority among others (par. 575), integrating these concerns into everyone's training (par. 576), preparing some talented men specifically for this work (par. 577), and establishing regional social centers of research and action in collaboration with the laity (par. 578).

Within hierarchical structures, the leader exerts enormous power. A universal council, however, convoked in union with the pope, such as Vatican II, carries the highest authority of the church to which even the pope is accountable. Likewise, the documents of general congregations represent the deliberations of representatives of the community worldwide, not simply the opinions of the general of the society. Nonetheless, Arrupe used his leadership position to influence and persuade others to promote the reform agenda, to deepen spirituality, and to link faith with justice. He used every opportunity for speaking and for promoting fully integrated contemplation in action, prophetic witness, and core themes from *The Spiritual Exercises* and from Ignatian spirituality.

In between these two general congregations, the social teaching of the church continued to unfold with sharper analysis of the modern world. The Thirty-first General Congregation was followed by yet another social encyclical, Paul VI's *Populorum progressio* (1967), by the Conference of Latin American Bishops (1968) in Medellin (which Arrupe attended), and by the synodal document *Justice in the World* (1971). Within a decade, official ecclesiastical documents articulated a growing awareness of global injustice embedded in social structures. Church teaching now recognized the limitations of a development model of economics in the third world and the relationship between faith and justice, between peace and justice, so that a form of integral liberation began to emerge. There was a reciprocal influence between the Society of Jesus and Pope Paul VI, whose encyclical *Evangelii nuntiande* (1975) expressed the role of religious life in evangelization along the lines articulated in the synod of 1971 and the Thirty-second General Congregation (O'Keefe 1998).

Influence of Liberation Theology

According to J. B. Libanio, a Brazilian Jesuit, "liberation theology starts from an option for the poor, with its ultimate motivation and inspiration in the gospel, aware that in the last resort it is grace. . . . The political and dialectical dimension is what makes it different from Ignatius's experience. It is dialectical in the sense of recognizing that the poor we meet in the Third World have been made poor. . . . It sees and asserts a causal connection between the existence of poor people and the accumulation of wealth by the rich" (1991, 54). "The political dimension of liberation theology's option for the poor is revealed in the importance it attaches to the poor person as the initiator of their [*sic*] own process of liberation from the situation of poverty and dehumanization" (55).

In 1972, Arrupe wrote an extensive commentary on the synodal document *Justice in the World*. His aim was to stir Christians worldwide to action on behalf of justice in response to the synod of 1971. In "Witnessing to Justice in the World," he called for a lived witness to justice originating in a deep concern for others rather than in a desire for power or prestige. He repeatedly stressed the credibility of life and action that inspires others to build a world based on justice. He strongly asserted that discernment was required for these choices. "Discernment means reading and interpreting the signs of the times. It means asking ourselves such questions as these? In the concrete, existential situation in which we find ourselves, what are the acts that have a bearing on the Gospel message of justice: the liberation of the oppressed, the defense of the poor, the safe-guarding of human rights, the promotion of human development?" (Arrupe 1980b, 119). This kind of discernment required the identification of appropriate means of action. Arrupe also recognized that conversion was a prerequisite for discernment—an open mind and heart: "This means getting rid of attitudes and prejudices that close one's mind and heart to everything except to the familiar, to what we are used to, to what has 'always been done;' and, also, getting rid of attitudes and prejudices that close one's mind and heart to everything except what is new, what is against 'tradition,' what is sensational, what is revolutionary" (1980b, 120).

He built on the papal theme "If you want peace, work for justice" (theme for the World Day of Peace in 1972) by describing the false peace that "in reality supports, maintains, and perpetuates a real disorder, and 'institutionalized violence;' that is to say, social and political structures which have injustice and oppression built into them. In such a situation, to bear witness to justice, to act for justice, may mean to engage in a hard and protracted effort to change such structures. . . . The outcome of any structural change should be a true liberation and not another type of oppression" (1980b, 107).

Dialogue and Discernment as a Way of Proceeding

In his style of governance, Arrupe sought to reconcile conflicts and to overcome resistance through consensus and dialogue. Ignacio Ellacuria, S.J., believed that the direction taken by the vice-province of Central America—which was inspired by the meeting in Medellin and embraced a theology of liberation—helped prepare the way for the Thirty-second General Congregation. In dealing with this community, Arrupe showed himself capable of real dialogue, seeking to understand the local situation and the varied responses of members of the society to it. Ellacuria said, "together we found the will of God in an interplay of representation and discernment carried out in the light of the strictest evangelical demands" (1986, 145). When the approaches to liberation and justice in Central America harmonized with the concerns of Arrupe and others in Rome, the outcome was very positive, according to Ellacuria and the Central American Jesuits:

> in spite of substantive differences, we Jesuits of Central America and Father Arrupe were able to attain a very high degree of consensus achieved by growth rather than imposition. We all learned in the process, and we all suffered with it; but the results were good: where there had hardly been any native vocations, these began to flower in an extraordinary manner; where theological reflection was practically nil, there emerged an important theological movement; where the best efforts of many were oriented towards undifferentiated development, they assumed a new direction toward the liberation of the popular majorities; where once people lived attracted by the powerful of this world, they began to feel harshly the vigors of persecution for the sake of the kingdom—even to martyrdom and the constant threat of death.
>
> Father Arrupe made all of this possible because, from his enormous evangelical richness, he knew how to approach with authority, humility, and immense love what was happening in these lands. (1986, 150–51)

Despite the developments in Central America, Arrupe was not convinced that the Society of Jesus as a whole had responded adequately to the pluriform agenda of renewal of life emerging from Vatican II and from the decrees of the Thirty-first General Congregation. Consequently, he called the Thirty-second General Congregation to develop a stronger consensus about the society's direction and a greater impetus to conversion and action. He sought the wisdom in the whole discerning group to deepen the reflection on the historical moment and to delineate the society's response. Nonetheless, he ardently supported the initial directions established in the Thirty-first General Congregation. Long before they voted on the key document of the Thirty-second General Congregation—Decree 4, "Our Mission Today: The Service of Faith and the Promotion of Justice"—he eloquently challenged the assembly on December 20, 1974: Were they willing to embrace the suffering that would surely follow should they continue the direction toward linking faith and justice? He spoke of misunderstanding, conflict, persecution from both church and civil authorities, even from one's own friends. According to Vincent O'Keefe, Ignatius himself believed persecution was a "sign of fidelity to Christ, a sign that we are not of this world" (1990, 63–64). In his travels throughout the world after the decree was passed, Arrupe tirelessly spoke about its implications. Three years later, at a meeting of the Congregation of Procurators, he expressed concern at the slowness of the society to implement the decrees of the Thirty-second General Congregation. He called for a more radical implementation of those decrees, and he linked this implementation to the Spirit breathing new life into the community and deeply desiring whole-hearted response (1985a, 21–42).

Vincent O'Keefe identifies Decree 4 from the Thirty-second General Congregation as the heart of the entire set of documents produced in this meeting (1990, 53). It states boldly: "The mission of the Society of Jesus today is the service of faith, of which the promotion of justice is an absolute requirement. For reconciliation with God demands the reconciliation of people with one another" *(Documents* 1977, par. 2). The subsequent paragraphs show continuity with the "Formula of the Institute" in the entirely new situation and challenges of the world today (par. 3). These challenges are named: a search for God by many who do not yet know Christ (par. 4), a complete loss of the sense of God by others (par. 5), and the reality of global interdependence. "There is a new challenge to our apostolic mission in a world increasingly interdependent but, for all that, divided by injustice: injustice not only personal but institutionalized: built into economic, social, and political structures that dominate the life of nations and the international community" (par. 6). This mission calls for a response that "must be total, corporate, rooted in faith and experience and multi-form" (par. 7).

The decree acknowledges that the modern world provides new tools as well as new challenges: "new and more effective ways of understanding man, nature and society; of communicating through image and feeling; of organizing action. These we must learn in the service of evangelization and human development" (par. 8).

The decree then calls for a "reassessment of all traditional apostolic methods, attitudes and institutions" in order to adapt them to a rapidly changing world (par. 39). To do this requires the discernment taught in the Exercises (par. 10).

The documents carefully integrate faith and justice, priestly ministry and social action, contemplative prayer, and service to others. Spiritual discernment, deep faith, and commitment to Christ are the primary spiritual resources. Discernment seeks to discover God's action in the world, in the hearts of contemporaries, and in changing structures as well as hearts.

Vincent O'Keefe, Arrupe's trusted assistant, reports, "The period following the 32nd General Congregation was a difficult one, and the new focusing of our mission on the service of faith and the promotion of justice caused tensions both in the Society and outside it. In numerous talks and writings, Father Arrupe worked to explain the true meaning of our mission today; he worked to overcome readings of decree 4 that he termed 'incomplete, slanted, and unbalanced' ('Rooted and Grounded in Love,' #67)" (1990, 55). Above all, Arrupe refused to allow justice and charity to conflict with one another or with the total mission of the society to evangelize others, proclaiming the totality of Christian faith and salvation. "Faith moves and is moved by charity, and that charity brings about and goes beyond justice" (Arrupe 1985c, no. 73). Arrupe believed that love overcomes all the apparent tensions and dichotomies. According to O'Keefe, Arrupe restored personal relationships within the society by his own "way of proceeding," which was "not only credible but infectious" (1998).

In 1981, the same year in which he gave the address "Rooted and Grounded in Love," Arrupe suffered a stroke from which he never fully recovered. When the Thirty-third General Congregation was finally convened in 1983 to elect his successor, and after Pope John Paul II had intervened in the ongoing governance of the society, the question uppermost in the minds of most Jesuits was whether the Thirty-third General Congregation would confirm the reinterpretation of the society's charism and mission arrived at in both the Thirty-first and Thirty-second General Congregations, as well as confirm the previous eighteen years of corporate life, reflection, and action so ardently inspired by Pedro Arrupe's leadership.

The Thirty-third General Congregation did so ratify these matters:

> the 33rd General Congregation readily receives the calls which the pope has made to the Society, and commits itself to a full and prompt response. At the same time we confirm the Society's mission expressed by the 31st and 32nd General Congregations particularly in the latter's decrees 2 and 4, which are the application today of the Formula of the Institute and of our Ignatian charism. They express our mission today in profound terms offering insights that serve as guidelines for our future responses:

—The integration of the service of faith and promotion of justice in one single mission [Decree 2, par. 8];

—the universality of the mission in the various ministries in which we engage [Decree 2, par. 9];

—the *discernment* needed to implement this mission [Decree 4, par. 10];

—the *corporate* nature of this mission [Decree 4, par. 62–69]. *(Documents* 1984, Part II, D.38)

The documents of the Thirty-third General Congregation also acknowledged "The decrees of General Congregation 31 (8, 13–17) and General Congregation 32 (2, 4, 11) as well as the writings of Father Arrupe have developed a spiritual doctrine at once profoundly rooted in the gospel and our tradition" (1984, 11). Arrupe's legacy was clearly accepted.

◆   ◆   ◆

The foregoing extended treatment of Pedro Arrupe and of his leadership of the Society of Jesus solidly demonstrates several themes introduced in the treatment of Ignatius of Loyola and the mysticism of service that he articulated and lived. The most compelling frame of reference for Arrupe's thought, action, and experience of the presence of God in a life-long process of personal conversion was one inspired by Ignatius. Both men gave evidence of ongoing mystical experience that "sent" them on significant missions. Theirs was a contemplation in action—a contemplation that included concrete situations and historical settings. They contemplated—pondered, considered, observed, noticed, beheld—the needs of the church, the desires of others, and the complex dynamics of their social worlds as a spiritual practice. They did this in the company of the Three Persons of the Trinity and of God's offer of salvation to the world. They asked, What have they done, are doing, and will do for Christ? They attempted to scrutinize "the signs of the times" for God's Spirit moving in them and in the church. When transposed into the new key of the twentieth century, this question was answered by Arrupe and the society within the context of careful social analysis by a commitment to transform society and themselves toward greater justice, charity, and human dignity.

Both Ignatius and Arrupe maintained a strong commitment to ongoing personal transformation in a process of action interpenetrated with contemplation and reflection. Both made their friendship with Christ the center of their lives. This friendship entailed not only intense periods of personal prayer, illumination, and mystical experience but also service to Christ in works of evangelizing, preaching, spiritual direction, and other forms of missionary activity. Both Ignatius and Arrupe allowed themselves to be transformed by the Spiritual Exercises and made them the center of all of their apostolic activity.

Both men consciously developed their service, social influence, and efforts at social change in response to and in support of the reforming efforts of the Roman Catholic Church of their day. Both led their communities, one as an innovative founder and the other as a courageous refounder. In the light of sociological theory, clearly Arrupe was one of the most important twentieth-century members of the Society of Jesus to contribute to the revitalization of the religious community and of the institutions the society runs in response to the mandates of the Thirty-first, Thirty-second, and Thirty-third General Congregations.

Both Arrupe and Ignatius were leaders of revitalization movements who attracted and inspired others to join together with them in their apostolic project. Just as the first fathers felt their union into a community was literally impelled by the Spirit and expected the Spirit to continue to inspire them in new directions, the twentieth-century Society of Jesus judged its reforming general congregations to be similar events of the Spirit. This was so much the case that Decree 2 of the Thirty-fourth General Congregation appropriated Arrupe's dream of uniting the whole body of the society with all of its spiritual and apostolic strength and talent in one mission for every Jesuit and all Jesuits:

> The Church, whose mission we share, exists not for itself but for humanity, bearing the proclamation of God's love and casting light on the inner gift of that love. Its aim is the realization of the Kingdom of God in the whole of human society, not only in the life to come, but also in this life. We exercise our Jesuit mission within the total evangelizing mission of the Church. This mission is "a single but complex reality which develops in a variety of ways:" through the integral dimensions of life witness, proclamation, conversion, inculturation, the genesis of local churches, dialogue and the promotion of the justice willed by God. Within this framework, in accordance with our charism, our tradition and the approval and encouragement of Popes through the years, the contemporary Jesuit mission is the service of faith and the promotion in the society of "that justice of the Gospel which is the embodiment of God's love and saving mercy." *(Documents* 1995, no. 24)

Both Ignatius and Arrupe knew how to influence and how to await a free response, empowered by God. Both men admirably succeeded in leaving behind a legacy of personal and social transformation rooted in their mystical experience.

7

Practical Mysticism

QUAKERS AND SOCIAL TRANSFORMATION

MARGARET BENEFIEL
and REBECCA DARDEN PHIPPS

Historians and theologians who study the spirituality of the Religious Society of Friends (Quakers) frequently locate that religious experience and unique method of silent worship within the mystical stream. Quaker religious vision and ethical values arise from and are formed by Friends' manner of corporate worship and worshipful living. Our intention is to offer some insight on mysticism and social transformation from a Quaker perspective, which we share. We augment the discussion by investigating the internal (mystical apprehension) and external (social transformation) processes of two Quakers whose mystical experiences in prayer and worship contributed to the prophetic witness of the Religious Society of Friends in England and the American colonies.

The individual and corporate Quaker experience of the immanent and transcendent presence of God in their lives, communities, and the world has led to significant, sustained acts of social conscience that have been characterized as affirmative, ethical, and practical mysticism. Historian Howard H. Brinton claims that Quakers practice a form of "group mysticism," apprehending religious truth through the immediate illumination of Jesus Christ, the Inward Teacher (1988, xiii). He maintains that the "full implications" of this form of mysticism "are demonstrated only in the course of historical development within a group of human beings who live according to its precepts" (1988, xiii). Douglas Steere describes the particular corporate character of Quaker religious experience as "the mystical witness to the active presence of the 'Beyond that is within' " (1984, 16). He asserts, in fact, that for Quakers, the outward expression of the mystical apprehension of the presence of God demonstrates "the living promise of transformation" (1984, 17).[1]

The Quaker experience in prayer and silent, expectant worship is characterized by listening to communication from God. Quaker journals historically demonstrate that Friends held complete confidence that God would communicate to them individually and corporately through the mediating inward presence of the Light Within (Jesus Christ). They experienced, therefore, tremendous clarity about their identity as God's prophetic witnesses to the True Light (John 1:9), which required persistent, compassionate confrontations with the social evils they believed God commanded them to address. Of particular importance in considering the Quaker religious phenomenon is the role of the community in discerning the authenticity of God's direction to them, called a *leading*. Considered a divine invitation or directive, a leading is methodically tested for its veracity both individually and corporately. Conflict with scriptural authority or with the community's religious values or with both would be evidence of a leading's lack of authenticity. Historically, once a leading was discerned as spiritually true, the community would go to great lengths to support an individual or members of the community in following the directive. In true Quaker style, the impetus and follow-through were very straightforward. Once a leading was received and tested, Friends would be faithful as a matter of course, whatever the opposition. These mystically apprehended directives or truths afforded great strength to the Friends as they discerned and supported spiritual authority.

The mystical "living promise of transformation" was realized in the prophetic witness of John Woolman (1720–72) and Catherine Payton Phillips (1727–94). In this essay, we consider their internal spiritual formation, their relationships to their particular communities of faith, and their involvement in social transformation. For Woolman and Phillips, these three aspects of their witness were all part of one spiritual process. As they wrote in their journals about their internal spiritual transformation, they could not separate that experience from their relationship with their community of faith, which had provided the context for their spiritual formation and the support for their following of leadings. Nor could they separate the process of internal spiritual transformation from their involvement in social action and transformation. Being obedient to God's chastening and healing work within them was part and parcel of yielding to God's moving through them to love, heal, and chasten the world.

---

1. John Copenhaver, who writes on prayer and social responsibility in the work of Douglas Steere (1992), and Philip Boroughs (1990), who writes on spiritual and social transformation in the life of John Woolman, explicitly link mysticism and social conscience.

John Woolman

"Great reformation in the world is wanting!" Woolman exclaimed in a journal entry dated "Fifth Month [May], 1772" (1989, 168). Writing on board the ship *Mary and Elizabeth* on a voyage from Philadelphia to London, he labored with inordinate concern for the physical and spiritual conditions of the seamen and apprentices who lived and worked in oppressive and corrupting circumstances. Despite the serious regard several members of the Religious Society, including the ship's captain, expressed for his well-being, Woolman insisted on traveling in steerage to be in righteous fellowship with the sailors. He had observed the "superfluities" of the finer lodgings of cabin passengers and "felt a scruple with regard to paying my money to defray such expenses" (1989, 164). Such extravagances, he believed, were maintained in the spirit of oppression, and he "could not find peace in joying in anything which I saw was against that wisdom which is pure" (1989, 165). After prayerful deliberation, he had discerned the "humbling hand of God upon me" and was "opened" in his mind to share the cramped and unhealthy accommodations of the poor sailors and cabin boys. Once settled on board, he "felt a satisfactory evidence that my proceedings were not my own will but under the power of the cross of Christ" (1989, 165). During the six-week journey across the Atlantic, Woolman engaged in companionable conversation, prayer, and worship with the sailors and lads, some barely out of childhood. He grew familiar with the rigors of their dangerous work and polluted living conditions, and understood clearly and regrettably who profited from their suffering. He concluded on his arrival in London that the seafaring life is so "full of corruption and extreme alienation from God" that he hoped

> Those acquainted with the pure gospel spirit may lay this case to heart, may remember the lamentable corruptions which attend the conveyance of merchandise across the sea, and so abide in the love of Christ that being delivered from the love of money, from the entangling expenses of a curious, delicate, and luxurious life—that we may learn contentment with a little and promote the seafaring life no further than that spirit which leads into all Truth attends us in our proceedings. (1989, 180)

Accounts by and about John Woolman, like this one, describe his compassion for others, his insight into the sources of injustice, his singular resolve not to contribute to systemic oppression, and his public pleas on behalf of the oppressed. His journal, a spiritual and literary classic since its publication in 1774, reveals an intimate, mystical relationship with God. His fellowship with the poor and the needy demonstrated the religious values and ethical principles he learned as a Quaker, notwithstanding the fact that he admonished many Friends to reform their lifestyles out of a Christian love of their fellow creatures. Here follows a brief summary of how Woolman's life and ministry were formed, with particular attention to the religious experiences and communitarian influences that characterized his practical or ethical mysticism.

Born in 1720 in rural New Jersey, near Philadelphia, Woolman was one of thirteen children in a pious Quaker family that made its living by farming and growing fruit. When he was a child, his consciousness developed within a close, conservative community that observed the Friends' testimonies of simple living[2] and of plain speaking and dress.[3] His family avoided worldly diversions, choosing instead practices that fostered Christian brotherhood. His family's Quaker lifestyle, based on Christian love and discipleship, required worshipful attentiveness to the revelations of "pure wisdom" within the Scriptures and from the Light Within (the Inward Christ). Woolman's attendance at Friends school and monthly meeting for worship[4] further instructed him in a tender-hearted regard for the spiritual and temporal welfare of others. His youthful nature, however, in significant part sociable, caused him painful conflict. He was drawn to both carefree, "wanton" companionship and a sober religious vocation (Woolman 1989, 25). Eventually, his tormented conscience and prayers for divine assistance enabled him to achieve a steadfast inward resolve:

> I kept steady to meetings, spent First Days afternoon chiefly in reading the Scriptures and other good books, and was early convinced in my mind that true religion consisted of an inward life, wherein the heart doth love and reverence God the Creator and learn to exercise true justice and goodness, not only toward all men but also toward the brute creatures; that as the mind was moved on an inward principle to love God as an invisible, incomprehensible being, on the same principle it was moved to love him in all his manifestations in the visible world. (1989, 28)

John Woolman left home at twenty-one years of age to work for a shopkeeper in the nearby town of Mount Holly. His religious convictions were

---

2. The testimony of simplicity is one's commitment to living simply in the manner of Christian discipleship, trusting God to provide the basic necessities of life and recognizing that the pursuit of luxuries is outside the wisdom of the Spirit.

3. Plain speaking means to speak the truth: "yes" means yes and "no" means no; also, "thee" is used to address all persons, rather than making a distinction between persons who deserve formal address ("thou"). Plain dress means wearing uniformly unadorned clothing, usually grey or black, with bonnets for women and hats for men.

4. A meeting for worship is the First Day (Sunday) worship.

soon challenged by enterprising colonialists absorbed in trade and the pursuit of profit. Some of his new responsibilities tested his conscience—for example, writing a bill of sale for a Negro woman his employer was selling to a purchaser, another Quaker. Woolman was deeply uneasy with "writing an instrument of slavery for one of my fellow creatures" and expressed to both his employer and the other Friend that he "believed slave keeping to be a practice inconsistent with the Christian religion" (1989, 32–33). The enslavement of humanity—with slaves and bonded servants bound in chains or unreasonable contracts, and with slave holders and masters bound to the cruel, unholy pursuit of comfort and profit—became an overriding concern for Woolman. His own early success in business demonstrated that he, too, earned returns and accumulated material goods out of proportion to his basic needs. At the age of twenty-six years, in obedience to his conscience, Woolman moderated his lifestyle and began working independently as a tailor; by the age of thirty-six years, he gave up retailing entirely and supported himself and his family as a tailor and orchardist.

Woolman's recognition of God "in all his manifestations" led to a universal embrace of all living persons and creatures. So sensitive was he to the suffering of others that he chose not to wear dyed clothing because the dyes were produced by slave labor. He readily perceived such connections between the consumption of commodities by the well-off and the suffering of persons whose hard labor made those commodities available:

> To see our fellow creatures under difficulties to which we are in no degree accessory tends to awaken tenderness in the minds of all reasonable people, but if we consider the condition of such who are depressed in answering our demands, who labour out of sight and are often toiling for us while we pass our time in fullness, if we consider that much less than we demand would supply us with all things really needful, what heart will not relent, or what reasonable man can refrain from mitigating the grief which he himself is the cause of, when he may do it without inconvenience? (1989, 244)

From his youth, Woolman experienced "gracious visitations" from God, which established an early reliance on divine communication and guidance (1989, 23). His recollections of prayer, inward and attentive listening, and mystical visions record a communion with God, whose "tender mercies" strengthened him. After one prayerful vision following a critical illness, he felt certain of his responsibility to prophesy, "And a trumpet was given me that I might sound for this language, that the children might hear it and be invited to gather to this precious habitation, where the prayers of saints, as precious incense, ariseth up before the throne of God and the Lamb. I saw this habitation to be safe, to be inwardly quiet, when there was [*sic*] great stirrings and commotions in the world" (1989, 160).

Woolman had complete confidence that God provided for his safety and necessities, as well as for all humankind, and he lived his life by that conviction. Others, too, recognized the sense that the Spirit was with him. During an occasion when Woolman worshiped with some American Indians, one chief waved away Woolman's interpreter, remarking, "I love to hear where the words come from" (1989, 133).

During his lifetime, Woolman was asked to serve the Religious Society of Friends as a public Friend,[5] itinerant minister,[6] and elder.[7] In codiscernment with the Quakers in his monthly, quarterly, and yearly meetings,[8] he heard and followed leadings to minister to individuals, meeting communities, and larger gatherings of Friends. With the support of his community, he traveled, on foot and horseback, thousands of miles to pray, worship, and counsel with Friends throughout the American colonies. A humble man, he continually prayed for strength and wisdom as he appealed to the tenderest feelings of respected Friends whom he believed had misapplied their power. He feared that "the seeds of great calamity and desolation are sown and growing fast on this continent" (1989, 129).

Assured of divine justification, Woolman tenaciously confronted the many social evils he witnessed: slavery, the oppression of the poor by the wealthy and ambitious, the encroachment on the territories of American Indians, war and the collection of war taxes, and the mistreatment of animals. He authored numerous essays and letters attempting to convince Friends to conduct their affairs righteously. Among his most well-known publications are "Some Considerations on the Keeping of Negroes" (in two parts), "A Plea for the Poor, or A Word of Remembrance and Caution to the Rich," and "Considerations on the True Harmony of Mankind." His ethical mysticism is reflected in his journal and inspired both Friend and non-Friend. Samuel Taylor Coleridge said, "I should almost despair of that man who could peruse the life of John Woolman without an amelioration of heart" (1956, 302).

John Woolman's contributions to social transformation were largely

5. A public Friend is a seasoned Friend who is appointed with responsibility for representing Friends at public gatherings.

6. An itinerant or traveling minister is a Friend with gifts in ministry whose meeting approves his or her traveling to other meetings, to start new meetings, or to visit other Friends on a concern.

7. An elder is a Friend recognized as spiritually seasoned or wise.

8. Monthly, quarterly, and yearly meetings are held at which Friends conduct business in the manner of worship: once a month (local); quarterly (regional); yearly (a larger region). There were also half-year meetings. A circular yearly meeting is held in different locations each year.

made through his prophetic ministry of spiritual reformation among Friends. In 1758, for instance, the Philadelphia yearly meeting formally urged Quakers to free their slaves, a move largely influenced by Woolman's advocacy. In 1776, Quaker slave holding was prohibited by that same body. He successfully encouraged Friends also to maintain their pacifist principles by calling for an act of civil disobedience: the refusal to pay taxes that would support the French and Indian War. Following the war and during a time of frontier violence, Woolman was led to visit American Indians. This outreach was representative of the historically peaceful relations Quakers maintained with American Indians in Pennsylvania and other colonies. His journal reflection on this visitation, conducted during a dangerous time, illustrates the mystical movements that inspired his ministry: "Love was the first motion, and then a concern arose to spend some time with the Indians, that I might feel and understand their life and the spirit they live in, if haply I might receive some instruction from them, or they be in any degree helped forward by my following the leadings of Truth amongst them" (1989, 127).

The preceding summary of John Woolman's life can only briefly reflect his mystical and ethical character. His manner of dying, in conformity with his principles, is equally illustrative. Just two months after arriving in England on the *Mary and Elizabeth*, Woolman contracted smallpox. As he lay near death, he refused medicines that might have alleviated his suffering because they were carried by stagecoaches and the "coach-boys and horses were badly exploited" (Ullman 1959, 92). He died in October 1772, nursed by several Friends, including Esther Tuke, who wrote of Woolman: "Though he appeared to us in some things singular, and the path he trod straiter [*sic*] than the liberty some of us have thought the truth gives, yet I say to thee, that I cannot help thinking it was the way truth led him. . . . I believe some hereaway will, and would be glad, perhaps, to find flaws in his singularity, to cover themselves, and stave off a narrower scrutiny and inspection into their own conduct and example" (Boroughs and Woolman 1991, 196).

Catherine Payton Phillips

Catherine Payton Phillips exhibited mystical inclinations from the beginning. Describing her experience of God as a young child, she reported in her *Memoirs*, "I cannot date the first dawn of divine light upon my soul; for with humble thankfulness I may say, that early in the morning of life I knew the Lord to be a God nigh at hand; convincing of evil, and raising breathings after the saving knowledge of his divine love and power" (Phillips 1797, 5). She spent much of her youth caring for her invalid father, a Friends minister himself, and reading him pious books, which she later regarded as the foundation of her spiritual formation. After a temporary rebellion as a teenager against the religion of her youth, Catherine Phillips once again embraced the ways of the Friends. At age twenty-two, after several years of "a season of deep distress" (1797, 13), she discerned God leading her to speak in her local meeting for worship. She delivered her first message, a brief prayer of supplication, convinced that faithfulness to speaking only what God had given her was more important than eloquence or lengthy discourse. A little more than a year after she first spoke in meeting, she felt called by God to travel in the ministry to Wales, where she and her companion, Lucy Bradley, traveled for seven weeks and attended numerous Friends' meetings. The journey to Wales marked the beginning of a long ministry of traveling to Friends' meetings in England, Scotland, Wales, Ireland, Holland, and America. From her first journey to Wales until nine years before she died, a period of thirty-six years, Catherine traveled "with little intermission" (1797, 307). Her journey through America lasted more than three years, in which she covered much of the 8,750 miles on horseback. In 1772, when Catherine was forty-six years old, she married William Phillips, her friend of twenty-three years, after a long and careful process of discernment. Before she felt "clear" to marry, she needed to know that the marriage would not "frustrate the intention of Divine wisdom respecting me" (1797, 208) by limiting her ability to follow faithfully any divine leadings to travel in the ministry.

Her journal primarily records her travels in the ministry and her mystical experiences during those travels. Her journal and letters together portray her deepening spiritual life and the ways in which it remained intimately connected to her faith community and to compassion for the world.

Corporate worship provided the context for most of Phillips's mystical experiences. From her local meeting at Dudley to the local meetings she visited in her traveling ministry, the opportunities[9] with Friends in their homes, the yearly meetings she visited, and the select meetings of ministers and elders,[10] Phillips tasted a wide range of meetings for worship. After each trip, she often recorded in her journal the number of meetings she had visited and the number of days she had been traveling. For example, in one trip around the north of England, she reported attending sixty-six meetings in sixty-two days, while traveling five hundred miles (1797, 229). Phillips frequently remarked on the spiritual state of a group of people—for example, commenting of New Garden Meeting in North Carolina, "We found a sincere-hearted remnant in this meeting, unto whom the Lord united us; but there was also a dead, for-

---

9. An opportunity is a gathering in a Friend's home to worship and seek God's presence there.

10. A select meeting of ministers and elders is a regularly scheduled gathering of Friends recognized for their pastoral (elder) and ministerial gifts, and appointed with those responsibilities.

mal, professing spirit, under which the living were sorely oppressed; as well as under a flashy wordy ministry" (1797, 79). Of her experience in Virginia she reported, "We had much suffering of spirit, for, although in many instances we were favoured with a good degree of strength and wisdom, to speak to the states of the people; yet could we not but sympathize with the seed of life, which in many of their souls was oppressed by a dark carnal spirit" (1797, 99).

In some cases, she found the meetings powerfully "gathered," and in these gathered meetings[11] she found her most profound experiences of God. One aspect of these experiences was finding herself and the group "searched" by Truth. At the half-year's meeting in Dublin in 1776, for example, she reported that the large gathering was "favoured with an awakening searching visitation" (1797, 230). And at Swansea Meeting in Wales, she reported that "a particular visitation of Truth was extended" (1797, 217) to some who had previously been part of the meeting but had drifted away.

At local meetings in Dublin, she observed God "opening fresh matter, suited to the several occasions" so thoroughly and with such searching of hearts "that it appeared as if every state and office in the society were ministered to" (1797, 231). A second aspect of these profound experiences of God was frequently being moved herself to offer vocal ministry. She found that a deeply gathered meeting drew the ministry out of her. "I was largely and livingly opened in [the Lord's] service" (1797, 218), she wrote after the circular yearly meeting held at Helston in 1772. In describing the select meeting of ministers and elders held at the yearly meeting in Gloucester in 1773, she stated that it was a "memorable opportunity" and then said, "Plentiful are the showers of gospel rain which often fall upon these occasions" (1797, 220).

Besides being the context for her most profound experiences of God, Phillips's faith community was intimately connected with her spiritual transformation in other ways. First, it shaped her. It emitted the spiritual air she breathed and from it flowed the spiritual water she drank. It formed her expectations of what God could do in her life and in the life of the meeting, of what the spiritual life could and should be.

Second, the community entered into her discernment process and thus taught her discernment in a number of ways. When she first felt led to travel in the ministry to Wales in 1749, she consulted her meeting. They prayed with her, discerned that this leading was indeed authentic, and provided her with a traveling minute indicating their support of her. She repeated this process each time a leading to travel in the ministry arose in her.

She usually traveled with another minister or elder—in her early years,

---

11. A gathered or covered meeting for worship is one in which the presence of the Spirit is deeply felt, where vocal ministry gathers Friends up in the Spirit.

with one more experienced than she. Training in discernment occurred naturally in this context. For example, when she heard of Mary Peisley's leading to travel in the ministry to America and felt led to accompany her, she wrote Mary asking for help in discernment: "I am almost at a loss to find terms to express the laborious thought which has possessed my soul; for it seems to me, that Providence designs I should accompany thee; . . . And now my dear friend, I intreat [*sic*] thee to weigh it well, and as disinterestedly as possible, and give me thy thoughts thereupon with all the freedom which our friendship, and the nature of the case, requires, not concealing one doubt" (1797, 50–51). After taking time to pray about Catherine's request, Mary wrote back, confirming Catherine's leading:

> [I]t springs on my heart to say, Thou art the woman, and I really believe the thing is of the Lord; . . . I can assure thee my dear friend, notwithstanding the love I have for thee in the truth, and the affection which I bear to thy person, with the likeness of souls I had discovered; yet, did I feel any obstruction or doubt in my mind of the thing's being right, I dare not conceal it from thee, nor take one step knowingly, out of the light and counsel of truth, in so important an affair. (Phillips 1797, 53–54)

Once on their journey, practice in discernment continued. They discerned together the spiritual condition of meetings they visited. They compared notes on their leadings to speak in meeting and helped one another know when they had discerned rightly and when they had "run ahead of their Guide." [12] Their being together twenty-four hours a day for more than three years with only rare breaks from one another—traveling 8,750 miles, riding horses through the wilderness, sharing the same bed (or sleeping on the ground in the forest together)—provided an intense school for spiritual formation.

Besides traveling with individual ministers and elders, Phillips was invited to join the regular corporate meetings of ministers and elders once they discerned her calling was genuine. This group also shaped her spiritually and ministerially, as she experienced deep worship with them and learned from their experiences in ministry, which they related to one another.

For Phillips, spiritual transformation was intimately connected with social transformation. God's leadings directed her to compassion for others in many forms: she insisted on holding a meeting for worship in steerage while she was on board a ship to America, even when the Anglican priest on board tried to dissuade her; after she addressed the "wreckers" in St. Agnes, they began saving the cargoes of the poor shipwrecked seamen off the North Sea coast in-

---

12. To run ahead of one's guide is to stray outside of a divine leading through self-will.

stead of stealing their goods (1797, 219); she took an interest in Friends' intervention in and the subsequent peaceful resolution of the American Indian wars; and she expressed her concern against slavery while in America. In all these instances, Phillips incarnated her understanding that God's compassion extended to all, especially to the poor and oppressed.

In 1792, Phillips published *Considerations on the Causes of the High Price of Grain* out of concern both for England's poor and for the country as a whole because she was convinced that a country whose poor suffer is headed for disaster. Two years before her death, when she could no longer travel in the ministry, she explained, "when active minds are confined in decrepid [*sic*] bodies, they naturally muse on many things" (1792, i). In this book, she offers sophisticated economic analysis regarding the high price of grain and other food. She calls upon her readers to address this problem, "for if the price of labour is not proportionably [*sic*] advanced, the poor, who till our lands, and support our manufactories, cannot live" (1792, ii).

Recalling the prices before 1756 (the first poor harvest in recent history), Phillips offers a detailed analysis of why the prices went up and stayed up, tracing the deprivation of the poor to the increasing penchant for luxury among the rich and middle classes. The seeds of poverty and violence, she believed, were sown in the taste for luxury. Further, she addresses the practice of enclosing common lands and points out the ways the poor were cheated in the process, as their cottages were eliminated. In describing the overcrowded housing that resulted from this policy, she writes: "A single room must serve a large family; . . . when putrid disorders attack them probably many lives are lost by it. Is it not shocking to humanity for the dead corps [*sic*] of an husband to lie on the same bed with a sick wife, and perhaps several children? Yet many such instances there are in this rich and proud nation; and where is the humanity of our senators, when they pass enclosing laws without protecting the poor cottagers?" (1792, 24). She then proposes a detailed and carefully constructed land-use policy, addressing the interests of the poor as well as of the legislators, the gentry, and the landlords, demonstrating her awareness of and sympathy with the needs of all concerned parties.

Always practical, Phillips also demonstrates extensive knowledge of agriculture, discussing such things as the use of oxen rather than horses for plowing, how to plow up the deeper soil rather than the poor overused topsoil, and the advantages of planting carrots rather than turnips. She anticipates objections to her land-use policy and uses her agricultural knowledge to suggest ways of making it work. Finally, she includes an appendix in which she gives detailed descriptions of seventeen plants and trees, suggesting how thoughtful placement of each of them might further the aims of her land-use policy, were it to be adopted.

In addition to *Considerations on the Causes of the High Price of Grain* to address her economic concerns, Phillips wrote *The Happy King*, a poem addressed to King George III, naming greed as the primary reason behind the injustice of slavery. She exhorts him:

> But why is slavery's galling yoke,
> Permitted to remain?
> When will th' oppressive chain be broke,
> Which does Europa stain?

> When all revere the Christian law's [*sic*],
> Freedom will be obtain'd,
> By every captive, and the cause
> Of slav'ry be explain'd.

> Then 'twill appear that sin and pride,
> Have strain'd the hateful cord;
> And avarice has open'd wide
> Her hands, and basely stor'd,
> The world with captives of all kinds;
> Who, to all nations sent;
> Do evidence their captor's crimes,
> On wicked traffic bent.

> "Oh cursed cruel thirst of gain,
> The source of every evil;"
> Which laws nor gospel do restrain,
> The offspring of the Devil. (1794, 29–30)

Toward the end of the poem, she requests King George to remove the Royal Stile, the royal seal of approval for commerce, from the Africa Slaving Company. She wanted him to stop supporting the slave trade and to support something that would help the Africans: the business interests of Sierra Leone.

> Now let me ask with def'rence due,
> Shall George for virtue fam'd,
> Support an antichristian crew,
> By being ignobly nam'd,

> The head of Britains [*sic*] trading throng,
> Who Afric's sons beguile;

Ah! Why is yet their charter strong,
Deck'd with the *Royal Stile?*

Efface it, saith the wise and good,
And grace therewith a trade;
Which when 'tis rightly understood,
Will Afric's people aid. (1794, 107)

She believed that if the king eschewed the slave trade and befriended African business, he and his empire would prosper and have peace:

Reflect oh King! on an apoch [*sic*],
Arising now in view;
Which may thy reign with lustre note,
And add a country new

To Britains [*sic*] empire vast and wide;
Which may extended be,
Without the sword's destructive pride,
Or dreaded misery.

By deeds of peace did pious Penn,
Well fix his peaceful state;
By deeds of peace it flourish'd when
It knew it's [*sic*] best estate. (1794, 109–10)

The abolition of the slave trade, then, would benefit not only the slaves but also the king and his nation. Freedom for the oppressed also meant freedom and peace for the oppressor.

❖   ❖   ❖

Friends today ask themselves, "What does the Lord require of me?" John Woolman and Catherine Payton Phillips serve as role models by demonstrating how two earlier Friends discerned the answer to this question in their own lives. This essay uncovers the mystical basis of the socially transforming ministries of Woolman and Phillips, and demonstrates how their worshiping communities served as the conduits through which God nurtured and developed the prophetic minister.

We are mindful, of course, of the particular spiritual and social dilemmas of eighteenth-century British and American society that provided the substance from which Woolman and Phillips discerned and responded to the Lord's requirements. We find, however, that the cultures in which twenty-first-century Friends find themselves offer remarkable parallels to Woolman and Phillips's concerns. The market practices of the world's wealthier nations and the consumerism of the affluent and middle classes continue to lead to poverty, violence, and forms of enslavement. May those in the present day take heart from the examples of Woolman and Phillips, and know that social transformation is possible when social action is grounded in personal spiritual transformation rooted in a deeply prayerful faith community.

8

Mystical Experience, Radical Subjectification, and Activism in the Religious Traditions of African American Women

JOY R. BOSTIC

Black women's social context in nineteenth-century North America was characterized by systematic attempts to subjugate Black people physically, psychologically, culturally, and spiritually. Legally or socially sanctioned forms of violence, intimidation, and exploitation—including rape, lynching, beating, and economic exploitation—were tools designed to control Black women. In naming the systemic forces that impeded Black women's lives, I use a term coined by Delores Williams—*demonarchy*. Williams defines demonarchy as the "demonic governance of black women's lives by white male and white female ruled systems using racism, violence, violation, retardation, and death as instruments of social control. . . . [D]emonarchy is a traditional and collective expression of white government in relation to black women" (1986, 52).

Demonarchy undermines and often denies altogether the very humanity and personhood of Black women. It is supported, perpetuated, and maintained by what Patricia Hill Collins calls the "matrix of domination" (1991). Collins's notion of the matrix of domination serves as a framework that helps us to understand the relationships among different forms of oppression affecting Black women's lives—that is, the ways in which these forms interlock and connect within a more general context of domination. This matrix is structured on multiple levels. Its axes include such dynamics as race, gender, and social class. However, persons experience and resist these types of oppression on various levels—personal, group or communal, and systemic. Historically, demonarchal ideologies, structures, and institutions based on the matrix of domination objectified Black women as the "Other." Black women not only had to struggle against the demonarchal attempts by Whites to control

143

and define them, but they also had to contend with the ways in which they themselves, as well as the institutions and members of their own communities, would internalize and perpetuate demonarchal values and ideologies.

Given the relative powerlessness of Black women in the nineteenth century and the predicament of Black people under demonarchy, how did Black women negotiate with and resist the matrix of domination? The spiritual autobiographies of Black women written during this period provide resources through which we can explore this question. These autobiographies constitute acts of witnessing. In them, Black women tell the stories of their spiritual journeys, of their "quests for spiritual perfection in an imperfect world" (Braxton 1989, 49). These literary works not only share the "trials, temptations, and triumphs" experienced by these women, but also "illuminate sex-specific aspects of black women's early intellectual history and [their] quest for self-definition and self-determination" (Braxton 1989, 50). They helped lay the "intellectual groundwork" for Black women's struggles to resist and challenge the demonarchal matrix of domination by asserting the humanity of Black women as persons chosen by God for salvation and called to engage in divine work (Braxton 1989, 50).

In this essay, I explore the spiritual autobiographies and narratives of four African American women: Jarena Lee, Sojourner Truth, Zilpha Elaw, and Rebecca Cox Jackson. These spiritual autobiographies constitute a specific type of literature Joanne Braxton identifies as "narratives of vision and power" (1989, 50). This genre is characterized by religious experiences involving direct encounters with God; the manifestation of ecstatic dreams; visions; spiritual gifts; profound feelings of love; and consciousness and knowledge of, as well as union with, a Holy Other.

In examining these texts, I explore how these women, by way of their religious experiences, were transformed into radical subjects despite attempts by others to control, define, and subjugate them as the "Other." I refer to this intellectual, spiritual, psychological, and theological transformation as the process of subjectification.[1] As a result of their subjectification or transformation, these women were able to assume roles as religious, social, and political activists that went beyond the roles assigned to them by the racist and sexist

---

1. See Jacquelyn Grant (1990). In this essay, Grant critiques dominant Christological discourse, arguing that those who are privileged because of race or gender or by both have constructed Christological definitions that have legitimized their power and at the same time objectified the marginalized. Grant uses the term *subjectification* to indicate the process by which the marginalized, particularly Black women, become the central subjects in Christological discussions, construct their own definitions of who Jesus is for them, as well as claim the power to define themselves.

culture in which they lived. Consequently, I look at how these women's mystical experiences informed their religious, social, and political activism. I also include a constructive discussion regarding the ways in which the testimonies of these women's lives might offer resistance strategies for contemporary African American women who continue to confront the demonarchal matrix of domination on personal, communal, and systemic levels.

Jarena Lee

Jarena Lee's *The Life and Religious Experience of Jarena Lee* was published in 1836. As the earliest known spiritual autobiography written by a Black female, Lee's narrative could serve as a foundational text for and an important resource in developing strategies for resistance to the demonarchal matrix of domination.

Lee was born in 1783 in the state of New Jersey. Because her family was poor, Lee began working at the age of seven as a "servant maid." She would continue to work as a domestic into her adult life. Lee's spiritual awakening occurred at an early age. Following this awakening, she was pursued by what she understood to be a demonic force that tempted her to commit suicide. As she continued to struggle with feelings of anxiety and fear for a period of four to five years, Lee was tempted on two more occasions to "destroy her life" (Andrews 1986, 30) just before her conversion. Recounting a vision, Lee described her spiritual, emotional, and psychological state.

> But notwithstanding the terror which seized upon me, when about to end my life, I had no view of the precipice on the edge of which I was tottering, until it was over, and my eyes were opened. Then the awful gulf of hell seemed to be open beneath me, covered only, as it were, by a spider's web, on which I stood. I seemed to hear the howling of the damned, to see the smoke of the bottomless pit, and to hear the rattling of those chains, which hold the impenitent under clouds of darkness to the judgment of the great day. (Andrews 1986, 30)

Jarena Lee relied heavily on prayer to alleviate or bring some resolution to her struggle. Finally, the day of her conversion came while she was sitting in a worship service.

> That instant, it appeared to me, as if a garment, which had entirely enveloped my whole person, even to my fingers' ends, split at the crown of my head, and was stripped away from me, passing like a shadow, from my sight—when the glory of God seemed to cover me in its stead.

> That moment, though hundreds were present, I did leap to my feet, and declare that God, for Christ's sake, had pardoned the sins of my soul. Great was the ecstasy of my mind. . . . For a few moments I had power to exhort sinners, and to tell of the wonders and of the goodness of him who had clothed me with his salvation. (29)

Through this encounter with the divine power of God, having stood on a spider's web suspended over the gulf of hell, Jarena Lee became intensely aware of the reality of human sin and the power of demonic forces. Lee conquered the "violence of the feelings" (32) she had struggled against and was liberated from the demonic influence that had tempted her to destroy her own life. This moment of conversion was a powerful experience of transformation in which the shadow self—the former, false self—was stripped away and vanished from her sight. A new reality, a new being had come forth clothed with the divine power of God.

The next stage of Lee's journey involved a new struggle that she described as a laboring of the mind. Lee wanted to "know more of the right way of the Lord" (33). The intellectual nature of this struggle testified to Lee's desire to obtain not only emotional and psychological freedom, but also spiritual and intellectual autonomy to understand the nature of God as well as her ethical responsibilities as a new creation "clothed" with God's salvation. Through her conversion, Lee was spiritually, psychologically, and emotionally liberated from the fear and anxiety she associated with human sin and the forces of evil. However, she desired a deeper communion with God. She retired "to a secret place" and prayed for God to do an even "greater work" in her life. As she prayed, she was overwhelmed by God's presence.

> That very instant, as if lightning had darted through me, I sprang to my feet, and cried, "The Lord has sanctified my soul!" There was none to hear this but the angels who stood around to witness my joy—and Satan, whose malice raged the more. That Satan was there, I knew; for no sooner had I cried out "The Lord has sanctified my soul," than there seemed another voice behind me, saying, "No, it is too great a work to be done." But another spirit said, "Bow down for the witness—I received it—*thou art sanctified!*" The first I knew of myself after that, I was standing in the yard with my hands spread out, and looking with my face toward heaven.
>
> I now ran into the house and told them what had happened to me, when, as it were, a new rush of the same ecstasy came upon me, and caused me to feel as if I were in an ocean of light and bliss.
>
> So great was the joy, that it is past description. There is no language that can describe it, except that which was heard by St. Paul, when he was caught up to the third heaven, and heard words which were not lawful to utter. (34)

Lee's ecstasy was so profound that she could not adequately describe her experience. She moved beyond her doubt regarding her relationship with God and into a deeper communion with and knowledge of God. This experience laid the foundation for the next stage of her spiritual journey: the call to preach the Gospel.

Four or five years after the liberating event described above, Lee testified that she heard a voice that said to her "Go preach the Gospel!" Lee's reply: "No one will believe me" (35). Determined not to be deceived by the voice of evil and wanting to know God's will concerning her calling, Lee went again to "a secret place" (35) to seek divine counsel. As she called upon God, Lee saw a vision of a pulpit with a Bible lying upon it. Lee records that the following night she actually "took a text" (35) and preached it in her sleep. Lee preached so powerfully that she and the rest of her family were awakened by the sound of her voice. Lee was then convinced that God in fact had called her to preach.

When Lee went to Richard Allen, one of the founders of the African Methodist Episcopal (A.M.E.) Church, to inform him of her calling, he dismissed her claim at first, saying that the Methodist Discipline did not "call for women preachers." [2] Lee was extremely apprehensive about accepting such a burdensome call, and so she was immediately relieved. But soon thereafter, "that holy energy which burned within [her], as a fire, began to be smothered" (36), and the contradictions regarding women's exclusion from ordained ministry became clear to her. Here, in the institution where she had been nurtured and had felt a sense of community, Lee's calling—her very personhood—was being denied.

Lee resisted and rejected this affront to her sense of personhood—this attempt to treat her as an object to be defined by institutional power and male leadership. In her spiritual autobiography, we have evidence that she asserted herself as a radical subject and simultaneously laid the intellectual and theological groundwork for the inclusion of Black women in ordained ministry. In a prophetic pronouncement, she warned the institutional church that its exclusion of women from the preaching ministry was tantamount to a betrayal of God's word.

---

2. Lee is recorded to have approached Allen to request the church's affirmation of her preaching ministry in 1809 at the Bethel African Methodist Church of Philadelphia. Before the African Methodist Episcopal Church adopted its own doctrine and disciplines, it was guided by the rules and Articles of Faith of the Methodist Episcopal Church, which did not allow for the ordination of women. Although her request was denied, Lee pursued her preaching ministry. Allen became bishop of the then newly organized African Methodist Episcopal Church and gave Lee permission to lead prayer meetings. He publicly affirmed Lee's preaching gifts after hearing her stand up and preach when the assigned preacher for the Bethel Church appeared to have "lost the spirit."

Oh how careful ought we to be, lest through our by-laws of church government and discipline, we bring into disrepute even the word of life. For as un-
seemly as it may appear now-a-days for a woman to preach, it should be
remembered that nothing is impossible with God. And why should it be
thought impossible, heterodox, or improper, for a woman to preach? seeing
the Savior died for the woman as well as the man.

> If a man may preach, because the Savior died for him, why not the
woman? seeing he died for her also. Is he not a whole Savior, instead of a half
one? as those who hold it wrong for a woman to preach, would seem to make
it appear. (36)

The logic and forcefulness of Lee's theological and biblical arguments attested
to the humanity of Black women and to the inclusive actions and intentions of
God and the Savior. This inclusivity was in contrast to the exclusionary practices of the church. Despite being rejected and not having her call formally
recognized by the institutional church, Lee remained confident regarding
what she perceived to be God's calling for her life. "As for me, I am fully per-
suaded that the Lord called me to labour according to what I have received, in
his vineyard. If he has not, how could he consistently bear testimony in favour
of my poor labours, in awakening and converting sinners?" (37).

It was her relationship with God and her experiences of visions, dreams,
and divine presence that gave Lee confidence to fulfill her call to preach. Not
only did Lee's religious experiences endow her with knowledge and the abili-
ties she needed to carry out this calling, but divine power was also manifested
in her ministry in a way that valorized her calling to others.

> During the exhortation, God made manifest his power in a manner suf-
ficient to show the world that I was called to labour according to my ability,
and the grace given unto me. . . .
> . . . I spoke to a large congregation of various and conflicting senti-
ments, when a wonderful shock of God's power was felt, shown everywhere
by groans, by sighs, and loud and happy amens. I felt as if aided from above.
My tongue was cut loose, the stammerer spoke freely; the love of God, and of
his service, burned with a vehement flame within me—his name was glorified
among the people. (44, 48)

Thus, although she was not formally recognized by the institutional church as
a preacher, her calling would not be denied, for Lee demonstrated such power
as she exhorted the masses and led prayer meetings that, eventually, Richard
Allen would be compelled to affirm her gifts publicly.

In carrying out her divine calling through extensive travels, Lee affected
the lives of individuals, changing their way of thinking about the humanity of

Black women. Her ministry facilitated the healing and conversion of many persons whom she encountered. She resisted and subverted the matrix of domination in a patriarchal institution that would have denied her identity and relegated her to roles it assigned to her. Once Lee overcame fear and the evil forces that tempted her to take her own life, her transformation resulted in her radical subjectification as a woman whose primary and ultimate authority was God. She defied and helped to transform the institutional church, opening the door for other women who would answer the call to preach.

Sojourner Truth

The life of Sojourner Truth (born a slave named Isabella around 1797) was certainly affected by the interlocking web of the matrix of domination. However, Truth challenged this matrix and entered into a process of subjectification that would result in a liberated identity. This process was rooted in Truth's theological development with respect to her understanding of God as well as to her becoming conscious of the oppressive realities of her sociohistorical condition.

As a slave, Isabella believed that her master was God. Believing that her master could see her at all times and knew everything that she did, she would confess when she felt she had done wrong because she thought that he would go easier on her. Her fear and awe of her master were so great that she deprived herself of sleep and worked endlessly to please him. When other slaves would speak contemptuously of slavery, Isabella would chastise them and even report them to the master. According to her narrative, she believed that slavery was "right and honorable" (Washington 1993, 21) In accepting her circumstances as normative, Isabella had deeply internalized the matrix of domination that undergirded the demonarchal system of slavery.

Isabella's consciousness grew regarding her sociohistorical condition as she continued to witness and to be subjected to her master's exploitation. As she attempted to make sense out of the contradictions of slavery, Isabella drew on the prayer tradition and on the understanding of God given to her by her mother, who taught her children that "there is a God, who hears and sees you," a God who lives in the sky; and "when you are badly beaten, or cruelly treated, or fall into any trouble, you must ask help" of God who will "always hear and help you" (7).

Isabella held on to this image of a God who would hear her prayers and help her in times of trouble. She would go daily to a "rural sanctuary" (44) and talk with God about the troubles and suffering she endured as a slave. As she prayed, Isabella would ask God whether "it was right" (45) that she was subjected to such suffering, and she would implore God to deliver her from evil. Previously so eager to please her master, John Dumont (believing him to have the power and omniscience of a god), she now came to understand the demonarchal nature of slavery and revolted against that unjust system by running away. This act of defiance and independence was in her view divinely authorized and sanctioned, for Isabella believed that it was God who gave her a plan to escape. In this way, God affirmed her humanity and declared the system of slavery unjust.

Isabella's understanding of God continued to evolve. During the festival of Pingster or Whitsuntide, while she was living with the Van Wagener family (for whom she had gone to work after she ran away from Dumont), Dumont appeared to take her back with him. Just as Isabella had resigned herself to go back, however, what she believed to be the true nature of God was revealed to her

> [w]ith all the suddenness of a flash of lightning, showing her, "in the twinkling of an eye, that he was *all over*"—that he pervaded the universe—"and that there was no place where God was not." [When] . . . her attention was once more called to outward things, she observed her master had left, and exclaiming aloud, "Oh God, I did not know you were so big," she walked into the house, and made an effort to resume her work. But the workings of the inward man were too absorbing to admit of much attention to her avocations. (49–50)

The power of this revelation compelled Isabella to be attentive to her own interiority, to the discovery of her own true identity as she rejected the culture's view of her as merely an objectified source of labor. Rather, she knew herself as a human subject, and as such, she engaged in theological reflection and contemplation that were critical to her own spiritual, psychological, and intellectual freedom and development.

It was as she struggled in prayer that Isabella was liberated from feelings of anxiety and dread, and experienced a profound sense of love when she encountered the Christian mediator in a vision. As a result of her experience, she was convinced that she had a divine friend and that she was assured of God's love and acceptance.

> She desired to talk to God, but her vileness utterly forbade it, and she was not able to prefer a petition. . . . now she began to wish for someone to speak to God for her. Then a space seemed opening between her and God. . . . At length a friend appeared to stand between herself and an insulted Deity; and she felt as sensibly refreshed as when, on a hot day, an umbrella had been interposed between her scorching head and a burning sun. But who was this friend?

"Who are you?" she exclaimed, as the vision brightened into a form distinct, beaming with the beauty of holiness, and radiant with love. She then
said, audibly addressing the mysterious visitant—"I *know* you, and I *don't*
know you." Meaning, "You seem perfectly familiar; I feel that you not only
love me, but that you always *have* loved me—yet I know you not—I cannot
call you by name" . . . "Who are you?" was the cry of her heart, and her
whole soul was in one deep prayer that this heavenly personage might be revealed to her, and remain with her. At length, after bending both soul and
body with the intensity of this desire, till breath and strength seemed failing,
and she could maintain her position no longer, an answer came to her, saying
distinctly, "It is Jesus." (50–51)

While living in New York City, Isabella became more and more conscious
of prevailing economic and social injustices. She "felt called in the spirit" (79)
to leave the city and travel east. This moment was significant with respect to I-
sabella's process of subjectification. It was at this time that she announced she
would no longer be called by her slave name. God had given her a new name:
Sojourner Truth, for God had called her to travel about and speak "truth" to
the people. As "Sojourner Truth," the woman born a slave named Isabella,
who once thought that her master was God and slavery was "noble and
right," had been transformed into a new self, a radical subject who had wres-
tled the authority to define who she was and her place in the world away from
agents of demonarchy.

> She was now fairly started on her pilgrimage; . . . her heart strong in
> faith that her true work lay before her, and that the Lord was her director;
> and she doubted not he would provide for and protect her, and it would be
> very censurable in her to burden herself with any thing more than a moder-
> ate supply for her then present needs. Her mission was not merely to travel
> east, but to "lecture," as she designated it; "testifying of the hope that was in
> her"—exhorting the people to embrace Jesus, and refrain from sin, the na-
> ture and origin of which she explained to them in accordance with her own
> most curious and original views. (80)

Despite her lack of economic resources and the fact that as a Black female
in the nineteenth century she was afforded little protection, Truth set out to
pursue what she perceived to be her calling. Her testimonies and challenges to
sin were informed by the many talks she had had with God about the injustices
she had suffered. She came to understand God as a God who not only stood
against injustice but also acted on behalf of those who suffered from injustice.
Truth claimed divine authority as an independent thinker who relied on
her own inner witness, her talks with God, and her ecstatic experiences of

dreams and visions as the ground and source of her knowledge and vocation. It was out of this sense of authority, this calling, and the belief that God would protect her that Truth became a formidable force in the struggles against the matrix of domination as an advocate for women's rights and racial equality.

Zilpha Elaw

Memoirs of the Life, Religious Experience, Ministerial Travels and Labours of Mrs. Zilpha Elaw, An American Female of Colour was first published in London in 1846. Elaw published *Memoirs* after a five-year preaching mission in Great Britain for the purpose of providing a "portrait of [her] regenerated constitution" (Andrews 1986, 51). She was born in Pennsylvania "of religious parents" (53), and she had two siblings—an older brother and an older sister. When Elaw was twelve, her mother died during her twenty-second pregnancy (only three of these pregnancies resulted in living infants). Following her mother's death, Elaw's father placed the children in the care of a Quaker couple. In her *Memoirs,* Elaw remarks how she did not receive much exposure to observable religious practices because the religious exercises of her guardians were "performed in the secret silence of the mind" (54). Later Elaw would become a member of the Methodist Church.

Zilpha Elaw describes "the divine work" on her soul as a "very gradual" process: her way was "prepared as the dawning of the morning" (55). The initial stirrings of Elaw's soul began when she was fourteen: after breaking a cardinal rule (not to use the Lord's name in vain), she had a dream.

> On that very night, after I had offended my heavenly Father by taking His name in vain, He aroused and alarmed my spirit, by presenting before me in a dream the awful terrors of the day of judgment, accompanied by its terrific thunders. I thought that the Angel Gabriel came and proclaimed that time should be no longer; and he said, "Jehovah was about to judge the world, and execute judgment on it." I then exclaimed in my dream, "Oh, Lord, what shall I do? I am unprepared to meet thee." I then meditated an escape, but could not effect it; and in this horrific dilemma I awoke: the day was just dawning; and the intense horror of my guilty mind was such as to defy description. I was now about fourteen years of age; and this dream proved an effectual call to my soul. (55)

Elaw became "distressed because of her sins," and although she stated that she never felt a fear or dread of hell, she experienced great sorrow because she believed that in her disobedience she had grieved God. As she attended Methodist meetings, Elaw grew in her religious knowledge. However, she did not feel confident that God had fully accepted her. Later, a vision provided her with the assurance she sought. "I distinctly saw the Lord Jesus approach me with open arms, and a most divine and heavenly smile upon his countenance. As He advanced towards me, I felt that his very looks spoke, and said, 'Thy prayer is accepted, I own thy name.' From that day to the present I have never entertained a doubt of the manifestation of his love to my soul" (56).

Following her conversion, Elaw came to know God as her protector, so her fears were allayed, and she came to know "the peace of God" (57). Through prayer and meditation, she experienced "communion" with God and a profound sense of love, particularly during times of "trials and tribulations." "At such times, an overflowing stream of love has filled my soul, even beyond my capacity to contain, and I have thought, when in such ecstasies of bliss, that I should certainly die under them, and go to my heavenly father at once, from an earthly to an heavenly transport; for I could not imagine it possible for any human being to feel such gusts of the love of God, and continue to exist in the world of sin" (58). Elaw continued to experience this love. When she was baptized, she was "so overwhelmed with the love of God that the self seemed annihilated," and she was "completely lost and absorbed in the divine fascinations" (61).

During the years following her conversion, Elaw engaged in the spiritual discipline of prayer as she grew in "grace and knowledge" (60). She strongly emphasized that her transformation and the source of her knowledge were "not by the aid of human instruments" (60). Rather, "it was by the Lord alone that [she] was upheld, confirmed, instructed, sanctified, and directed" (60). Awakened to the source of her being—the love of God—Elaw did not embrace the externally imposed definitions and expectations of Black women's roles in society. Instead, she relied on her inward resources and communications with God as the authoritative sources for her identity and calling. At a Methodist camp meeting, she received a "redoubling" of her assurance that God was the ultimate source of her identity.

> It was at one of these meetings that God was pleased to separate my soul unto Himself, to sanctify me as a vessel designed for honour, made meet for the master's use. . . . I became so overpowered with the presence of God, that I sank down upon the ground, and laid there for a considerable time; and while I was thus prostrate on the earth, my spirit seemed to ascend up into the clear circle of the sun's disc; and, surrounded and engulfed in the glorious effulgence of his rays, I distinctly heard a voice speak unto me, which said, "Now thou art sanctified." . . . When I recovered from the trance or ecstasy into which I had fallen . . . I clearly saw by the light of the Holy Ghost, that my heart and soul were rendered completely spotless—as

clean as a sheet of white paper, and I felt as pure as if I had never sinned in all
my life; a solemn stillness rested upon my soul. (66–67)

After receiving this assurance, Elaw began her public ministry of prayer and
preaching in spite of family opposition and obligations. Elaw's husband was
very hostile toward religion, and he directed his hostility at his wife because of
her fervent religious commitment. She also had to wrestle with her parental
obligations and to struggle through poverty and debt (particularly after the
death of her husband).[3] To pursue her calling, Elaw had to go against the societal expectations that she fulfill her role as a mother, and so she arranged for
the care of her daughter. She followed the Spirit's direction to visit the sick,
the poor, the rich, and even those who held high political offices in the state.
Eventually through her many travels in ministry, she ministered to Black communities of faith (including those in slaveholding states in the South), and
later she traveled to England to preach and minister to predominantly White
audiences. Elaw had to contend with the matrix of domination as she faced resistance and intimidation as well as the threat of physical violence by those
who were opposed to Black and female ministers.

Elaw believed that God blessed her labors. She would sometimes have
doubts about her calling or about the direction of her travels and ministry,
but through visions, dreams, and "walking and talking" with God, she received direction, knowledge, and power to carry out the will of God despite
poverty, racism, sexism, and family constraints. Furthermore, the knowledge
she gained through visions and dreams, and the power that was evident in
her life through the manifestation of charisms legitimized Elaw's authority,
even among those who opposed her because she was Black or because she
was female.

Rebecca Cox Jackson

Rebecca Cox Jackson was born in 1795 in the Philadelphia area. Jackson's autobiography begins with an account of her spiritual rebirth. The year was
1830, and she was thirty-five years old. Similar to Lee and Truth, Jackson also
suffered from fears and anxieties. She sought relief through prayer. As she was
praying, she had a religious experience that enabled her to overcome her fear
of lightning. Subsequently, she welcomed lightning as a revelation of divine
glory.

---

3. Jarena Lee had to deal with some of the same issues after her husband died and she was left
with two children.

And in this moment of despair the cloud bursted, the heavens was clear, and the mountain was gone. My spirit was light, my heart was filled with love for God and all mankind. And the lightening, which was a moment ago the messenger of death, was now the messenger of peace, joy, and consolation. And I rose from my knees, ran down stairs, opened the door to let the lightning in the house, for it was like sheets of glory to my soul. (Humez 1981, 72)

Imbued with feelings of profound love, joy, peace, and acceptance, Jackson was emotionally empowered and spiritually transformed, and thus liberated from the anxieties and fears that had seized her in the past.

During this period of what Jean Humez calls "awakening and early gifts" (1981, 69), Jackson was visited by many dreams and visions and received what she herself described as "gifts of power" (Humez 1981, 96). For her, these dreams, visions, and gifts were her primary sources of knowledge and authority. Jackson rejected the authority of others to act as mediators of knowledge. She wrote that "there was no mortal that I could go to and gain instruction, so it pleased God . . . to teach me in dreams and visions and revelations and gifts" (96). Moreover, in exercising these gifts throughout her life, she was able to influence her external environment. In one instance, she successfully petitioned God to stop a rainstorm so that she could attend a prayer meeting. As she prayed, she heard a voice saying to her, "Do you know what you have done? You have climbed to the heaven and have taken hold of the clouds . . . if thou can climb to the heaven and take hold of the clouds, which are above thy reach, and have power over them, then thou can have power over thy light and trifling nature, and over thy own body also. Thy make must be unmade and remade, and thou must be made a new creature" (98).

Jackson's spiritual gifts not only enabled her to change her environment, but also gave her the ability to claim authority as a subject and to discover her own voice and identity. With her inner voice as her ultimate authority, she overcame her fears and anxieties, and asserted a new sense of identity beyond the control of familial and church institutions. This assertion placed her in great conflict with her husband and brother as well as with the male leadership in the A.M.E. Church, which accused her of trying to break up the church and of usurping male authority. Eventually her marriage ended, and she broke with the institutional church.

Jackson joined the Shakers because she sought a religious community that valued and promoted the theological and ethical understandings she had developed under the tutorship of the Spirit.[4] However, she once again felt com-

---

4. Jackson felt that the Shakers' beliefs were most consistent with her own. She was particularly concerned with being a part of religious community that supported a celibate lifestyle.

pelled to follow her inner voice, which called her to minister to the needs of her own people. When the Shaker elders refused to support this ministry, Jackson left the Shaker community to fulfill what she believed to be her calling. Later, she returned, and the elders gave their support to her work. She fulfilled her vision of building a Shaker community made up of mostly Black women and was given the title "Mother" Jackson as a leader among the Shakers.

Jackson relied primarily on divine direction and instruction as well as "gifts of power" (96) as sources of authority to carry out her religious activism. Thus, she was adamant about the need to distinguish the voice of God from other voices: she relied on the inner voice that spoke to her in her encounters with God through dreams and visions, and she rejected any voice or authority that was not consistent with the inner compulsion she felt in her own spirit.

◆   ◆   ◆

In the spiritual autobiographies of Jarena Lee, Sojourner Truth, Zilpha Elaw, and Rebecca Cox Jackson, we hear testimonies of women who broke the grip of anxiety and fear caused by the uncertainty of their spiritual and material lives within the web of the matrix of domination. Through her religious experiences, Jarena Lee conquered the demonic forces that would have destroyed her life, was transformed into a new being, and went on in her religious activism to bring about healing for many converts. Sojourner Truth evolved in her understanding of God, developed a critical consciousness concerning race and gender oppression, and became an advocate for justice. Zilpha Elaw believed she was instructed and set apart by God in spite of societal pressures and role expectations, and thus pursued a public ministry in the deep South as well as among Whites in Europe. In response to God's call, she risked physical harm and endured sexist and racist opposition to her religious work. And Rebecca Cox Jackson, whose radical obedience to her inner voice led to her religious activism, established a Black Shaker community. These extraordinary women can provide resources for contemporary African American women's resistance to and transcendence of the demonarchal oppression that continues to affect our lives and the lives of our communities.

The women represented in these narratives of vision and power had internalized in various ways the ideologies, values, and assumptions of demonarchy. They had to contend with the anxiety and fear arising out of the uncertainties in their spiritual and material circumstances and futures. However, they were able to engage in a process of subjectification through their encounters with God and were thereby invested with the ability to reject and cast off the oppressive chains of spiritual and material bondage. These women claimed authority in a culture where they were often denied authority, and by the power of God they received a new sense of identity.

These women's personal resistance and transformation constituted acts of social transformation in and of themselves. In becoming radical subjects, they changed the course of history by rejecting, defying, and transcending the oppressive realities of their own sociohistorical circumstances and by subverting the demonarchal designs on their lives. In carrying out their vocations, they brought about social transformation as they also resisted, defied, and transformed communal institutions—as they confronted and challenged demonarchy itself.

They valued the workings of God through ecstatic experiences as sources of knowledge, power, and authority in a culture that denied them access to traditional modes of power and to formal education. In challenging and resisting demonarchy, they literally looked into the pit of hell and not only survived, but also conquered the demonic forces that sought to take their very lives. They understood God to be a God who stood against injustice, a God who could see their suffering and who heard their prayers. The God of these African American women protected them and provided them with the resources they needed to resist demonarchy and to fulfill their callings.

The lives of these women can serve as resources for identifying and constructing resistance strategies that reflect the religious traditions of African American women. Lee, Truth, Elaw, and Jackson demonstrated in their lives and work a *holy boldness*[5] rooted in their belief that God gave them the authority and the power to carry out their vocations. Here, I use the notion of holy boldness to capture a religious, sociopolitical stance and practice arising out of Black women's religious experiences—to characterize how these women acted as radical subjects to engage in social transformation. I contend that this notion of holy boldness is an effective heuristic device as well as a hermeneutic through which to explore African American women's religious traditions. Holy boldness characterizes the ways in which Black women have claimed divine authority to resist, defy, and transform the existing religious institutions, doctrines, and polity, as well as the sociohistorical conditions and power relations perpetuated by demonarchy and its matrix of domination as it is either externally imposed on African Americans or internalized by them. Holy boldness is a stance and a practice that values ecstatic experiences as sources of knowledge and power, and that also assumes a critical conscious-

---

5. *Holy boldness* refers to persons who possess spiritual power, confidence, and audacity. It is used within the Black church tradition. See, for example, Cheryl Townsend Gilkes (1986), whose article also appears in Black women's literature. See also Toni Cade Bambara (1980).

ness toward oppressive systems and the urgency to confront and to challenge demonarchy and the matrix of domination that supports it.

Further exploration of African American women's religious traditions through this notion of holy boldness certainly will uncover and highlight diverse resistance strategies employed by Black women as they have assumed and exercised this religious sociopolitical stance and practice. This exploration will yield implications for developing rituals, pedagogies, theologies, and ethical frameworks that will affirm and empower African American women who still must confront the matrix of domination.

PART THREE

Emerging Contemporary Approaches

9

Awakening for All Beings

BUDDHISM AND SOCIAL TRANSFORMATION

DONALD ROTHBERG

Violence never ceases through hatred. It is only through love that it ceases. This is an ancient law.

—Gautama Buddha,
the *Dhammapada*

The essence of nonviolence is love. Out of love and the willingness to act selflessly, strategies, tactics, and techniques for a nonviolent struggle arise naturally. . . . Other struggles may be fueled by greed, hatred, fear or ignorance, but a nonviolent one cannot use such blind sources of energy, for they will destroy those involved and also the struggle itself. Nonviolent action, born of the awareness of suffering and nurtured by love, is the most effective way to confront adversity.

—Thich Nhat Hanh,
Love in Action

The mercy of the West has been social revolution; the mercy of the East has been individual insight into the basic self/void. We need both. They are both contained in the traditional three aspects of the Dharma path: wisdom *(prajñā)*, meditation *(dhyāna)*, and morality *(śīla)*. Wisdom is the intuitive knowledge of the mind of love and the clarity that lies beneath one's ego-driven anxieties and aggressions. Meditation is going into the mind to see this for yourself—over and over again, until it becomes the mind in which you live. Morality is bringing it back out in the way you live through personal example and responsible action, ultimately toward the true community *(saṇgha)* of "all beings."

—Gary Snyder,
Earth House Hold

Parts of this chapter have been modified from a 1992 article by Donald Rothberg entitled "Buddhist Responses to Violence and War: Resources for a Socially Engaged Spirituality," *Journal of Humanistic Psychology* 32, no. 4: 41–75.

Buddhism and the Contemporary Prospects
of Connecting Mysticism and Social Transformation

The core teaching of the Buddha, expressed in the Four Noble Truths, supposedly communicated soon after his full enlightenment, is that there is profound suffering or unsatisfactoriness in life; that the roots of such suffering are in greed, hatred, and delusion; that it is possible to end suffering, to uproot greed, hatred, and delusion; and that there are clear, practical ways to transform suffering through and into wisdom and love. In this fundamental teaching, there is no limiting of the transformative process to separate individuals, even if Buddhist teachings have often been interpreted in a more individualistic way, including in the contemporary West. Hence, many contemporary "socially engaged" Buddhists, both Asian and Western, although firmly based in traditional teachings and practices, have explicitly attempted to connect individual and social (or "inner" and "outer") transformation, and to understand the often dialectical relationship between individually and collectively based suffering and liberation.

In this essay, I suggest that Buddhists bring vital resources for the contemporary linking of individual and collective transformation—for the integration, in the context of this book, of mysticism and social transformation. Yet such an integrative effort meets immediately a host of difficulties related to the common and deeply rooted split between individual (particularly mystical) transformation and collective action, a split found in different ways in both Western and Asian settings. Hence, a starting point, explored in the second section of this essay, must be to consider some of the various sources of this split and particularly its expression in specific Western frameworks and practices. Then, in the third section, I analyze some aspects of the relationship between individual and social transformation in Buddhism, also discussing Buddhist versions of the split. I focus on early Buddhism, but bring in some treatment as well of the later Mahāyāna ("Great Vehicle") movement. Finally, in the fourth section, I present some of the resources as well as challenges of contemporary socially engaged Buddhism, both in Asia and the West, in terms of connecting individual and social transformation.

The Western Opposition of Mysticism and Social Transformation

The split or polarization between mysticism and social transformation is deeply entrenched both in twenty-five hundred years of Western thought and practice and in distinctively modern conceptual and institutional structures. This split historically has taken the form of an opposition between the supposedly timeless, absolute, and otherworldly quality of mysticism and the suppos-

edly historical, contingent, and this-worldly quality of social action (Woods 1996).

The roots of this opposition go back as least as far as the separation made between *theōria* and *praxis* by Aristotle in the *Nicomachean Ethics*. For Aristotle, the clearly superior "contemplative" life of *theōria* requires a suspension from the duties and constraints of practical, active life in the *polis*. In *theōria,* we become like the gods, Aristotle thinks, using the divine aspect of our intelligence and being unconcerned with actions: "Anything that concerns actions appears trivial and unworthy of the gods" (1178b, 16–17; Aristotle 1985, 289). As Plotinus suggests in continuing this view, "The point of action is contemplation. . . . Contemplation is therefore the end of action" *(Enneads* III, 8 [30], 6; in O'Brien 1981, 167). Such contemplation stands in relation to the eternal and the necessary, whereas the life of *praxis* is concerned with the time bound and the contingent (Arendt 1958). Furthermore, the contemplative knows the eternal only individually, outside of Plato's cave, apart from the constraints of the human community, or, in Plotinus's words, "as the flight of the lone to the Alone" *(Enneads,* VI, 9 [9], 11; in O'Brien 1981, 88). Indeed, the very concept of mysticism itself (from the Greek, related to the term *to close)* and the practice of Western mysticism have been commonly embedded within versions of the distinction of *theōria* and *praxis,* and specifically linked with the qualities of *theōria*.

The fundamental distinction of *theōria* and *praxis* has, with modernity, been transmitted in secular form through the core polarities of theory and practice, contemplation and action, intellectual and activist, and so on. These distinctions still in large part structure our basic concepts and current understandings of mysticism, social transformation, and their relationship. Much of the contemporary literature on mysticism, for example, especially stresses the introvertive mystical experience—that is, the experience of undifferentiated unity beyond the senses, following the work of Walter Stace (1960). Such experience is distinguished from the extrovertive mystical experience of unity or interpenetration within normal sense experience and activity. In fact, a number of contemporary writers prefer to limit the term *mysticism* to the former, introvertive types of experiences, distinct both from "visionary" experiences and from such extrovertive experiences (Forman 1990a).

Similarly, many of the modern traditions related to social transformation have been explicitly antireligious and antimystical, whether in the Enlightenment critiques of religion as oppressive and authoritarian or in the Marxist analysis of religion as fundamentally escapist, a kind of opiated inner refuge from the brutal realities of social life. These social critics have often rejected and reversed the primacy of *theōria* in favor of the primacy of *praxis* or practical reason. Marx comments, for example, in the seventh of the "Theses on

Feuerbach": "All social life is essentially *practical*. All the mysteries which lead theory into mysticism find their rational solution in human practice and in the comprehension of this practice" (Kamenka 1983, 157, emphasis in original). In this context, it is commonplace for modern secular social activists to consider mysticism as necessarily "inner" and at best an irrelevant escape, at worst a fundamental delusion, and to emphasize institutional (rather than individual) transformation—the transformation of economic, social, judicial, and political institutions.[1]

Such a contemporary opposition between mysticism and social transformation is also closely related to the differentiation in the modern worldview between the "natural" (or "objective"), "social," and "subjective" worlds that Weber and Habermas analyze (Habermas 1984). In such a worldview, religion and spirituality are increasingly interpreted (where they are not simply rejected) as subjective and private, and separated from what is seen as the objective world of nature studied by the empirical sciences and the social or public world of intersubjectivity (Bellah et al. 1985, 220–24; Kovel 1991, 204–12; Rothberg 1993). The subjective world of personal values and visions is resolutely separated from the social world and deemed a matter of private choice and preference. Inner experiences are typically seen as idiosyncratic and particular, not capable of the objectivity or intersubjectivity characteristic, respectively, of the objective and social worlds (Rothberg 1986). In this context, it is common to separate (secular) individual transformation, often interpreted psychologically, from collective transformation (Jacoby 1975), although there are many exceptions, such as critical social theory and some approaches to feminism.

Here, ironically, we have come full circle from the Platonic and neo-Platonic perspectives that mysticism brings us into contact with what is most real and objective (e.g., for Plato, the "Forms"). Now mysticism is deemed incapable of leading us to the real and universal, leaving us only with the subjective and particular, at best—as we in our society often say, "real *for me*." Such a dramatic turn, however, may obscure the commonality between the classical and modern perspectives in regard to how mysticism is understood and the fact that both approaches *share* versions of the split between theory and practice, thereby perpetuating a split between mysticism and social action.

Yet, at the present time, these very modern conceptual and institutional

---

1. To be sure, the lives of many mystics (Buddha, Isaiah, Jesus, Joan of Arc, the Baal Shem Tov, and Gandhi, to name a few) have led to often dramatic and far-reaching social transformations. Plato, after all, had the philosopher who had left the cave return to the cave following "enlightenment" in order to serve humanity. Yet the dominant contemporary tendency is nonetheless to distinguish radically mysticism and social transformation.

structures that make difficult or impossible the integration of mysticism and social transformation are increasingly viewed as problematic, whatever their achievements, as are many aspects of their ancestry. A host of critics link such structures with a series of conceptual, epistemological, ethical, social, political, and ecological issues and problems, and many point to the need for large-scale change and the development of "postmodern" worldviews (e.g., Berman 1981; Bordo 1987; Foucault 1980; Habermas 1975; Merchant 1980; Taylor 1989; West 1982). As I have argued elsewhere (Rothberg 1993), such postmodern worldviews can be developed, and characteristically modern problems can be addressed by questioning the split of individual and collective development, by exploring the integration of mysticism and social transformation, or by more broadly developing what I have called a contemporary "socially engaged spirituality." One possible outcome, for example, of the now almost relentless critique of modernity is to reimagine subjectivity (and the mystical depths of subjectivity) both as having its own "objectivity" and as fundamentally interwoven with the natural and social worlds (e.g., Abram 1996; Griffin 1988a; Griffin 1988b; Wilber 1995). Such changes in many of our fundamental concepts and practices might facilitate rather than hinder an integration of mysticism and social transformation. They may help us not only to be more open to mysticism in general, but also *not* to interpret and articulate mysticism (including Buddhist mysticism) within the old framework— that is, in an overly individualistic and "subjective" way, organized by the basic splits between theory and practice, inner and outer, individual and collective.

Individual and Social Transformation in Buddhism

The "path" of transformation that leads to the end of suffering and ignorance, and to *nirvāṇa* (Sanskrit; Pali: *nibbanā*) is commonly understood in Buddhism as a threefold training, designed to replace the repetitive cycles of greed, hatred, and delusion (the sources of suffering or *dukkha*) with generosity, loving kindness, and wisdom. This training emphasizes (1) ethical integrity in action and interaction *(śīla)*; (2) the meditative development of mind and heart (usually grouped under the heading of *samādhi* or "concentration"); and (3) insight and wisdom (Pali: *paññā;* Sanskrit: *prajñā*). As we shall see, socially engaged Buddhist approaches can also be understood as following this threefold training. The general form of Buddhist training can be expressed in a way that is slanted neither to individual transformation nor to social transformation, although in this section I speak primarily of the individual emphasis of early (and later, Theravāda) Buddhism.

Ethical training is based initially on ethical guidelines, encompassing more than two hundred main rules and many other minor rules for the Buddhist monk or nun, which are intended to proscribe actions and ways of life that encourage greed, hatred, or delusion in oneself and in others. They are especially intended to help one become more calm, balanced, and equanimous so as to be able to deepen concentration, mindfulness, and wisdom. The most fundamental ethical precepts—for instance, the five interrelated precepts specified for lay people in the Theravāda Buddhism of South Asia—are very similar in content to some of the Judaic Ten Commandments, involving guidelines to abstain from killing, from stealing, from "false" speech, from improper sexuality, and from intoxicants that cloud the mind. However, the precepts are understood very differently from the way that the biblical commandments are commonly interpreted. They are not pronouncements by an external authority to be taken as absolutes to which one must adhere. Rather, Buddhist precepts are understood as training guidelines, as recommendations that can never be fulfilled absolutely, but that can help one to learn and develop. Although the ethical precepts may serve as an initial foundation in training, they also may help guide one's more active and interactive life as a field of spiritual practice just as fundamental as formal meditative practice and may eventually become the spontaneous expression of a wise and compassionate being and way of life.

The second component of Buddhist training—meditative development—involves many forms, of which several main ones can be mentioned here. Through concentrative meditation (samatha)[2], one is able to focus enough attention to cut through automatic, reactive patterns (such as those rooted in greed, anger, and hatred) and to achieve a stability in consciousness. Such concentration can be developed to great depth in the jhana practices, leading to profound rapture, stillness, and a wide range of extraordinary states of consciousness. Yet even on the basis of a minimal level of concentration and awareness, the meditator can then examine, in "insight" (vipassanā) meditation, the varied contents of experience more directly in an increasingly continuous and present-centered way (King 1980; Nyanaponika 1962; Solé-Leris 1986). In the early Buddhist teaching of the Foundations of Mindfulness, for instance, the meditator is encouraged to direct attention to bodily sensations; to the "feeling-tones" (vedanā) of a given experience as either pleasant, unpleasant, or neutral; to mental-emotional events such as anger, fear, love, and so on; and to experience in the light of traditional Buddhist teachings (for a recent translation, see Naṇmoli and Bodhi 1995, 145–55). The meditator may also cultivate particular qualities or virtues, such as loving-kindness (mettā) or compassion (karuṇā), in yet other forms of meditation.

2. In what follows in this section, all terms are from the Pali language, except in the discussion of the Mahāyāna bodhisattva.

The third component of Buddhist training, the cultivation of wisdom, involves study and practice oriented by the Buddha's teachings and insights about liberation. The account of Dependent Arising, for example, which many have seen as the central Buddhist teaching (Kalupahana 1975; Macy 1991) and which the Buddha reportedly formulated on the evening of his enlightenment, provides an analysis of a set of twelve interrelated factors that together are responsible for suffering and its perpetuation. According to this analysis, there is a close mutual conditioning of spiritual ignorance *(avijjā)*, craving or desire (or aversion), grasping (or pushing away, *upādāna*), and suffering. For instance, spiritual ignorance is understood most basically as the deep (and generally unconscious) belief or assumption that there is a separate, independent self and separate, independent others. Based on this belief, individuals attempt to gain lasting happiness *(sukha)* by manipulating self and others in order to produce pleasant experiences and avoid (or deny) unpleasant experiences for this supposedly separate self.

For Buddhists, such a belief in a separate self is false. As is revealed most fully in the deeper understanding attained by the Buddha in the "mystical" experience of *nibbanā* and accessible through training, there is no separate and independent self; all beings and all phenomena are interrelated.[3] Furthermore, all experiences (including that of wisdom!) are transient, impermanent. There can be no lasting happiness from pleasant experiences or from the absence of unpleasant experiences. In fact, as long as this core belief leads one to look for happiness in this way, there actually is bound to be the opposite of happiness—that is, suffering—because pleasant experiences will always eventually end or change. Indeed, because there cannot be deep or permanent satisfaction from pleasant experiences, there is commonly greed, an unbounded and sometimes psychologically addicted pursuit of pleasant experiences.

Such ignorance is not easily uncovered or transformed. It manifests itself as a confusion or basic delusion about reality, as a lack of awareness about the

---

3. Of course, we have to ask to what extent the Western concepts of mysticism and social transformation correspond to Asian (particularly premodern) Buddhist traditions. Are Buddhist teachings and practices, for example, "mystical"? There appears to be a broad phenomenological similarity between the examples of the experiences of introvertive mysticism given by Stace and the descriptions of the experience of *nibbanā (nirvā ṇa)* in early Buddhist tradition (Stace 1960, 123–27). To be sure, the interpretive issues are rather subtle and require a much longer discussion than is possible here (see Griffiths 1990 and the recent discussions of the relationship of mystical experience ad cultural context in Forman 1990b; Katz 1978, 1983, 1992; Rothberg 1990). There is also a common emphasis on "nondualistic" or "enlightened" experience of the phenomenal world in many Buddhist traditions that seems to fit well within the model of extrovertive mysticism. Although the category of mysticism may not be analogous to any Buddhist terms and carries considerable baggage, it seems at least plausible to speak of Buddhist mysticism.

whole process. It is connected with "automatic" or unconsciously "driven" behavior, and it has not only cognitive but also physical and emotional dimensions. When such ignorance exists, there are strong unconscious dispositions to act on the mistaken beliefs about reality and happiness—that is, to continue in ignorance. In the context of human experience, these dispositions are related to continual craving or desire for what is taken to be pleasant and continual aversion to or hatred for what is taken to be unpleasant. Related to such desire or aversion is an endless set of activities in which there is a grasping after what is desired and a pushing away of whatever is hated or linked with aversion. Such activities might involve an attempt to control a situation or people in a certain way, or to possess desired resources or commodities, or to strike back in anger when one feels uncomfortable after someone else has directed anger or hatred at oneself. But acting in this way perpetuates the entire cycle, reinforcing the ignorance as well as future desire and aversion, and future grasping and pushing away. The result is what the Buddha called *samsara,* a "vicious circle" of ignorance about reality and suffering, and a lack of deep peace and happiness. *Samsara,* unlike the perfume of the same name, has little to do with "a taste of serenity," as the ads would have it.

But to what extent is such a threefold spiritual training linked with *social* transformation in early Buddhism? First of all, it must be said that the teachings and practices of the Buddha were for the most part addressed to the monks *(bhikkhus)* and nuns *(bhikkhunis)* who were the followers of the Buddha rather than to lay persons or to the society as a whole. However, there was arguably not the kind of sharp distinction between spiritual practice and social involvement that has led some commentators, such as the eminent sociologist Max Weber (1958, 213ff.), to claim that early Buddhism was "asocial" and "otherworldly." The early Buddhist *bhikkhus* and *bhikkhunis* were not strictly separated from laypeople, not cloistered like many Christian monks and nuns (and some later Buddhist monastics). Rather, like many of their contemporary Buddhist counterparts in southeast Asia, they constantly intermingled with laypeople, generally on an everyday basis. Individual transformation always thus took place in the context of *sangha* (or community), whether the more narrow monastic community or the wider community made up of monastics and lay supporters. The *sangha* was and is essentially, we might say, a kind of transformative community dedicated to spiritual development. Yet it is *a community of transformation, in which the social structures remain generally constant,* following, on the one hand, the guidelines for monastic life and, on the other, the ancient patterns of Asian village life.

Second, despite the Buddha's focus on the lives of monks and nuns, it is clear that the Buddha was interested in social life outside the monastic community. He expressed concern many times about the conditions for peace, social justice, and the roots of social harmony in economic well-being. At times, he counseled kings on nonviolence, several times intervening to prevent wars (Rahula 1988, 107), although he apparently did not take sides in most of the conflicts of his day (Chakravarti 1987, 172). The Buddha also clearly suggested that lay followers should follow the ethical guidelines as much as possible.

Nonetheless, the clear focus of the Buddha's analysis and teaching was on *individual* transformation in the monastic *social* context, which was conceived of as separate from the *political* world of kings and power—a separation, by the way, which was unlike the Brahmanic connection of the political and religious spheres (Chakravarti 1987, 170ff.). The monk or nun was explicitly prohibited from being involved in political affairs, and talking about the king was considered as objectionable. Indeed, "danger from kings" was deemed more significant for a monk or nun than danger from robbers, fire, water, and beasts of prey (Sarkisyanz 1965, 78)!

Hence, the teachings given by the Buddha to the monastic community were strongly influenced by a separation between the spiritual and political spheres, although the spiritual was not separated from the social sphere as such. The various suggestions made by the Buddha to kings and even the discussions of the righteous ruler *(cakkavatti)* are all extensions of these "nonpolitical" teachings. In fact, the Buddha once stated that he was not interested in the problems of war and conquest, or in the victories and defeats of kings (Chakravarti 1987, 170). Many scholars conclude that the Buddha himself did not take a serious, systematic interest in the political realm and its transformation (Ling 1973, 152; Gombrich 1988, 81), even if later Buddhists have done so. Nor was there an explicit account in the early teachings of a social transformation or evolution that might parallel individual transformation.

The basic teachings, such as those of the Four Noble Truths or Dependent Arising, are clearly presented in a more psychological and individual form. The workings of ignorance, craving and aversion, grasping and pushing away, spiritual practice and liberation are analyzed on the level of the individual. There is no analysis of the extent to which these factors are supported, increased, decreased, manipulated, or exploited on the level of social, political, economic, and ideological systems, even though the Buddha did at times recognize systemic influences, especially systems producing poverty, as I mentioned earlier.[4]

In the centuries following the life of the Buddha, the political and spiri-

4. However, some contemporary engaged Buddhists have given systemic readings of the analysis of Dependent Arising, the Four Noble Truths, and other basic Buddhist teachings. See, for example, Santikaro 1997.

tual spheres were less strictly separated in many Buddhist societies, with a number of different consequences. In some cases, Buddhism became identified with particular rulers and peoples, and later with nation-states. The famous ruler Asoka of the third century B.C.E. implemented a number of beneficent edicts based on his understanding of Buddhist teachings, including a ban on capital punishment and even the killing of animals (Ling 1973, 151–74; Thurman 1988). Other rulers, however, sometimes used Buddhism to justify self-defensive wars (e.g., in Sri Lanka) and aggression, notably in twentieth-century Japan (Heisig and Maraldo 1995; Rothberg 1992; Sharf 1995).

In terms of our interest in mysticism and social transformation, one of the most notable later developments was the dramatically increased importance that the later Mahāyāna movement (which emerged during the first century B.C.E.) gave to the figure of the bodhisattva or "enlightenment being" (P. Williams 1989). The Sanskrit term *bodhisattva* (Pali: *bodhisatta*), used in early Buddhism to refer to the Buddha before his full enlightenment—i.e., as a "Buddha-to-be"—came to characterize the most spiritually developed being (other than the Buddha) according to the Mahāyāna teachings. The bodhisattva was juxtaposed to the early Buddhist figure of the arhat, who was criticized as embodying an overly individualistic (and subtly selfish) ethos. The arhat practices ideally in solitude, as part of a wider community, yet seeks his or her own liberation. The bodhisattva, on the other hand, vows to save all other beings before his or her own final enlightenment. The vow "Sentient beings are innumerable; I vow to save them all" is repeated every day, for instance, in Zen monasteries. The bodhisattva perfects "skillful means" *(upāya)* that can help awaken the varieties of beings. In some Mahāyāna texts and traditions, the bodhisattva is a layperson; for example, in the *Vimalakīrtinirdesa Sutra* (Thurman 1976), the lay bodhisattva Vimalakīrti is portrayed as instructing monks, skillfully expounding subtle philosophies, and engaging in numerous activities in the world designed to help beings awaken spiritually.

Much Mahāyāna spiritual practice, especially in China and Japan, was also somewhat more social than practice in the early Indian Buddhist context (although how much such a change is due to cultural rather than doctrinal factors is unclear). Monks and nuns commonly meditated together (rather than generally alone, as in India) and often did agricultural work together (which was not the case in southern Buddhism). However, despite the Mahāyāna injunction to liberate all beings, Mahāyāna practices commonly did not extend to projects of social transformation. Mahāyāna meditators might have radiated compassion for all beings and practiced individually to remove barriers between self and other, but they still saw the source of greed, hatred, and delusion—i.e., the source of suffering—in the individual rather than (also) in social structures.

Contemporary Engaged Buddhism and Social Transformation

Much of the project of contemporary engaged Buddhists can be understood as a further questioning of any strict split between Buddhist practice and social and political involvement, and as an attempt to develop a clearer and more explicit connection between individual spiritual (or mystical) development and social transformation (Foster 1988; Jones 1988). In some cases, it is also an attempt to develop the potential of the bodhisattva ideal in ways not open, for various reasons, in the earlier Mahāyāna contexts and to question an exclusive focus on understanding the individual sources of suffering and on individual transformation.

The idea of an *engaged* Buddhism (a phrase apparently coined by the Vietnamese Zen teacher, poet, and activist Thich Nhat Hanh) has at least two main interrelated senses.[5] The first has to do generally with bringing Buddhism into contemporary *everyday life* in all its aspects, including the contexts of families, interpersonal relationships, communities, work and economics, social and political relationships, and ecosystems. The second sense (and the focus in this section), often identified by speaking of *socially engaged* Buddhism, covers a range of approaches unified by the notion that Buddhist teachings and practices might be particularly applied to larger-scale social, political, economic, and ecological institutions and systems, and to their associated philosophies (see Rothberg 1998 for a more extended discussion of the roots of the term).

A number of varieties of engaged Buddhism have developed both in Asia and in the West: some emphasizing grassroots activism leading to political activity; some more oriented to social service; some (in Asia) attempting to deal with problems of development through establishing alternative models combining the best in traditional culture with democratic strategies and modern technologies; some (especially in the West) more concerned with issues of war and peace, ecology, gender, power, authority, and everyday life; some explicitly nonhierarchical, democratic, and decentralized; some (a minority) more hierarchical and nondemocratic (Jones 1989, 227–88; Kotler 1996; Queen and King 1996).

---

5. Interestingly, Vietnamese Buddhism in many ways seems to integrate the teachings of early Buddhism (preserved in the Theravāda tradition of south and southeast Asia) and Mahāyāna teachings more fully than any other Buddhist culture.

A fundamental claim of these engaged Buddhists is that spiritual and social transformation are not separate. Resolving social crises requires going to the roots of the difficulties in the (socially conditioned) human predicament—that is, going to the level of the fear, greed, hatred, and delusion that lead to conflict, violence, and suffering. For some engaged Buddhists, resolving individual suffering requires likewise going to its roots in the social structures that condition fear, greed, hatred, and delusion; happiness, as Nhat Hanh often suggests, is not really purely individual.[6] To bring spiritual intention to the social and political aspects of one's life is often to acknowledge that spiritual transformation cannot be partial or fragmented (i.e., deal with only *some* general aspects of one's experience).

Engaged Buddhists have begun to approach the traditional categories of the three-fold Buddhist training in ethics, meditative practice, and wisdom in ways that cultivate this ambitious project to integrate personal and social transformation as, in the context of this essay, a mystical path. For instance, Nhat Hanh (1987a, 85–102; 1987b), Sulak Sivaraksa (1988, 49–82; 1992a; 1992b, 73–79), A. T. Ariyaratne (Macy 1985), Robert Aitken (1984), and Ken Jones (1989) have all attempted to generate a social ethics by extending the meaning of Buddhist training precepts beyond the usual understanding of their scope as limited to personal and face-to-face relationships. For instance, the precept to refrain from killing may be followed by acting on the assumption of responsibility for the violent actions of one's government and on the Mahāyāna bodhisattva's vow to help liberate all beings. Nhat Hanh's version of this precept reads, "Do not kill. Do not let others kill. Find whatever means possible to protect life and prevent war" (1987a, 98). Sulak Sivaraksa has interpreted this precept as a counsel not to live wastefully while others are dying of starvation and to inquire into the systemic roots of violence and killing in political and economic structures (1992a). Similarly, it is possible to extend the meaning of precepts having to do with stealing, lying, sexuality, and intoxicants to include our participation in systems in which exploitation, misinformation, propaganda, and the domination of women are commonly perceived as normal. Sivaraksa concludes: "The way out of our predicament is for all of us to recognize that the problems on earth are our own personal problems and our personal responsibility" (1992a, 134). The important implication, which I examine below, seems to be that as participants in complex social systems, we can speak in a meaningful way of our intentions and responsibility for states of affairs, actions, and consequences that we do not influence in an immediate face-to-face manner.

6. Recently, Nhat Hanh has written that the next Buddha may "not be just one person, but . . . a community, a community of love" (1998, 141).

There has also been some development of forms of engaged meditative training to complement this expanded sense of ethics. One key seems to be to expand the notion of mindfulness while nonetheless remaining rooted in the traditional meditative practice. For instance, Nhat Hanh and others have encouraged the cultivation of mindfulness in a number of social situations usually beyond the scope of the traditional monk or nun, including family and social service situations. Nhat Hanh has also suggested a number of reflections that bring attention to situations in the world beyond our immediate experience, to the consequences of our actions, and to the web of relationships in which we live and act. This extension of the meaning of mindfulness was part of a considered response to the war in Vietnam in the 1950s and 1960s (Khong 1993). As Nhat Hanh notes:

> When I was in Vietnam, so many of our villages were being bombed. Along with my monastic brothers and sisters, I had to decide what to do. Should we continue to practice in our monasteries, or should we leave the meditation halls in order to help the people who were suffering under the bombs? After careful reflection, we decided to do both—to go out and help people and to do so in mindfulness. We called it engaged Buddhism. Mindfulness must be engaged. Once there is seeing, there must be acting. . . . We must be aware of the real problems of the world. Then, with mindfulness, we will know what to do and what not to do to be of help. (1991, 91)

Another application of the traditional tools of mindfulness to social contexts has been pioneered by Joanna Macy, who has developed a Buddhist-based training that involves bringing attention to participants' unexplored "pain for the world"—their anger, despair, grief, sadness, fear, etc. (1983, 1991). Her work (sometimes called workshops in "despair and empowerment") thus helps to give a broader understanding of investigating the first Noble Truth of Buddhism—i.e., the reality of suffering or unsatisfactoriness. Through innovative (and traditional) techniques, interactive exercises, and social rituals, participants are able to access the often deeply buried yet immensely powerful and painful emotions connected with violence and with collective suffering, whether the unhealed suffering from past generations of oppression according to religion, race, ethnicity, gender, or sexual orientation; a recent murder or situation of abuse in one's community; the state of ecological crisis in general; or a particular case of clear-cutting. As in the teaching of the Four Noble Truths, close familiarity with suffering is a starting point for practice, framed within a new way of understanding and being, and linked with pragmatic steps to work with and transform the pain, moving toward effective action in the world.

Others have attempted to bring attention and mindfulness to experiences of more complex social, political, and economic relationships. In the context of rural self-development projects in Sri Lanka, A. T. Ariyaratne and his coworkers in the Sarvodaya movement have connected traditional Buddhist teachings with awareness of the dynamics of relevant social and economic systems. In such settings, they have applied the Four Noble Truths (including the Eightfold Path), the traditional ethical precepts, and the practices of the four "divine abodes" (or *brahmavihāra,* the four "immeasurables" in Mahāyāna tradition): loving kindness *(mettā)),* compassion *(karuṇā),* rejoicing in others' good fortune *(muditā),* and equanimity *(upekkhā).* To know *dukkha* (unsatisfactoriness or suffering) and the cause of *dukkha* may be in part to know the dynamics of "development" models encouraged by Western powers. Traditional notions of mindfulness may be expanded to include awareness of community needs and issues of justice, as is suggested by this report of a Sarvodaya trainer: "Right mindfulness—that means stay open and alert to the needs of the village. . . . Look to see what is needed—latrines, water, road. . . . Try to enter the minds of the people, to listen behind their words. . . . Is the food enough? are the people getting wet? are the tools in order? is anyone being exploited?" (Macy 1985, 37). In this context, mindfulness may be seen not just as an ancient tool for self-knowledge and peace, but as a fundamentally radical act in that directly paying attention to given social phenomena often requires cutting through numerous layers of denial, fear, projection, and conditioning.

Closely related to the expansion of traditional teachings of ethics and mindfulness has been an attempt to develop an expanded sense of what wisdom and deep understanding entail—a sense that would integrate the traditionally highly psychological Buddhist analyses with cultural, social, political, economic, and ecological analyses and strategies. Although such an integration is still in its early stages among socially engaged Buddhists, I can point briefly to what I take to be some of the basic principles at the core of this expanded sense of wisdom.

A first principle of such an engaged Buddhism is that it emanates (as much as possible) from and refers back to the core enlightenment experience and understanding of the Buddha—in other words, to what we might call the Buddha's mystical experiences. In this sense, the deepest experiences of wisdom, loving-kindness, compassion, nonduality, and interdependence provide the basic reference points for social action and for understanding. There is an explicit questioning of more dualistic, self-centered ways of action and understanding that are oriented to the strategic manipulation of things and other beings.

A second, more specific principle is that what we call "inner" (personal or individual) and what we call "outer" (collective or social) are deeply connected. When we look deeply, especially on the basis of Buddhist training, we find that we cannot separate ourselves from others, nor can we separate our "inner" states from what is supposedly "outer." There is no private, independent "self"; our thoughts, our emotions, and even our suffering are not purely personal and separate, but rather expressions of a greater whole. As the English meditation teacher and activist Christopher Titmuss suggests, "People are beginning to see that personal pain and global pain are not two separate factors, but very much interrelated. Some people experience inside of themselves what they conceive of as being the pain of the world, but in a way it's the pain of themselves. There are others who experience inside of themselves what they conceive of as being purely personal pain. In a way, it's the pain of the world" (1988, 184). Making a similar point, Thich Nhat Hanh once responded to a question about whether there was some special collective karma of the people of Vietnam. He suggested that the suffering connected with the war in Vietnam was felt by the entire world.

That there is a reciprocal relationship between inner experience and social structures suggests again the possibility of integrating psychology (Buddhist and Western) and social analysis, as well as Buddhist practices and some of the Western strategies and techniques for social transformation. In Buddhist terms, it seems possible to identify the extent to which existing social ideas, institutions, and systems are both rooted in and support greed, hatred, and ignorance, as well as to develop social structures that are rooted in and support more virtuous activities.

A third principle, based on understandings of interdependence and the interconnection of inner and outer, concerns what we might call *coresponsibility* with others for the state of things—recognizing in particular that problems cannot simply be attributed to others, to scapegoats, or to those who are somehow "bad" or "evil." Greed, hatred, delusion, and the roots of violence are found in all beings. Particularly if we access, especially with the help of meditation, our own "shadow" and negativity—our anger, fear, greed, confusion, sadness, readiness to act violently, and so on—there is less of a tendency to project this negativity outward and to maintain ourselves as fundamentally different and separate from others whom we call "evil." Indeed, we may come to see that a basic root of war and violence is a kind of self-ignorance in which we fearfully hate the other upon whom we have projected our own negative qualities, qualities often unknown to ourselves. In an essay beginning with the line "The root of war is fear," Thomas Merton suggests, "It is not only our hatred of others that is dangerous but also and above all our hatred of ourselves:

particularly that hatred of ourselves which is too deep and too powerful to be consciously faced. For it is this which makes us see our own evil in others and unable to see it in ourselves" (McDonnell 1974, 276).

A fourth principle, familiar to students of nonviolence, is that the means are just as significant as the ends and in fact *are* the ends. This principle is closely connected to the traditional Buddhist emphasis on intention as more central than consequences. The key, in Nhat Hanh's language, is to *be peace* rather than to work for some imagined future peace through means that are not in themselves peaceful—i.e., that involve greed, hatred, and delusion. The tool of moment-to-moment mindfulness as a basic means of transformation is here especially important in helping to avoid a separation between the experiences of the participants in social action and the desired changes, between the process of change and the intended results. The experiences and the intentions of those working for change are not to be seen as secondary or unimportant. In particular, Nhat Hanh questions the ultimate depth and efficacy of movements for change motivated by anger and hatred, even if they are nonviolent in terms of tactics. He believes that engaged Buddhist perspectives might bring a fresh approach to the Western peace movements through an emphasis on process and through the cultivation of joy and happiness among those often attending to horrors and injustices.

A fifth principle is that the aim of social action and social transformation is most basically reconciliation and harmony, rather than the victory by one side of a polarized situation. The most basic work is therefore not to fight and defeat the enemy, so to speak, but, as in more individual meditation, to heal and transform violence, anger, hatred, and ignorance—especially through mindfulness, and openness—and, as much as possible, to renounce actions rooted in anger and hatred. In this sense, the work of transformation is conceived as the same on all levels—intrapsychic, interpersonal, communal, social, political, and ecological—with tools appropriate for each level.

Whatever the promise and attractiveness of this approach, socially engaged Buddhism—or what we might call the contemporary Buddhist-based integration of mysticism and social transformation—is still at an early stage of development. Elsewhere (Rothberg 1998), I have identified three main challenges for its continued evolution. First, there is a need to formulate analyses of contemporary cultural philosophies and social structures in Buddhist terms, making use of the best of contemporary non-Buddhist resources. How can sexism, racism, consumerism, ecological crisis, or the breakdown of community, on the one hand, and visions of a "dhammic society" or a "Buddhist economics" (E. F. Schumacher's term), on the other, be understood and addressed? (For initial responses to these questions, see, for example, Jones 1989, and Watts, Senauke, and Santikaro 1997.) Here, there are some very important parallels, for example, with the Western tradition of critical social theory (the Frankfurt school), whose theorists (Horkheimer, Adorno, Marcuse, Habermas) have attempted to integrate (Freudian) depth psychology with cultural, social, and economic analyses inspired especially by Weber and Marx.

Second, there needs to be a much more sophisticated approach to transformative strategy. How might engaged Buddhists ally with other like-minded persons and groups in the contemporary Western setting? What are the contemporary skillful means necessary in the social field? What are the optimal ways to give energy to social transformation?

Third, and perhaps most crucially, there is a need to articulate more fully the nature of an engaged Buddhist path—in other words, the nature of a Buddhist mystical path of individual and collective transformation. What does it mean on an everyday basis to use as a contemporary *koan,* or as a guide, questions such as, "How can we end racism?" or "How can I respond to the (increasing) gap between rich and poor?" or "What shall I do about ecological devastation?" What kinds of individual and group practices need to be developed to help explore such a territory? How might such practices rest in newly articulated Buddhist understandings, for example, of racism or of economic ideologies and structures or of the roots of ecological problems? How might such freshly developed practices and teachings be grounded in traditional Buddhist models of transformation? Again, there is much in non-Buddhist activism and social theory that might be integrated with such a conception of an engaged Buddhist path.

◆   ◆   ◆

Engaged Buddhists have a special role to play, I believe, in the contemporary integration of mysticism and social transformation, whatever the terms we use to describe such a connection of individual and collective learning and response to suffering. The Buddhist understandings and practices concerning *individual* transformation are, I believe, among the most highly articulated expressions of mysticism in human history. Furthermore, they are expressed in language and with an underlying nondogmatic philosophy that can arguably be well integrated within a pragmatic, scientific, and (generally) democratic culture perhaps as well as or better than any other ancient mystical approach. Witness, for example, the very active integration of Buddhism and psychotherapy (Epstein 1995; Rubin 1996); a parallel integration with the Western social justice traditions is at the heart of Western (and some Asian) forms of socially engaged Buddhism.

As I suggested at the outset, to connect individual and collective transformation goes very much against the grain of several thousand years of Western culture (and against much of the grain of Asian culture) and is a difficult quest. Nonetheless, such a quest is also, I would maintain, a large part of the healing of contemporary culture East and West—as I suggested in the second section, a large part of the healing of modernity and the birthing of a post-modernity that truly reflects learning and growth. New healings, new births, are always difficult in some ways, yet they may also call for great creativity and forms of life yet unimaginable. Buddhists—established on the firm foundations of "no-self," compassionate action, and the bodhisattva's vow to save all beings—may play a vital role in helping us to imagine and to actualize the unimaginable.

10

The Transcendence of Justice and the Justice of Transcendence

MYSTICISM, DEEP ECOLOGY, AND POLITICAL LIFE

ROGER S. GOTTLIEB

Humanity's responses to the perils and pains of existence give rise to many attempts to see the sources of our suffering, to escape or transcend our limits, and to form or recognize communities of solidarity—both with other people and with beings who are not people. The cry of the heart has gone out to gods and goddesses, to totem animals and sacred mountains, and to those with whom we would join on the barricades. In the desperate time of the present, as cynics celebrate the end of alternatives to global capitalism, global industrialism, and global techno-addiction, those of us who are not entranced by the prospect of a fully administered society search for something else. Sensing the bleak and poisonous prospects around us, we shrink from pollution that is physical, psychic, and moral. Surely we believe (as people have always believed) that there is some other choice we can make. Surely we can find some wisdom with which to confront the soulless intelligence of modernity and the amoral cyberchic of postmodernity. Surely we can touch with our living hearts the Heart of the World and listen to the secret revelations of its unending beat. Surely, at least as individuals, we do not have to be bound by the endless commodification of the living world. Surely, if we cannot defeat or change, then we can *transcend* that which surrounds us.

One name for that transcendence is mysticism. It has for thousands of years signified the attempt to move beyond the confines of society and history—to break the bounds of normal human interaction, normal conscious-

This essay was first published in the *Journal of the American Academy of Religion* 67, no. 1 (Mar. 1999) 149–66. It is reprinted here by permission.

ness, and normal physical reality. It has been, or has been claimed to be, the foundation for a wisdom beyond—or hidden beneath—"this world." Yet, as we shall see in relation to the present, the world has a way of persisting in the face of the most transcendent of wisdoms. The struggle between transcendence and the social world, and the dangers that attend each are the subjects of this essay.

Mysticism

The term *mysticism* is used to describe a variety of at times overwhelming, often life-defining experiences, encounters that give rise to fundamental shifts in how we sense the nature of both the universe and our own personal identity. For many, those experiences are the heart of the world's religions. Beyond details of dogma, institutional organization, or even ethical teachings, the direct encounter with the divine seems to make possible a temporary release from the boundaries of the social ego and the socially constructed understanding of the body. This encounter provides an alternate possibility to constricted forms of self-definition and challenges merely local claims about who we are, what we owe each other, and what we can be. The truth contained in mystical experiences seems to dwarf parochial understandings. People see these experiences as "perennial" (as in "the perennial wisdom"), to be hidden from people not mature enough to grapple with the insights that mystical experience can confer, and even containing a hint of danger if misunderstood or misappropriated (as in the yogic warnings about the perils of developing psychic powers without the appropriate ethical development).

Mystical experiences are celebrated in every religious tradition. Consider, for example, the arhat, the type of the sage in the original form of Buddhism, which has come to be known as Theravāda. In his religious practices, the arhat seeks an end to the psychic confinement caused by mistaken identification with a self bound to desires and attachments. Intellectually, the arhat has come to believe that this identification is the source of great pain (as the Buddha taught in the first of the Four Noble Truths). Yet intellectual acceptance of the first Noble Truth does not necessarily produce a sense of self (or "nonself") that is actually free of attachment. The question arises: Is it in fact possible to be alive as a human being and *not* identify with a conventionally understood self, a collection of desires, aversions, and so on? This question is answered—and what we might call mystical wisdom arises—when the student directly experiences a state of mind in which identification with self dissipates. As one early practitioner is reputed to have said when questioned by a fellow seeker,

"During my meditation I reached a point where I had no thought that 'I am this; this is mine; this is my self.' "[1]

Consider the prophet Elijah. Fleeing for his life from Jezebel's wrath after he put to death the prophets of Baal, he encounters God not in a mighty wind, an earthquake, or a fire, but in a "still, small voice" (1 Kings 19:11–12). The voice is "inside him." It is a source of ultimate knowledge or, in the case of what is typically stressed in Jewish scriptures, of ultimate moral responsibility—a responsibility that takes precedence over all merely social or merely conventional customs or forms of authority. The experience of God's voice provides an ultimate ethical arbiter that releases us from any conflicting obligations to social powers.

Consider the poet William Blake's seeing Christ suspended in air, dancing outside his window; or the states of ecstatic no-self produced by Sufi dancing or tribal chanting; or the transformations of consciousness that come on a Native American Vision Quest, prepared for by days of fasting and isolation. Or consider the feminist image of a divine interconnection and sharing and mingling of mind, emotion, and body—an interconnection in which God does not speak from the heavens or even within our hearts, but emerges in the sacred spaces that both separate and connect us.[2]

In all these instances (and the legion more that could be discussed), we find the wisdom of mysticism. This wisdom provides an end or at least a temporary alternative to the ego's twisted identification with a psychic condition of permanent dissatisfaction, insecurity, and violence. From attachment to a particular social role, we move to an identification with a cosmic harmony for which possessions, status, or social group become merely relative, merely historical, essentially contingent. From attachment to our particular, personal, self-owned pains and pleasures, we move to a celebration of the infinite fields of energy that move through us. As in the case of Elijah, we develop a deeply altered and often highly critical sense of the meaning and validity of social life: of its teaching about what is important, of its norms of human interaction, and of its models of success or adequacy.

Perhaps most importantly, although the intensity of the experience fades and may be difficult even to remember at times (it is said that Pascal, having had an experience of God, sewed an image of the sun or a phrase beginning "fire, fire" into his clothes to remind himself), the wisdom of mysticism opens the receiver up to a clarity of understanding about what is of lasting impor-

1. For this account of Buddhism and others in this paper, see, for example, Conze 1951 and Stryk 1969.

2. For a feminist account, see Heyward 1992.

tance in the realms of everyday, nontranscendent life. Variously known as love, grace, peace, or care, the wisdom of mysticism releases us from the bondage to patterns of emotion that ultimately serve neither ourselves nor others. The demands that we earn a great deal of money, that we be beautiful, that we make war on our "enemies," that we believe the government, that we manage to be successful at being "men" or "women"—these snarling dogs of desire ("fires" the Buddha called them) become the tame lapcats of tamed desire. We escape—initially only for a moment, but then for much longer if we are able to maintain the power of the memory of that moment—the demands, evaluations, and definitions of our social existence. Maintaining this memory requires stern but rewarding discipline, described in detail in the mystical traditions. If we follow these paths of prayer, meditation, fasting, study, retreat, knowledge, and service, the traditions promise, we will be ever more released from the bondage of false attachments.

It is in just this promise that the danger lies: the place where mysticism can betray itself and deteriorate into self-deception, folly, and escapism, for mysticism can be and has been used simply to evade that which is frightening, confusing, or difficult *in* the social realm. In such cases, it is motivated by an inability to face what is threatening in the world as it is, and what the mystic really seeks is escape. In such cases, the mystic claims to have experienced— and at times to offer to others—the Truth of the Whole, but is really simply avoiding what is distasteful.

For instance, we become entranced by, even addicted to, the *experience* of the mystical state. It is so lofty, so sweet, such a relief from how awful we feel most of the time. And when we are under it or in it or up to it, we do not have to take seriously our suffering, anyone else's suffering, or the ways in which not only what Buddhists would call the folly of individual attachment but also social evil that causes that suffering.

This danger of mysticism is that it becomes in Kierkegaard's sense merely "aesthetic": merely a series of experiences that do not contribute to the formation of an ethical and spiritual character; merely something that, in the end, is another titillation, another object of desire, another way to pacify a self that has not been transformed, but only thrilled or sedated.

Put another way, the danger of mysticism is that it can become an escape from concerns about other people. Entranced by the cosmic oneness of it all, we end up forgetting or ignoring the other people in the room, on our block, or on our globe. Feeling cared for by an infinite source of love, we forget (inadvertently? to some extent intentionally?) that it is up to us to manifest as well as receive that love and that if we do not, our own access to the source will become more and more strained, desperate, and attenuated.

Many years ago a teacher of yoga and meditation instructed me: "Do not be distracted by sounds in your practice, but use them. For instance, if you are meditating and you hear a loud siren outside your window, instead of feeling interrupted, you can simply take in that energy, move it up your spine to your crown chakra, and use it to further your practice."

A useful tip I thought at first. But then I thought further and asked him: "Sir, this sounds like a fine idea if, for instance, the siren is simply from an ambulance on its way to a nearby hospital. But what if it is the siren of the police vans that in Amsterdam took Jews to be transported to the death camps? When is the sound a source of energy to be incorporated into the meditation, and when is it an indication that we need to end the meditation, look outside ourselves, and act in resistance to help innocent people who are being murdered? And what is the source of an ability to discern between the two?"

What I am saying here is not meant to discredit mysticism. Although my questions include elements that resemble Marx's or Nietzsche's critiques of religion, I do not accept their fundamental antagonism to spiritual life. Unlike them, I believe that mystical experience contains the possibility of *Great Truth. And* I am suggesting that it also contains the chance of *Real Error.* In fact, it is just because mystical experience contains the *Powers* of *Truth*—relief from suffering, transcendence of social limitations, insights into Connectedness, Grace, Gaia, or God—that we can use those experiences as distractions, painkillers, or excuses to *Look* the *Other Way.*

The danger that mysticism may become (merely) aesthetic or serve as a spiritual by-pass of the moral and the political is not unknown in religious culture. In traditional Judaism, one does not approach the mysticism of the Cabala until one is established in family and community relationships, typically not until the age of forty. The entire history of Buddhism is marked by a split over precisely the nature of mystical enlightenment and the role of the enlightened person in the community. Whereas Theravāda Buddhism saw the sage as ultimately no more than a person who provides an example to others that enlightenment is possible, Mahāyāna Buddhism arose partly out of the critique of what it took to be the selfish and ultimately self-defeating character of that ideal. In its place, the Mahāyāna offered the image of the bodhisattva, who refuses ultimate enlightenment in order to help all other sentient beings to achieve it. Such a person is like a strong young man who, when his household is lost in a dangerous forest, stays with the group to help them all to safety rather than making his own way home.

Yet the awareness of these traditions is itself suspect in part because of the duality of all mystical encounters: at once a communion with energies that transcend society *and also* with experiences processed, understood, and described in words by socially situated human beings. The pervasive sexism of even the most mystically founded traditions should remind us that although

God or Goddess may touch us directly, our response to that touch will necessarily bear some imprint of our contingent selves. For example, it was not in fact simply a "person" who, when suitably mature, was allowed by the rabbis to study the Cabala. It was always and only men. The claim that we speak with truth about, as opposed to simply that we have experienced, a *Truth Beyond Question* has too often been a strategy for *Power over the Uninitiated*.

In our time, the dangers of mysticism are especially real because much of mysticism in the advanced industrial societies is disconnected from tradition, community, and personal responsibility. It was, after all, in great measure the widespread use of psychedelic drugs that brought an interest in ecstatic states back into a society defined by professionalism, technology, and television. The power of these drugs—for many people an instant revelation—was precisely their impotence. Because nothing had prepared us for what they offered—and we had not seriously prepared ourselves—the next day's psychic life was often no more holy than the day before. At best, the drug experience was a signal that there was more to life than was dreamed of at Harvard Business School or the National Science Foundation. At best, it served only as a beginning to a long and difficult search.

Further, since the cavalier cultural raids on ancient and tribal traditions of the 1980s, one can learn the secrets of a South American shaman for the cost of a weekend's time and a few hundred dollars. (This experience will be wonderful, and next month we can learn witchcraft or perhaps the mysteries of the Druids.) The consequence is that far from becoming an alternative to the limitations of social life, mystical experience becomes one more commodity—with no more ultimate spiritual meaning than anything else that can be bought or sold.

In short, although the actual truths disclosed by mystical experience may in fact be just those truths all of us need to know, our access to them has always been (and perhaps are now even more so, given the depth and extent of the presence of society) conditioned by the social setting in which they unfold.

In fact, it is precisely that social setting that has led to a return—on something approaching a mass scale—of a mysticism that takes the earth and all its life as an ultimate truth.

Deep Ecology

The crucial fact of our time is that we may be destroying the very support systems that make human life possible. With less uncertainty, we can say that we have *already* extinguished countless species, poured millions of tons of toxic wastes into the air, earth, and water, and altered the earth's atmosphere and climate.

A variety of environmental movements and philosophies have arisen in response to this crisis. From the heart of the spiritual impulse and the memories of countless generations in which forest and grassland, bird and wolf and salmon were our home and family and intimate enemy, comes deep ecology.

The deep ecology of which I speak here is not the version presented in the technical language of philosophical ethics, where debates about varieties of intrinsic, as opposed to instrumental, value take place. Rather, I speak of a passionate, spiritually oriented, mystical communion with the earth and its many beings—a recognition of kinship with those beings, which no more requires philosophical justification than does the connection we feel with our parents, our pets, or our lovers. As such, deep ecology is a spiritual philosophy, and the deepest experiences that animate its adherents are profoundly mystical.[3] What is "deep" about this perspective is the experience—and the conviction—that our surroundings are essential to what we are, not just because they are useful, but because we are indeed tied to them by invisible threads of longing, teaching, learning, connection, struggle for existence, and memory. Sky and earth, bird and fish, each leaf on each tree—all these mirror who and what we are; indeed, without them, we could not be ourselves.

This deep ecology is not, nor could it possibly be, a recent creation. As humans have evolved physically, cognitively, culturally, and spiritually in a setting bounded by beings who are not people, so a recognition of our delight in them and affinity with them has been present in all human cultures throughout our history.

There is a midrash (a Jewish spiritual story that aims to enlighten rather than legislate) that speaks of trees: "When a tree that bears fruit is cut down, its moan goes round the world. Yet no sound is heard." Or even more poignantly, in the words of the eighteenth-century Hasidic Rebbe Nachman: "If a person kills a tree before its time, it is like having murdered a soul." The medieval Catholic Hildegard of Bingen saw God in the physical world: "I, the fiery life of divine essence, am aflame beyond the beauty of the meadows, I gleam in the waters, and I burn in the sun, moon, and stars. . . . I awaken everything to life." The Qu'ran was confident that "the creation of the heavens and the earth is greater than the creation of humankind; yet most people understand not." And the World Council of Indigenous Peoples stated in 1977 that in their past, "The earth was our nurturing mother, the night sky formed our common roof, the Sun and the Moon were our parents."[4]

This recognition is also found in nondenominational, often explicitly

---

3. There are many sources here: e.g., Macy 1994; Devall and Sessions 1985.

4. For these quotations as well as for many sources on contemporary and traditional writings on religion and nature, see Gottlieb 1996.

nonreligious, nature writing that celebrates a luminous moment of seeing in which the natural world speaks to us. In her celebrated essay "Living Like Weasels," Annie Dillard describes a moment when she came face-to-face with a weasel: "our eyes locked, and someone threw away the key. Our look was as if two lovers, or deadly enemies, met unexpectedly on an overgrown path when each had been thinking of something else" (1982, 14). Similarly, Aldo Leopold, one of the inspirations of the deep ecological turn in contemporary environmental ethics, speaks of seeing a "fierce green fire" in the eyes of a dying wolf he had himself shot and of never again thinking of wolves or mountains or wilderness in the same way (1949, 130).

Considered as a form of spirituality—as a way of moving beyond the conventional social understanding of the self or of the social construction of the body—deep ecology articulates a powerful and pervasive sensibility. It unifies and expands our childhood love for an animal, the times as adolescents when only the woods or fields seemed to understand us, the moments of grace we feel watching a sunrise or light glinting over ice-covered branches, or hearing birds sing on a surprisingly warm day in March. Knitting together these moments, a deep ecological perspective simply says: "You are more than your profession and race and religion and even gender. In your cells and sinews and even your atoms there is a tie to all that surrounds you. Open yourself up to this source of grace and peace and love. More importantly, open yourself up to the love you feel for it."

Deep ecology also, as Joanna Macy (1994) observes, signals something of our capacity to love and of the reality of our connections to other beings across space and time. Our sadness for the burning rainforests and casually eliminated species is a sign that despite everything, we can still love—and mourn. As deep ecology sings of the joy we feel in our delight of nature, so it must also have us join in the requiem for what we have ourselves helped to kill. Our pain is not simply that things will be inconvenienced—that recreation will be interfered with because the forest has been cut down, that a potential cancer cure has been lost as the rainforest burns, that forty thousand people in Newfoundland's fishing communities have lost their jobs because mechanized trawlers strip-mined the cod fishery. The earth is not just being polluted, deep ecology suggests; it is being *desecrated*. Something more than useful, something more than physically pleasing, something *holy* is being torn to bits for what are typically the most trivial, thoughtless, or downright cruel of reasons. Thus, deep ecology highlights the limitations of a purely instrumental attitude toward nature, an attitude that reduces nonhuman nature to quantities of stuff to be measured, mastered, and commodified. As a philosophy based in powerful emotional experiences, deep ecology expresses simply and directly what many people feel: a love and concern for the natural world. Just as more familiar mystical experiences alter our attitudes toward death, our fear of the unknown, or our petty insecurities, the realization of our kinship with the earth confirms the need to question any unquestioned trashing of our dear relations. The insights of deep ecology can teach us to see the familiar in a new way, challenging our taken-for-granted beliefs, practices, and institutions.

Deep ecology, like all forms of mysticism, comprises knowledge as well as emotionally meaningful experiences. It reminds us of truths that industrial civilization and many forms of patriarchy have obscured: for example, that we are physical beings, made of the same stuff as earth and stream and air; or that we need the wilderness because, as Edward Abbey observed, we ourselves are wild animals (1977). As Paul Shepard has argued, we develop a good deal of our language, our sense of ourselves, our understanding of morality, and our very sensory apparatus from direct or symbolic lessons from the natural world (1983). And as David Abram suggests, the boundaries between the human and the nonhuman are the sources of knowledge about balance and integrity for the human community (1996); for a time, out-of-mind wisdom was sought beyond those boundaries and seen as vested in the shamans, priestesses, and prophets who journeyed there.

Finally, an identification with nature can be the source of deep pleasure and deeper calm. Just as people who hear the voice of God may feel a little differently about a flat tire or being passed over for a promotion, so a felt connection with a tree or a bird can soothe the anxieties and relieve the sense of overwhelming pressure to achieve or possess in the social realm. Such a connection might even, if we let it, help us learn not to be quite so (desperately, compulsively) busy. Experiencing ourselves as natural as well as social, part of a cosmos as well as a community, we can find a remedy for the kinds of neurosis that typically are not part of the lives of ants, birches, or elks.

Even my anxiety over the fate of the environment can be soothed by the experience of connection with it. I can, for instance, see the rainforest not only as an object I am trying to save, but, in John Seed's words, "See myself as *part* of the rainforest trying to save itself" (Seed, Macy, and Fleming 1991, 8). And I can then realize that even desperation to save nature need have no place in my life. Like the leaves on the trees that I love, I can only do my bit and then drift gently down to the forest floor and make way for more life.

Once again, here is where the dangers arise, for deep ecology (just as other forms of mysticism) can slide too easily into the attempt to escape society or to bring into the social realm one of the more pernicious forms of religious ideology and practice. In fact, at least four central dangers face deep ecology in this regard.

First, mystical experience can give rise to fundamentalism. Given the long history and the present resurgence of religiously motivated violence and narrow-mindedness, this prospect is bleak indeed. Although deep ecology is a powerful critic of modernist scientific and economic reductionism, it is, as Michael Zimmerman has argued, always quite difficult to transcend the limitations of the Enlightenment while simultaneously keeping its accomplishments (1995). We see the consequences of the rejection of those accomplishments in religious totalitarianism of all stripes. Political notions of individual rights and a spiritual understanding that mystical knowledge is essentially metaphorical are both foreign to any form of fundamentalism. The mullahs of whatever faith are sure they know what God wants, and they have the whips and chains to put that knowledge into practice.

Of course, deep ecology remains too institutionally marginal for it to face an exactly comparable danger. However, its form of fundamentalism, I believe, would take the shape of attempting to escape society, to see "nature" as a realm in which people are absent and in the celebration of which people can be ignored. Yet if it is truly nature we love, we must not forget people, for they, too, are born of the earth.[5] If we would commune with plants, we must not (as Aldo Leopold himself suggested) forget the weeds in a city vacant lot. We must also show some concern for those kids playing in the city lot—at risk from broken glass and drug dealers, and generally lacking the physical or cultural access to the wilderness we seek to preserve.

Second, in another area, we can recognize that the special virtue of non-fundamentalist contemporary spirituality is its ability to synthesize spiritual insights across traditions. Buddhists talk to Jews, Christians study yoga, and everybody wants to know a little bit about shamanism. The wonderful opportunities of this openness are obvious, but the danger is that certain principles will be lost. Although every tradition can be clearly seen for its virtues and powers, spiritual deep ecologists will lose their thread if they let certain clarities be obscured: the equality of men and women, a recognition of the past and present effects of racial domination, the need to frame spiritual truths in the context of a worldwide economy and culture. If these clarities are neglected, the integrity of deep ecology will diminish, and it may devolve into a sect of spiritually and thus socially irrelevant bird-watchers.

Third, all attachment to truth provides the opportunity to hate error. There is thus the possibility—which at times has been realized in practice—of deep ecologists erecting a sharp divide between themselves and other kinds of environmentalism. Surely grounds for an alliance exist between deep ecologists and those who (merely) think of the world as deserving of care because it is God's creation and not in itself sacred. Surely the deep ecologists have

5. This critique is developed more extensively in Gottlieb 1995.

enough in common with the stewards of nature to make common cause with them against the pure despoilers. On a practical level, only a mass movement can motivate the government to constrain global capitalism and to demand international, national, and local programs to recover what we have lost and to clean up the mess we have made. Such a movement will require environmentalists of all stripes, and participation will necessitate a long view in which tactical compromise with less-radical elements will be necessary to secure the basis of an ongoing collective and effective movement. As they relate to others in the struggle to protect nature, spiritual deep ecologists should remember that, in our own time, we encounter the wilderness with the very accomplishments of our society riding on our back. As E. O. Wilson (1983) observed, no matter how much the naturalists love the jungle, they had better be very well equipped, or before long a host of jungle dwellers will break them down into their constituent amino acids. Every deep ecologist goes to the wilds with a pair of vibram boots, a nylon backpack, and a Swiss army knife. With all that stuff along, there is little room for arrogance.

What all this adds up to is that just as we experience the mystical touch of God as socially situated individuals, so we come to "nature" through social life. We bring our historically defined expectations and needs. We have a concept of nature (as benign or threatening, comfortable or forbidding, infinitely powerful or dangerously at risk) that is very much the product of our own society's level of technological development. Especially in our own time, we only *go* to the wilds with the very particular accomplishments of our society riding on our back.

Thus, there is, fourth, also the problem that at times the bland images of nature that emerge from deep ecology distort what nature really is like. For example, our mystically based love of life will not extend to the AIDS virus, and our wariness at tampering with the sacred character of nature may well be suspended when it comes to using genetic engineering to cure cystic fibrosis. Ghetto rats will probably escape the purview that holds all of life as sacred, as might the black flies that cause widespread blindness in Africa. Adopting a deep ecological perspective will not eliminate the hard choices we face—choices about how much to take for ourselves and how much to leave for others, how much to exercise the control we increase day by day, and how much to surrender. It will not turn the real world into a PBS special on butterflies or dolphins. The love we feel for the nonhuman is not a love that can erase the realities of struggle and conquest—of nature as one long and frequently quite painful food chain.

There is an old Buddhist tale about two monks who stand on top of a mountain, surveying all of nature. "How horrible!" says one, with tears in his eyes. "They are all eating each other." "Don't be so upset," the other comforts him. "Really, they are feeding each other." The point, of course, is that both are correct.

Social Transformation

In human history, the long counterpoint to the ecstasy that takes us out of our social setting is the longing for justice within it. Morality and transcendence are the twin axes along which authentic personal and communal existence develop, and our success at both is the criteria for measuring the adequacy of a humane form of life. This longing for a more just social order can be found in the cautionary words of prophets, social reformers, and revolutionaries. In contrast to the claims of mysticism, the pursuit of justice is very much an awareness of just how socially situated we are and of how our concerns with making things better center on the alteration and improvement of this situation that defines us, grounds us, and sets our tasks.

This pursuit of justice exists, among other things, as a needed corrective to the ahistorical pretensions of mystical traditions—their claims to provide doctrines that originate outside of the social order. From a viewpoint that originated in politics, rather than spirituality, we are able, for instance, to critique the sexist teachings of early Buddhism. For all its self-understanding as a source of truth beyond the ego, it maintained the idea of women's social and spiritual inferiority. Although the Buddha may have seen his way clear of the imposed caste system and the empty formalities of ritual sacrifices, he could not escape his own attachment to patriarchy. What source could there be for even recognizing this failing except a socially based political critique? Such a source only rarely emerges from transcendent visions but rather typically stems from the cries of the oppressed themselves. Ultimately, as I mentioned above, the danger here is that mystical *experience* is used as a support for *social authority*. It is then that, inevitably, veracity is claimed not simply for the experience, but for one particular discursive and institutional expression of it. And this expression will *always* give rise to structures of power and privilege—which will be defended with all the typical violence and deceit that hierarchies of power always employ.

In our own time, deep ecology in particular and the conservation movement in general have been the subject of extensive critiques: for ignoring the social basis of their own perspectives; for emphasizing the wilderness and forgetting toxic waste dumps; for loving the trees and lacking concern for children. These criticisms have helped move deep ecologists toward an understanding that environmentalism needs to embrace the concern of environmental justice: an awareness of and resistance to the unfair distribution of responsibility for and suffering from humanity's attacks on the environment. The radioactive dumps on native lands, the toxic wastes flowing into the poor neighborhoods, the outlawed chemicals exported to the third world: Can we really love nature if these things escape our vision?[6]

Finally, it must be stressed that for many people, the struggle for justice is *itself* a form of connection that can break the bonds of the ego. Although social movements too often have devolved into the brutal tyrannies of a Stalin or the crass appeal to group hatred of a Farrakan, at their best they provide experiences in which political solidarity blossoms into a kind of selfless love. At times, people struggling for justice are freed from the usual petty isolations, jealousies, and fears. In the very struggle, they find the joy of service and the spiritual clarity that comes from knowing the ultimate rightness of what they are doing.

And Yet . . .

Too often, confidence in one's ultimate rightness has led political movements into dogmatic violence. The history of too many revolutions is the history of the replacement of one autocracy by another. The history of too many groups on the left reveals sectarianism, verbal violence, and exclusion of others who deserve solidarity. We have seen the fundamental wisdom of the struggle for justice be obscured by rage, pompous posturing, or simple careerism.[7]

Thus, just as a political perspective is necessary for both a grounding and a critique of mysticism and deep ecology, so their spiritual insights and resources can be a corrective to the excesses of politics.

Mysticism in general can offer relief from identification with theories, rigidly held "positions," and the pursuit of institutional power. An emphasis on compassion, on empathy even for the guilty, on service rather than on the acquisition of personal status within the "movement"—these values can be forthcoming from a direct experience of the holy, for from that experience, once again, we may learn that the ego-bound concerns that motivate us toward arrogance and violence, even in the service of justice, are not the only reality. To make the point, we need only compare Lenin's practice of threatening to expel any party leader who disagreed with him to Gandhi's insistence that comrades vote against him if that was what their own inner wisdom dictated. Coercion is clearly a product of any kind of fundamentalism, whether of a religious or a secular kind. Control or cooperation, manipulation

6. Two accounts of these matters are in Gedicks 1993 and Bullard 1994.

7. For an extensive critique of these defects in the history of European and American left movements, see Gottlieb 1987 and 1992.

or trust, the Grand Inquisitor and Lenin or Gandhi and Aung San Suu Kyi Sang Soo Sy—these choices face any collection of human beings, any institutional structure, any attempt to bring truth into the world.

From deep ecology in particular the world of conventional human-oriented politics also has much to learn. For one thing, deep ecology's emphasis on the value of the nonhuman offers a measure and a limit of what we are seeking when we pursue an improved "standard of living." The notion of a "sustainable" form of life begins to condition what we are after; it becomes an essential defining element along with justice and freedom. And (as difficult as it is to find the right way of putting this) we have before us the prospect that the true subjects of political life are not just people, but people, animals, plants, ecosystems, and perhaps the biosphere itself. Thus, new questions arise for social activities of all kinds. What is the ultimate worth of this construction project, these jobs, this or that commodity? Whose needs or wants deserve to be satisfied? And which should be altered?

In the same vein, a mystical identification—or deep relationship—with the natural world allows us to orient political struggle away from entitlement and rage, and in a direction not tied (or at least less tied) by a psychic addiction to the very social system that destroys us. As Marcuse observed, by rooting personal identity in the ownership of things, the consumer society binds its subjects to the principles of ever-increasing production and consumption (1967). The recognition of spiritual values in general and the value(s) of nature in particular gives us a way out of the ecocidal cul-de-sac of the endless mall. We develop, in short, an alternative sense of self. This alternative allows the possibility of a withdrawal of psychic energy from a cultural and economic system that threatens all those subject to it.

In more strategic political terms, concern for nature is a value that can provide the basis for a new kind of solidarity. We might remember that whatever else divides us as human beings, we all need to breathe. Virtually all of our hearts rejoice to the sounds of spring. These commonalties may save us when the divisions of race, class, gender, ethnicity, or sexuality leave us deeply suspicious of each other.

Although those individuals getting very rich from causing pollution or those people whose most immediate livelihood depends on exploitation of their surroundings are not likely to be convinced, we have already seen cross-class, cross-race, and cross-national coalitions doing serious political work. An enormous dam project slated for India—supported by the World Bank and liable to destroy the habitat of endangered species and indigenous people alike—was stopped by a transcontinental alliance of local people, environmental activists, lawyers, and concerned citizens from India, Switzerland, and the United States (Rich 1994, 44–47). In Wisconsin, white activists have helped native peoples fend off multinational mining interests (Gedicks 1992). These examples show only a few of the arenas of cooperation based on a joint concern for the human and the nonhuman world.

It may actually be that care for the environment will continue and will flourish as one of the main motivating forces of politics in the twenty-first century. The abatement signaled in the United States by the Republican victories of the mid-1990s is, I believe, a temporary development. In any event, the "working class," as Andre Gorz observed many years ago, is not likely to mount a serious challenge to the established social order to get a 10 percent increase in pay (1990, 218). Concern for the environment—a concern motivated both by "self-interest" and by interest for nature that we love and long for—*could* be a significant element in a major social transformation. If people can truly see what is at stake, they may yet rise to the challenge. The spiritual understanding of this concern has been and will continue to be an essential element in the process. We have seen it already in the spiritual motivation of the radical ecology group Earth First! as well as in the convention-challenging claims of the new earth-oriented ecotheology coming out of mainstream religions and in the politicized versions of spiritual ecofeminism.

Finally, and perhaps most surprisingly, there is in a general deep ecological orientation a cognitive corrective to the distortions of centralized, reductionist, commodified knowledge and social practice. In agriculture, for instance, the belief that modernized science and technology can replace the fertility of the earth or the expertise of local groups has led to a series of disasters. As Vandana Shiva has described it, the imposition of "advanced," commodity-oriented monocultures has erased a wide variety of crops, seeds, productive uses (for food, fodder, herbs, local consumption as well as sale), and ultimately peoples (1993). The result has been polluted soils, drastically increased water consumption, less-productive land use, and violent social dislocation. In this approach, there is respect neither for the earth nor for the people who have sustainably managed their fields and forests for centuries. A perspective that sees communion with nature as having spiritual as well as instrumental value might look very carefully at any attempt to supplant either natural processes or long-established local forms of culture and practice. Thus, just as a spiritual view of the ultimate value of persons can provide an orientation for social life (though clearly not a simple way to resolve its conflicts and contradictions), so a spiritual view of nature can offer at least the beginning of an orientation toward production, consumption, and development.

Paradoxically, the wisdom of a mystical deep ecology can augment the powers and promises of the secular drive for just social transformation. Their mutual support is necessary, I suspect, if the environmental crisis is not to erode the conditions for human life on earth and simultaneously erode our very confidence in our right to exist on it. If we are to be truly touched by the Holy Spirit, our own spirit of holiness must reach out to the enormous family of life that surrounds us, shapes us, and gives us our own particular place in the vastness of time and space.

◆   ◆   ◆

The vision of mysticism offered here will not satisfy everyone. It is a particularly *nonmetaphysical* view, in which ultimate reality is pretty much exhausted by "ordinary" reality. Of course, when illuminated by the sparks of mystical experience, ordinary reality can shine pretty brightly (as in the old Zen story that identifies true enlightenment with simply seeing "a mountain as a mountain and a river as a river"). But what is absent here is any confidence that the pains of injustice and loss will be compensated for by any Grand Plan, Protecting All-Powerful Source, or Cosmic Pattern of Growth and Development. Speaking quite personally, I never could feel any of those possibilities; I believe we just have what we have. Mysticism, in my view, does not mean transcendence, but (again) illumination: not to believe in something else, but to see more clearly (and more brightly) what we have and who we are. In the end, the work of mysticism is to join us to what we have: in delight, in grief, in life and death. Sometimes that joining will have the force and pleasure of a sexual climax, sometimes the utter peace of a spring flower or the caress of a child's hand. Sometimes it will be the knowledge that we can join with what is only by resisting it and that "acceptance" must mean that we fight back in our struggle for justice. At such times, we fully realize our desire to transcend the falseness of our social world not by finding some other realm, but by performing acts of solidarity and resistance, by transforming the emotional, moral, and therefore spiritual meaning of the falseness of our social world.[8]

8. This perspective on the relation between spiritual life and resistance is developed in my book *A Spirituality of Resistance: Finding a Peaceful Heart and Protecting the Earth* (Gottlieb 1999).

Works Cited

Abbey, Edward. 1977. *The Journey Home*. New York: Penguin.

Abram, David. 1996. *The Spell of the Sensuous: Perception and Language in a More-than-Human World*. New York: Pantheon.

Aitken, Robert. 1984. *The Mind of Clover: Essays in Zen Buddhist Ethics*. San Francisco: North Point.

Alonso Cortés, Narciso. 1946. "Pleitos de los Cepeda." *Boletín de la Real Academia Española* 25: 85–110.

Andrews, William L., ed. 1986. *Sisters of the Spirit*. Bloomington: Indiana Univ. Press.

Aquinas, Thomas. 1964a. *Summa theologica*. Vol 18. Edited by Blackfriars, translated by Thomas Gilby. New York: McGraw Hill.

————. 1964b. *Summa theologica*. Vol 46. Edited by Blackfriars, translated by Jordan Aumann. New York: McGraw Hill.

Arenal, Electa, and Stacey Schlau. 1989. *Untold Sisters: Hispanic Nuns in Their Own Works*. Translated by Amanda Powell. Albuquerque: Univ. of New Mexico Press.

Arendt, Hannah. 1958. *The Human Condition*. Chicago: Univ. of Chicago Press.

Aristotle. 1985. *Nicomachean Ethics*. Translated by Terence Irwin. Indianapolis: Hackett.

Armstrong, Edward A. 1973. *Saint Francis, Nature Mystic: The Derivation and Significance of the Nature Stories in the Franciscan Legend*. Berkeley: Univ. of California Press.

Armstrong, Regis J. 1985. "Clare of Assisi: The Mirror Mystic." *The Cord* 35: 195–202.

————, ed. and trans. 1993. *Clare of Assisi: Early Documents*. St. Bonaventure, N.Y.: Franciscan Institute.

Armstrong, Regis, and Ignatius C. Brady, eds. and trans. 1982. *Francis and Clare: The Complete Works*. New York: Paulist.

Arrupe, Pedro, S.J. 1980a. "Address to General Congregation 32." 1974. Reprinted in *Justice with Faith Today: Selected Letters and Addresses II*, edited by Jerome Aixala, S.J., 317–20. St. Louis: Institute of Jesuit Sources.

————. 1980b. "Witnessing to Justice in the World." 1972. Reprinted in *Justice with Faith Today: Selected Letters and Addresses II*, edited by Jerome Aixala, S.J., 79–120. St. Louis: Institute of Jesuit Sources.

————. 1985a. "Final Address of Father General to the Congregation of Procurators." 1978. Reprinted in *The Spiritual Legacy of Pedro Arrupe, S.J.*, 21–42. Private publication by the New York Province.

———. 1985b. "The Trinitarian Inspiration of the Ignatian Charism," an address at the Center for Ignatian Spirituality, Feb. 8, 1980. In *The Spiritual Legacy of Pedro Arrupe, S.J.*, 87–144. Private publication by the New York Province.

———. 1985c. "Rooted and Grounded in Love." 1981. Reprinted in *The Spiritual Legacy of Pedro Arrupe, S.J*, 145–95. Private publication by the New York Province.

———. 1986. *One Jesuit's Spiritual Journey: Autobiographical Conversations with Jean-Claude Dietsch, S.J., and Selected Letters and Addresses.* Translated by Ruth Bradley. St. Louis: Institute of Jesuit Sources.

Asseldonk, Optatus van. 1991. "The Spirit of the Lord and Its Holy Activity in the Writings of Francis." *Greyfriars Review* 5, no. 1: 105–58.

———. 1993. "Sorores Minores e Chiara d'Assisi a San Damiano: Una scelta tra clausura e lebbrosi?" *Collectanea Franciscana* 63, 3–4: 595–633.

Babinsky, Ellen L. 1993. "Introduction" and "Notes" in *Marguerite Porete: The Mirror of Simple Souls*, 5–61. Classics of Western Spirituality. New York: Paulist.

Bambara, Toni Cade. 1980. *The Salt Eaters.* N.Y.: Vintage.

Bartoli, Marco. 1992. "Historical Analysis and Psychoanalytical Interpretations of a Vision of Clare of Assisi." *Greyfriars Review* 6, no. 2: 189–209.

———. 1993. *Clare of Assisi.* Translated by Sister Frances Teresa. Quincy, Ill.: Franciscan.

Beer, Francis de. 1983. *We Saw Brother Francis.* Translated by Maggi Despot and Paul Lachance. Chicago: Franciscan Herald.

Bellah, Robert, Richard Madsen, William Sullivan, Ann Swidler, and Steven Tipton. 1985. *Habits of the Heart: Individualism and Commitment in American Life.* New York: Harper and Row.

Berger, Peter L., ed. 1981. *Other Side of God: A Polarity in World Religions.* Garden City, N.Y.: Doubleday.

Berger, Peter, Brigitte Berger, and Hansfried Kellner. 1973. *The Homeless Mind: Modernization and Consciousness.* New York: Random House.

Berman, Morris. 1981. *The Reenchantment of the World.* Ithaca, N.Y.: Cornell Univ. Press.

Bernard of Clairvaux. 1979. *On the Song of Songs III.* Translated by Kilian Walsh and Irene Edmunds. Kalamazoo, Mich.: Cistercian.

Bilinkoff, Jodi. 1988. "The Social Meaning of Religious Reform: The Case of St. Teresa and Avila." *Archiv für Reformationsgeschichte* 79: 340–57.

———. 1989. *The Avila of Saint Teresa: Religious Reform in a Sixteenth-Century City.* Ithaca: Cornell Univ. Press.

Bloch, Maurice. 1989. *Ritual, History, and Power: Selected Papers in Anthropology.* London: Athlone.

Bobin, Christian. 1997. *The Secret of Francis of Assisi: A Meditation.* Translated by Michael H. Kohn. Boston: Shambhala.

Boff, Leonardo. 1982. *St. Francis: A Model for Human Liberation*. Translated by John W. Diercksmeir. New York: Crossroad.

Bordo, Susan. 1987. *The Flight to Objectivity: Essays on Cartesianism and Culture*. Albany: State Univ. of New York Press.

Boroughs, Philip, and John Woolman. 1991. *Spirituality and Social Transformation in Colonial America*. Ann Arbor, Mich.: Univ. Microfilms International.

Bourdieu, Pierre. 1991. *Language and Symbolic Power*. Cambridge, Mass.: Harvard Univ. Press.

Braxton, Joanne M. 1989. *Black Women Writing Autobiography: A Tradition Within a Tradition*. Philadelphia: Temple Univ. Press.

Brinton, Howard H. 1988. *Friends for 300 Years*. 1952. Reprint. Wallingford, Penn.: Pendle Hill.

Brueggemann, Walter. 1978. *The Prophetic Imagination*. Philadelphia: Fortress.

Bruneau, Marie-Florine. 1998. *Women Mystics Confront the Modern World: Marie De l'Incarnation (1599–1672) and Madame Guyon (1648–1717)*. Albany: State Univ. of New York Press.

Brunette, Pierre. 1994. "Claire et François d'Assise: Leur relation d'après les sources." Colloque: Claire d'Assise: Féminité et Spiritualité, Université de Montréal, May 11–13.

———. 1995. "François et Claire." In *Sainte Claire d'Assise et sa postérité*. Actes du Colloque de l'U.N.E.S.C.O., Sept. 29–Oct. 1, 1994, edited by Geneviève Brunel-Lobrichon, Dominique Dinet, Jacqueline Gréal, and Damien Vorreux, 87–100. Paris: Publication du Comité du VIIIe Centenaire de sainte Claire.

———. 1997. *Francis of Assisi and His Conversions*. Translated by Paul Lachance and Kathryn Krug. Quincy, Ill.: Franciscan.

Bryant, Gwendolyn. 1984. "The French Heretic Beguine: Marguerite Porete." In *Medieval Women Writers*, edited by Katharina M. Wilson, 204–26. Manchester: Manchester Univ. Press.

Bullard, Robert D., ed. 1994. *Unequal Protection: Environmental Justice and Communities of Color*. San Francisco: Sierra Club.

Bynum, Caroline Walker. 1991. *Fragmentation and Redemption: Essays on Gender and the Human Body in Medieval Religion*. New York: Zone.

Carney, Margaret. 1993. *The First Franciscan Woman: Clare of Assisi and Her Form of Life*. Quincy, Ill.: Franciscan.

Certeau, Michel de. 1986. *The Mystic Fable*. Translated by Michael B. Smith. Chicago: Univ. of Chicago Press.

Chakravarti, U. 1987. *The Social Dimensions of Early Buddhism*. Delhi: Oxford Univ. Press.

Chesterton, Gilbert K. 1924. *St. Francis of Assisi*. New York: George H. Doran.

Coleman, John A., S.J. 1997. "Exploding Spiritualities: Their Social Causes, Social Location, and Social Divide." *Christian Spirituality Bulletin* (spring 1997): 9–15.

Coleridge, Samuel Taylor. 1956. *Collected Letters of Samuel Taylor Coleridge*. Vol. 1. Edited by Earl Leslie Griggs. London: Clarendon.

Colledge, Edmund. 1968. "Liberty of Spirit: The Mirror of Simple Souls." In *Theology of Renewal 2,* edited by L. K. Shook, 100–117. Montreal: n.p.

———. 1981. "Historical Introduction." In *Meister Eckhart: The Essential Ser-mons, Commentaries, Treatises, and Defense,* edited and translated by Edmund Colledge and Bernard McGinn, 5–23. Classics of Western Spirituality. New York: Paulist.

Collins, Patricia Hill. 1991. *Black Feminist Thought: Knowledge, Consciousness, and the Politics of Empowerment.* New York: Routledge.

Constable, Giles. 1997. "The Interpretation of Mary and Martha." In *Three Studies in Medieval Religious and Social Thought,* 3–41. Cambridge: Cambridge Univ. Press.

The Constitutions of the Society of Jesus and Their Complementary Norms. 1996. A Complete English Translation of the Official Latin Texts. St. Louis: Institute of Jesuit Sources.

Contreras, Jaime. 1992. "Aldermen and Judaizers: Cryptojudaism, Counter-Reformation, and Local Power." In *Culture and Control in Counter-Reformation Spain,* edited by Anne J. Cruz and Mary Elizabeth Perry, 93–123. Hispanic Issues, vol. 7. Minneapolis: Univ. of Minnesota Press.

Conwell, Joseph F., S.J. 1997. *Impelling Spirit: Revisiting a Founding Experience, 1539 Ignatius of Loyola and His Companions.* Chicago: Loyola Univ. Press.

Conze, Edward. 1951. *Buddhism: Its Essence and Development.* New York: Harper.

Copenhaver, John D., Jr. 1992. *Prayerful Responsibility: Prayer and Social Responsibility in the Religious Thought of Douglas Steere.* Lanham, Md.: Univ. Press of America.

Cornet, Bernard. 1995–97. "Le *'De Reverentia Corporis Domini,'* exhortation et lettre de saint François." *Études Franciscaines* 6: 65–91, 167–80; 7: 28–35, 35–58, 155–71; 8: 35–53.

Cousins, Ewert. 1983. "Francis of Assisi and Bonaventure," and "Francis of Assisi: Christian Mysticism at the Crossroads." In *Myticism and Religious Traditions,* edited by Steven L. Katz, 163–90. Oxford and London: Oxford Univ. Press.

Cruz, Anne J., and Mary Elizabeth Perry. 1992a. "Introduction: Culture and Control in Counter-Reformation Spain." In *Culture and Control in Counter-Reformation Spain,* edited by Anne J. Cruz and Mary Elizabeth Perry, ix–xxiii. Hispanic Issues, vol. 7. Minneapolis: Univ. of Minnesota Press.

———. 1992b. *Culture and Control in Counter-Reformation Spain.* Hispanic Issues, vol. 7. Minneapolis: Univ. of Minnesota Press.

Cupitt, Don. 1998. *Mysticism after Modernity.* Malden, Mass: Blackwell.

Dante Alighieri. 1973. *The Divine Comedy: Purgatorio, Text and Commentary.* Bollingen Series 80. Princeton: Princeton Univ. Press.

Derrida, Jacques. 1967a. *De la grammatologie.* Paris: Minuit.

———. 1967b. *L'écriture et la différence.* Paris: Seuil.

———. 1972a. *Marges de la philosophie.* Paris: Minuit.

———. 1972b. *La dissémination.* Paris: Seuil.

———. 1976. *Of Grammatology.* Translated by Gayatri Chakravorty Spivak. 1967. Baltimore: Johns Hopkins Univ. Press.

————. 1978. *Writing and Difference.* Translated by Alan Bass. 1967. Chicago: Univ. of Chicago Press.

————. 1982a. *Margins of Philosophy.* Translated by Alan Bass. 1972. Chicago: Univ. of Chicago Press.

————. 1982b. *Dissemination.* Translated by Barbara Johnson. 1972. Chicago: Univ. of Chicago Press.

————. 1986. *Schibboleth.* Paris: Galilée.

————. 1987. *Psyché: Inventions de l'autre.* Paris: Galilée.

Devall, Bill, and George Sessions. 1985. *Deep Ecology: Living As If Nature Mattered.* Salt Lake City: Peregrine Smith.

Dijk, Willibord-Christian van. 1996. "A Prayer in Search of an Author." *Greyfriars Review* 10, no. 3: 257–64.

Dillard, Annie. 1982. *Teaching a Stone to Talk.* New York: HarperCollins.

Documents of the 31st and 32nd General Congregations of the Society of Jesus. 1977. An English Translation of the Official Latin Texts of the General Congregations and of Accompanying Papal Documents. St. Louis: Institute of Jesuit Sources.

Documents of the 33rd General Congregation of the Society of Jesus. 1984. An English Translation of the Official Latin Texts of the General Congregation and of Related Documents. St. Louis: Institute of Jesuit Sources.

Documents of the 34th General Congregation of the Society of Jesus. 1995. St. Louis: Institute of Jesuit Sources.

Dronke, Peter. 1984. *Women Writers of the Middle Ages.* Cambridge: Cambridge Univ. Press.

Dunne, John S. 1969. *The Search for God in Time and Memory.* New York: MacMillan.

Eckhart, Meister. 1936. *Meister Eckhart: Die deutschen und lateinischen Werke.* Edited by Josef Koch and Josef Quint. Stuttgart and Berlin: W. Kohlhammer.

————. 1981. *Meister Eckhart: The Essential Sermons, Commentaries, Treatises, and Defense.* Translated by Edmund Colledge and Bernard McGinn. New York: Paulist.

————. 1986. *Meister Eckhart: Teacher and Preacher.* Translated by Bernard McGinn with Frank Tobin and Elvira Borgstädt. New York: Paulist.

Egan, Harvey D., S.J. 1976. *The Spiritual Exercises and the Ignatian Mystical Horizon.* St. Louis: Institute of Jesuit Sources.

————. 1984. *Christian Mysticism: The Future of a Tradition.* New York: Pueblo.

Egan, Robert J., S.J. 1987. "Discernment, Cultural Analysis, and Social Transformation: On Letting Love Make History." Unpublished address for the Ignatian Spirituality Institute, sponsored by the Oregon Province of the Society of Jesus, Portland, Oregon, Aug. 11–14.

————. 1990. "God in All Things: Ignatian Spirituality in the Situation of Postmodern Culture." Comprehensive Examination Paper, Graduate Theological Union, Berkeley.

————. 1991a. "Ignatian Spirituality: Finding God in Everything." Toronto: Regis College.

————. 1991b. "Ignatian Spirituality and Social Justice." Toronto: Regis College.

Eichendorff, Joseph. n.d. "Der Einsiedler." In *Eichendorff's Werke in vier Teilen,* vol. 1, edited by Ludwig Krahe. Berlin: Deutsches Verlagshaus Boug.

Ellacuria, Ignacio, S.J. 1986. "Pedro Arrupe, Innovator of Religious Life." In *Pedro Arrupe, S.J., As They Knew Him,* edited by Stefan Bamberger, S.J., and translated from the Spanish by Yolanda de Mola, S.C., 1992–93, 141–74. N.p.: n.p.

Epstein, Mark. 1995. *Thoughts Without a Thinker: Psychotherapy from a Buddhist Perspective.* New York: Basic.

Erickson, Victoria Lee. 1993. *Where Silence Speaks: Feminism, Social Theory, and Religion.* Minneapolis: Fortress.

Farley, Wendy. 1996. *Eros for the Other: Retaining Truth in a Pluralistic World.* University Park: Pennsylvania Univ. Press.

Flood, David. 1989. *Francis of Assisi and the Franciscan Movement.* Quezon City, Philippines: Franciscan Institute of Asia.

"Florence, Maurice" [Michel Foucault]. 1994. "Foucault, Michel, 1926." In *The Cambridge Companion to Foucault,* edited by Gary Gutting. Cambridge: Cambridge Univ. Press.

Forman, Robert. 1990a. "Introduction: Mysticism, Constructivism, and Forgetting." In *The Problem of Pure Consciousness: Mysticism and Philosophy,* edited by Robert Forman, 3–49. New York: Oxford Univ. Press.

———. 1990b. *The Problem of Pure Consciousness: Mysticism and Philosophy.* New York: Oxford Univ. Press.

Foster, Nelson. 1988. "To Enter the Marketplace." In *The Path of Compassion: Writings on Socially Engaged Buddhism,* 2d ed., edited by Fred Eppsteiner, 47–64. Berkeley, Calif.: Parallax.

Foucault, Michel. 1980. *Power/Knowledge: Selected Interviews and Other Writings, 1972–1977.* Edited by Colin Gordon. Ithaca, N.Y.: Cornell Univ. Press.

Fox, Matthew. 1995. *Wrestling with the Prophets: Essays on Creation Spirituality and Everyday Life.* San Francisco: Harper.

Frugoni, Chiara. 1993. *Francesco e l'invenzione delle stimmate: Una storia per parole e imagine fino a Bonaventura e Giotto.* Turino: Enaudi.

Gadamer, Hans-Georg. 1975. *Truth and Method.* Translated by Garrett Barden and John Cumming. New York: Crossroad.

Galilea, Segundo. 1980. "Liberation as an Encounter with Politics and Contemplation." In *Understanding Mysticism,* edited by Richard Woods, 529–40. Garden City, N.Y.: Doubleday.

Gallant, Laurent. 1995. "Francis of Assisi: Forerunner of Interreligious Dialogue?" Paper presented at the symposium "Franciscan Mission and Interreligious Dialogue." Thirtieth International Congress on Medieval Studies, May 8–11, Western Michigan University.

Gedicks, Al. 1993. *The New Resource Wars: Native and Environmental Struggles Against Multinational Corporations.* Boston: South End.

Gilkes, Cheryl Townsend. 1986. "The Role of Women in the Sanctified Church." *Journal of Religious Thought* 43, no. 1: 24–41.

Glendinning, Simon. 1998. *On Being with Others: Heidegger, Derrida, Wittgenstein.* New York: Routledge.

Godet, Jean-François. 1985. "Il progetto evangelico di Chiara oggi." *Vita Minorum* 56: 198–301.

———. 1991. *Clare of Assisi: A Woman's Life.* Chicago: Haversack.

Gombrich, Richard. 1988. *Theravada Buddhism: A Social History from Ancient Benares to Modern Colombo.* London: Routledge and Kegan Paul.

Gorz, Andre. 1990. "Socialism and Revolution." In *An Anthology of Western Marxism: From Lukacs and Gramsci to Socialist-Feminism,* edited by Roger S. Gottlieb, 218–32. New York: Oxford Univ. Press.

Gottlieb, Roger S. 1987. *History and Subjectivity: The Transformation of Marxist Theory.* Philadelphia: Temple Univ. Press.

———. 1992. *Marxism 1844–1990: Origins, Betrayal, Rebirth.* New York: Routledge.

———. 1995. "Spiritual Deep Ecology and the Left." *Capitalism, Nature, Socialism* 6, no. 4 (fall): 1–21. Reprinted in Roger S. Gottlieb, *This Sacred Earth: Religion, Nature, Environment.* New York: Routledge, 1996.

———, ed. 1996. *This Sacred Earth: Religion, Nature, Environment.* New York: Routledge.

———. 1999. *A Spirituality of Resistance: Finding a Peaceful Heart and Protecting the Earth.* New York: Crossroad.

Grant, Jacquelyn. 1990. "Subjectification as a Requirement for Christological Construction." In *Lift Every Voice: Constructing Christian Theologies from the Underside,* edited by Susan Brooks Thistlethwaite and Mary Potter Engel, 201–14. New York: Harper San Francisco.

Greenburg, Moshe. 1983. *Biblical Prose Prayer as a Window to the Popular Religions of Ancient Israel.* Berkeley: Univ. of California Press.

Griffin, David. 1988a. *The Reenchantment of Science.* Albany: State Univ. of New York Press.

———. 1988b. *Spirituality and Society.* Albany: State Univ. of New York Press.

Griffiths, Paul. 1990. "Pure Consciousness and Indian Buddhism." In *The Problem of Pure Consciousness: Mysticism and Philosophy,* edited by Robert Forman, 71–97. New York: Oxford Univ. Press.

Guilhem, Claire. 1979. "L'Inquisition et la dévaluation des discours féminins." In *L'Inquisition espagnole: XV–XIX siècle,* edited by Bartolomé Bennassar, 197–240. Paris: Hachette.

Gutiérrez, Gustavo. 1973. *A Theology of Liberation: History Politics, and Salvation.* 1972. Translated by Caridad Inda and John Eagleson. Maryknoll, New York: Orbis.

———. 1988. *We Drink from Our Own Wells: The Spiritual Journey of a People.* Translated by Matthew J. O'Connell. Maryknoll, New York: Orbis.

Gutiérrez Nieto, Juan Ignacio. 1983. "El proceso de encastamiento social de la Castilla del siglo XVI: La respuesta conversa." In *Congreso Internacional Teresiano, 4–7 Octubre 1982,* edited by Teófanes Egido Martínez, Victor García de la

Concha, and Olegario González de Cardenal, 1: 103–20. Salamanca: Universidad de Salamanca.

Habermas, Jurgen. 1975. *Legitimation Crisis*. Translated by Thomas McCarthy. 1973. Boston: Beacon.

———. 1984. *The Theory of Communicative Action, Vol. 1: Reason and the Rationalization of Society*. Translated by Thomas McCarthy. 1981. Boston: Beacon.

Habig, Marian, ed. 1973. *St. Francis of Assisi: Writings and Biographies. English Omnibus of Sources for the Life of St. Francis*. Chicago: Franciscan Herald.

Hadewijch. 1980. *Hadewijch: The Complete Works*. Translated by Mother Columba Hart, O.S.B. Classics of Western Spirituality. New York: Paulist.

Hadot, Pierre. 1995. *Philosophy as a Way of Life*. Edited by Arnold I. Davidson. Oxford: Blackwell.

Halperin, David. 1995. *Saint Foucault: Towards a Gay Hagiography*. New York: Oxford Univ. Press.

Haskins, Susan. 1993. *Mary Magdalene: Myth and Metaphor*. New York: Harcourt Brace.

Heiler, Friedrich. 1997. *Prayer: A Study in the History and Psychology of Religion*. 1932. Reprint. Rockport, Maine: One World.

Heisig, James, and John Maraldo, eds. 1995. *Rude Awakenings: Zen, the Kyoto School, the Question of Nationalism*. Honolulu: Univ. of Hawaii Press.

Heschel, Abraham J. 1955. *God in Search of Man: A Philosophy of Judaism*. New York: Farrar, Strauss, and Giroux.

Heyward, Carter. 1992. *Touching Our Strength*. San Francisco: Harper.

Hollywood, Amy. 1994. "Beauvoir, Irigaray, and the Mystical." *Hypatia* 9, no. 4: 158–85.

———. 1995. *The Soul as Virgin Wife: Mechthild of Magdeburg, Marguerite Porete, and Meister Eckhart*. Notre Dame: Univ. of Notre Dame Press.

Humez, Jean McMahon, ed. 1981. *Gifts of Power: The Writings of Rebecca Jackson, Black Visionary, Shaker Eldress*. Boston: Univ. of Massachusetts Press.

Idigoras, Jose Ignacio Tellechea. 1994. *Ignatius of Loyola: The Pilgrim Saint*. Translated, edited, and with a preface by Cornelius Michael Buckley, S.J. Chicago: Loyola Univ. Press.

Ignatius of Loyola. 1991. *Ignatius of Loyola: Spiritual Exercises and Selected Writings*. Edited by George Ganss, S.J., with the collaboration of Parmananda R. Divarkar, S.J., Edward Malatesta, S.J., and Martin E. Palmer, S.J. Mahwah, N.J.: Paulist.

Irigaray, Luce. 1993. *Sexes and Genealogies*. Translated by Gillian C. Gill. New York: Columbia Univ. Press.

Jacoby, Russell. 1975. *Social Amnesia: A Critique of Conformist Psychology from Adler to Laing*. Boston: Beacon.

James, William. 1961. *The Varieties of Religious Experience: A Study in Human Nature*. 1902. Reprint. Introduction by Reinhold Niebuhr. New York: Macmillan, Collier.

————. 1982. *The Varieties of Religious Experience.* 1903. Reprint. New York: Penguin American Library.

Jantzen, Grace M. 1994. "Feminists, Philosophers, and Mystics." *Hypatia* 9, no. 4: 186–206.

————. 1995. *Power, Gender, and Christian Mysticism.* Cambridge: Cambridge Univ. Press.

Johnson, Timothy. 1994. "Image and Vision: Contemplation as Visual Perception in Clare of Assisi's Epistolary Writings." *Greyfriars Review* 8, no. 2: 202–17.

Jones, Ken. 1988. "Buddhism and Social Action: An Exploration." In *The Path of Compassion: Writings on Socially Engaged Buddhism,* 2d ed., edited by Fred Eppsteiner, 65–81. Berkeley, Calif.: Parallax.

————. 1989. *The Social Face of Buddhism: An Approach to Political and Social Activism.* London: Wisdom.

Kagan, Richard L. 1990. *Lucrecia's Dreams: Politics and Prophecy in Sixteenth-Century Spain.* Berkeley: Univ. of California Press.

Kalupahana, David. 1975. *Causality: The Central Philosophy of Buddhism.* Honolulu: Univ. of Hawaii Press.

Kamenka, Eugene, ed. 1983. *The Portable Karl Marx.* New York: Penguin.

Katz, Steven, ed. 1978. *Mysticism and Philosophical Analysis.* New York: Oxford Univ. Press.

————, ed. 1983. *Mysticism and Religious Traditions.* New York: Oxford Univ. Press.

————, ed. 1992. *Mysticism and Language.* New York: Oxford Univ. Press.

Khong, Chan. 1993. *Learning True Love: How I Learned and Practiced Social Change in Vietnam.* Berkeley, Calif.: Parallax.

King, Winston. 1980. *Theravāda Meditation: The Buddhist Transformation of Yoga.* University Park: Pennsylvania State Univ. Press.

Knowles, Elizabeth, ed. 1999. *The Oxford Dictionary of Quotations.* 5th ed. New York: Oxford Univ. Press.

Kotler, Arnold, ed. 1996. *Engaged Buddhist Reader.* Berkeley, Calif.: Parallax.

Kovel, Joel. 1991. *History and Spirit: An Inquiry into the Philosophy of Liberation.* Boston: Beacon.

Kristeva, Julia. 1984. *Revolution in Poetic Language.* Translated by Margaret Waller. 1974. New York: Columbia Univ. Press.

Lambert, Malcolm. 1992. *Medieval Heresy: Popular Movements from the Gregorian Reform to the Reformation.* 2d ed. Oxford: Blackwell.

Lane, Dermot. 1996. *Keeping Hope Alive: Stirrings in Christian Theology.* Mahwah, N.J.: Paulist.

Leclercq, Eloi. 1961. *Wisdom of the Poverello.* Translated by Marie-Louise Johnson. Chicago: Franciscan Herald.

————. 1977. *The Canticle of Creatures, Symbols of Union: An Analysis of St. Francis of Assisi.* Chicago: Franciscan Herald.

Leclercq, Jean. 1996. "St. Clare and Nuptial Spirituality." *Greyfriars Review* 10, no. 2: 171–78.

Leclercq, Jean, Louis Bouyer, François Vandenbroucke, and Louis Cognet. 1968. *The Spirituality of the Middle Ages: A History of Christian Spirituality II*. New York: Seabury.

Leopold, Aldo. 1949. *A Sand County Almanac*. New York: Oxford Univ. Press.

Lerner, Gerda. 1993. *The Creation of Feminist Consciousness*. New York: Oxford Univ. Press.

Lerner, Robert. 1972. *The Heresy of the Free Spirit in the Later Middle Ages*. Berkeley: Univ. of California Press.

Libanio, J. B. 1991. "St. Ignatius and Liberation." Translated by Francis McDonagh. *The Way Supplement* 70: 51–63.

Ling, Trevor. 1973. *The Buddha: Buddhist Civilization in India and Ceylon*. New York: Charles Scribner's Sons.

Lonergan, Bernard J. F. 1958. *Insight: A Study of Human Understanding*. New York: Philosophical Library.

Macy, Joanna. 1983. *Despair and Personal Power in the Nuclear Age*. Philadelphia: New Society.

———. 1985. *Dharma and Development: Religion as Resource in the Sarvodaya Self-Help Movement*. Rev. ed. West Hartford, Conn.: Kumarian.

———. 1991. *Mutual Causality in Buddhism and General Systems Theory: The Dharma of Natural Systems*. Albany: State Univ. of New York Press.

———. 1994. *World as Lover, World as Self*. Berkeley: Parallax.

Manselli, Raoul. 1988. *St. Francis of Assisi*. Translated by Paul Duggan. Chicago: Franciscan Herald.

Marcuse, Herbert. 1967. *One-Dimensional Man*. Boston: Beacon.

Matura, Thaddée. 1985. "Introduction." *Claire d'Assise: Ecrits*. Paris: Les Editions du Cerf.

———. 1997. *Francis of Assisi: The Message in His Writings*. Translated by Paul Barrett. St. Bonaventure, N.Y.: Franciscan Institute.

McDonnell, Ernest W. 1969. *The Beguines and Beghards in Medieval Culture*. New York: Octagon.

McDonnell, Thomas, ed. 1974. *A Thomas Merton Reader*. Rev. ed. Garden City, N.Y.: Doubleday.

McGinn, Bernard. 1981a. "The God Beyond God: Theology and Mysticism in the Thought of Meister Eckhart." *Journal of Religion* 61: 1–19.

———. 1981b. "Theological Summary." In *Meister Eckhart: The Essential Sermons, Commentaries, Treatises, and Defense,* translated by Edmund Colledge and Bernard McGinn, 24–61. New York: Paulist.

———. 1991. *The Foundations of Christian Mysticism*. Vol. 1 of *The Presence of God: A History of Western Christian Mysticism*. New York: Crossroad.

———. 1994. *The Growth of Mysticism: Gregory the Great through the Twelfth Century*. Vol. 2 of *The Presence of God: A History of Western Christian Mysticism*. New York: Crossroad.

———. 1998a. *The Flowering of Mysticism: Men and Women in the New Mysticism*

(1200–1350). Vol. 3 of *The Presence of God: A History of Western Christian Mysticism*. New York: Crossroad.

———. 1998b. "Quo Vadis? Reflections on the Current Study of Mysticism." *Christian Spirituality Bulletin* 6, no. 1: 13–21.

McIntosh, Mark. 1998. *Mystical Theology*. Malden, Mass.: Blackwell.

McNamara, Jo Ann. 1973. *Gilles Aycelin: The Servant of Two Masters*. Syracuse, N.Y.: Syracuse Univ. Press.

Mechthild of Magdeburg. 1990–93. *Mechthild von Magdeburg, "Das fliessende Licht der Gottheit": Nach der Einsiedler Handschrift in kritischem Vergleich mit der gesamten Überlieferung*. Edited by Hans Neumann. Munich: Artemis.

Menestō, Enrico, ed. 1984. *Frate Francesco d'Assisi*. Atti del XXI Convegno Internazionale, Assisi. Spoleto: Centro Italiano di Studi Sull'Alto Medioevo.

Menestō, Enrico, Stefano Brufani, Giuseppe Cremascoli, Emore Paoli, Luigi Pellegrini, and Stanislao da Campagnola, eds. 1995. *Fontes Franciscani*. Assisi: Edizioni Porziuncola.

Merchant, Carolyn. 1980. *The Death of Nature: Women, Ecology, and the Scientific Revolution*. San Francisco: Harper and Row.

Metz, Johann Baptist. 1998. *A Passion for God: The Mystical-Political Dimension of Christianity*. Translated and edited by J. Matthew Ashley. Mahwah, N.J.: Paulist.

Miccoli, Giovanni. 1989. "Francis of Assisi's Christian Proposal." *Greyfriars Review* 3, no. 2: 127–72.

Mieth, Dietmar. 1969. *Die Einheit von Vita Activa und Vita Contemplativa in den deutschen Predigten und Traktaten Meister Eckharts und bei Johannes Tauler*. Regensburg: Friedrich Pustet.

———. 1986. "Die theologische Transposition der Tugendethik bei Meister Eckhart." In *Abendländische Mystik im Mittelalter*, edited by Kurt Ruh, 63–79. Stuttgart: J. B. Metzlersche.

Milbank, John. 1996. "Stories of Sacrifice." *Modern Theology* 12, no. 1: 27–56.

Moore, R. I. 1987. *The Formation of a Persecuting Society*. Oxford: Blackwell.

Münzter, Thomas. 1967. "Die Fürstenpredigt." In *Theologische-Politische Schriften*, edited by G. Franz. Stuttgart: Reclam.

Naṇmoli, Bhikkhu, and Bhikkhu Bodhi, trans. and eds. 1995. *The Middle Length Discourses of the Buddha: A New Translation of the Majjhima Nikaya*. Boston: Wisdom/Barre Center for Buddhist Studies.

Naranjo, Claudio, and Robert Ornstein. 1971. *On the Psychology of Meditation*. New York: Viking.

Netanyahu, B[enzion]. 1995. *The Origins of the Inquisition in Fifteenth Century Spain*. New York: Random House.

Nguyen-Van-Khanh, Norbert. 1994. *The Teachings of His Heart: Jesus Christ in the Thought and Writings of St. Francis*. Translated by Ed Hagman. St. Bonaventure, N.Y.: Franciscan Institute.

Nhat Hanh, Thich. 1987a. *Being Peace*. Berkeley, Calif.: Parallax.

————. 1987b. *Interbeing: Commentaries on the Tiep Hien Precepts.* Berkeley, Calif.: Parallax.

————. 1991. *Peace Is Every Step.* New York: Bantam.

————. 1993. *Love in Action: Writings on Nonviolent Social Change.* 1969. Berkeley, Calif.: Parallax.

————. 1998. *Teachings on Love.* Translated by Mobi Warren and Annabel Laity. Berkeley: Parallax.

Nicholas, Antonio De. 1986. *Powers of Imagining: Ignatius de Loyola.* Albany: State Univ. of New York.

Nyanaponika, Thera. 1962. *The Heart of Buddhist Meditation.* London: Rider.

O'Brien, Elmer, ed. 1981. *The Essential Plotinus* 2d ed. Indianapolis: Hackett.

O'Keefe, Vincent T., S.J. 1990. "Jesuit Spirituality: A Resource for Ministry Now and in the Future." In *Jesuit Spirituality,* with John W. O'Malley, S.J., and John Padberg, S.J. Chicago: Loyola Univ. Press.

————. 1998. Personal interview by Janet K. Ruffing, New York City, Sept. 24.

O'Malley, John W., S.J. 1993. *The First Jesuits.* Cambridge, Mass.: Harvard Univ. Press.

Ostriker, Alicia. 1985. "The Thieves of Language: Women Poets and Revisionary Mythmaking." In *New Feminist Criticism: Essays on Women, Literature, and Theory,* edited by Elaine Showalter, 314–38. New York: Pantheon.

Ozment, Steven E. 1973. *Mysticism and Dissent: Religious Ideology and Social Protest in the Sixteenth Century.* New Haven: Yale Univ. Press.

Peers, E. Allison. 1944–46. *The Complete Works of Teresa of Avila,* 3 vols. London: Sheed and Ward.

Peterson, Ingrid J. 1993. *Clare of Assisi: A Biographical Study.* Quincy, Ill.: Franciscan.

————. 1995. "Clare of Assisi's Mysticism of the Poor Crucified." *Greyfriars Review* 9, no. 2: 163–92.

Petroff, Elizabeth Alvida, ed. 1986. *Medieval Women's Visionary Literature.* Oxford: Oxford Univ. Press.

Pfeiffer, Franz, ed. 1962. *Deutsche Mystiker des vierzehnten Jahrhunderts.* Vol. 2 of *Meister Eckhart, Predigten und Traktate.* Aalen, Germany: Scientia.

Phillips, Catherine Payton. 1792. *Considerations on the Causes of the High Price of Grain.* London: J. Phillips.

————. 1794. *The Happy King.* London: J. Phillips.

————. 1797. *Memoirs.* London: J. Phillips.

Porete, Marguerite. 1993. *Marguerite Porete: The Mirror of Simple Souls.* Translated, introduction, and notes by Ellen Babinsky. Classics of Western Spirituality. New York: Paulist.

Pozzi, Giovanni. 1990. *"The Canticle of Brother Sun:* From Grammar to Prayer." *Greyfriars Review* 4: 1–21.

Queen, Christopher, and Sallie King, eds. 1996. *Engaged Buddhism: Buddhist Liberation Movements in Asia.* Albany: State Univ. of New York Press.

Rahner, Karl. 1963. *Visions and Prophecies.* Translated by Charles Henkey and Richard Strachan. New York: Herder.

————. 1964. *The Dynamic Element in the Church.* Translated by Walter J. O'Hare. New York: Herder.

Rahula, Walpola. 1988. "The Social Teachings of the Buddha." In *The Path of Compassion: Writings on Socially Engaged Buddhism,* 2d ed., edited by Fred Eppsteiner, 103–10. Berkeley, Calif.: Parallax.

Rich, Bruce. 1994. *Mortgaging the Earth: The World Bank, Environmental Impoverishment and the Crisis of Development.* Boston: Beacon.

Ricoeur, Paul. 1976. *Interpretation Theory: Discourse and the Surplus of Meaning.* Fort Worth, Tex.: Christian Univ. Press.

Rothberg, Donald. 1986. "Rationality and Religion in Habermas' Recent Work: Some Remarks on the Relation between Critical Theory and the Phenomenology of Religion." *Philosophy and Social Criticism* 11: 221–43.

————. 1990. "Contemporary Epistemology and the Study of Mysticism." In *The Problem of Pure Consciousness: Mysticism and Philosophy,* edited by Robert Forman, 163–210. New York: Oxford Univ. Press.

————. 1992. "Buddhist Responses to Violence and War: Resources for a Socially Engaged Spirituality." *Journal of Humanistic Psychology* 32, no. 4: 41–75.

————. 1993. "The Crisis of Modernity and the Emergence of Socially Engaged Spirituality." *ReVision* 15, no. 3: 105–14.

————. 1998. "Responding to the Cries of the World: Socially Engaged Buddhism in North America." In *The Faces of Buddhism in North America,* edited by Charles Prebish and Kenneth Tanaka, 266–86, 334–41. Berkeley: Univ. of California Press.

Rubin, Jeffrey. 1996. *Psychotherapy and Buddhism: Toward an Integration.* New York: Plenum.

Rückert, Fredrich. n.d. "Du bist die Ruh, der Friede mild." In *Rückert Werke,* edited by Franz Schubert. Leipzig: Bibliografisches Institut.

Ruffing, Janet K. 1995. " 'The World Transfigured:' Kataphatic Experience Explored Through Qualitative Research Methodology." *Studies in Spirituality* 5: 232–59.

Ruh, Kurt. 1993. *Geschichte der abendlèndischen Mystik.* Munich: C. H. Beck.

Runciman, Steven. 1954. *The Kingdom of Acre.* Vol. 3 of *A History of the Crusades.* Cambridge: Cambridge Univ. Press.

Saint-Säens, Alain. 1996. "A Case of Gendered Rejection: The Hermitess in Golden Age Spain." In *Spanish Women in the Golden Age: Images and Realities,* edited by Alain Saint-Säens and Magdalena S. Sánchez, 56–65. Westport, Conn.: Greenwood.

Sandmel, Samuel, M. Jack Suggs, and Arnold J. Tkacik, eds. 1976. *The New English Bible with the Apocrypha.* Oxford Study Edition. New York: Oxford Univ. Press.

Santikaro, Bhikkhu. 1997. "The Four Noble Truths of Dhammic Socialism." In *Entering the Realm of Reality: Towards Dhammic Societies,* edited by Jonathan Watts, Alan Senauke, and Santikaro Bhikkhu, 89–161. Bangkok: International Network of Engaged Buddhists.

Sarkisyanz, E. 1965. *Buddhist Backgrounds of the Burmese Revolution.* The Hague: Martinus Nijhoff.

Scarry, Elaine. 1985. *The Body in Pain: The Making and Unmaking of the World.* Oxford: Oxford Univ. Press.

Schillebeeckx, Edward. 1968a. "The Church as Sacrament of Dialogue." In *God the Future of Man,* 115–40. Translated by N. D. Smith, 115–40. New York: Sheed and Ward.

———. 1968b. "Church, Magisterium, and Politics." In *God the Future of Man,* 141–66. Translated by N. D. Smith. New York: Sheed and Ward.

Schmucki, Octavian. 1989. "The Mysticism of Saint Francis in the Light of His Writings." *Greyfriars Review* 3, no. 3: 242–66.

———. 1992. *The Stigmata of St. Francis.* St. Bonaventure, N.Y.: Franciscan Institute.

Schneiders, Sandra. 1986. "Theology and Spirituality: Strangers, Rivals, or Partners?" *Horizons* 13, no. 2: 253–74.

Schulz, Frieder. 1996. "The So-Called Peace Prayer of St. Francis." *Greyfriars Review* 10, no. 3: 237–55.

Schürmann, Reiner. 1978. *Meister Eckhart: Mystic and Philosopher.* Bloomington: Indiana Univ. Press.

Seed, John, Joanna Macy, and Pat Fleming. 1991. *Thinking Like a Mountain: Towards a Council of All Beings.* Philadelphia: New Society.

Sells, Michael A. 1994. *The Mystical Languages of Unsaying.* Chicago: Univ. of Chicago Press.

Sensi, Mario. 1994. "Chiara d'Assisi nell'Umbria del Quattrocento." *Collectanea Franciscana* 64, nos. 1–4: 215–37.

Sharf, Robert. 1995. "The Zen of Japanese Nationalism." In *Curators of the Buddha: The Study of Buddhism under Colonialism,* edited by Donald Lopez, 107–60. Chicago: Univ. of Chicago Press.

Shepard, Paul. 1983. *Nature and Madness.* San Francisco: Sierra Club.

Shiva, Vandana. 1993. *The Violence of the Green Revolution.* London: Zed.

Sivaraksa, Sulak. 1988. *A Socially Engaged Buddhism.* Bangkok: Thai Inter-Religious Commission for Development.

———. 1992a. "Buddhism and Contemporary International Trends." In *Inner Peace, World Peace: Essays on Buddhism and Nonviolence,* edited by Kenneth Kraft, 127–37. Albany: State Univ. of New York Press.

———. 1992b. *Seeds of Peace.* Berkeley, Calif.: Parallax.

Slade, Carole. 1995. *St. Teresa of Avila: Author of a Heroic Life.* Berkeley: Univ. of California Press.

Snyder, Gary. 1969. *Earth House Hold.* 1964. New York: New Directions.

Solé-Leris, Amadeo. 1986. *Tranquility and Insight: An Introduction to the Oldest Form of Buddhist Meditation.* Boston: Shambhala.

Sorell, Roger D. 1988. *St. Francis of Assisi and Nature: Tradition and Innovation in Western Christian Attitudes toward the Environment.* New York: Oxford Univ. Press.

Stace, Walter. 1960. *Mysticism and Philosophy.* London: Macmillan.

Steere, Douglas V. 1984. *Quaker Spirituality.* New York: Paulist.

Strayer, Joseph R. 1980. *The Reign of Philip the Fair.* Princeton: Princeton Univ. Press.

Stryk, Lucien, ed. 1969. *World of the Buddha.* New York: Anchor.

Taylor, Charles. 1989. *Sources of the Self: The Making of the Modern Identity.* Cambridge, Mass.: Harvard Univ. Press.

Teresa of Avila. 1944–46. *The Complete Works of Teresa of Avila,* 3 vols. Translated by E. Allison Peers. London: Sheed and Ward.

———. 1976–85. *The Collected Works of St. Teresa of Avila.* 3 vols. Translated and edited by Kieran Kavanaugh and Otilio Rodríguez. Washington, D.C.: Institute of Carmelite Studies.

Théry, Gabriel. 1926. "Édition critique des pièces relatives au procès d'Eckhart contenues dans le manuscrit 33b de la Bibliothèque de Soest." *Archives d'Histoire Littéraire et Doctrinal du Moyen Âge* 1: 129–268.

Thurman, Robert. 1976. *The Holy Teaching of Vimalakīrti.* University Park: Pennsylvania State Univ. Press.

———. 1988. "Edicts of Asoka." In *The Path of Compassion: Writings on Socially Engaged Buddhism,* 2d ed., edited by Fred Eppsteiner, 111–19. Berkeley, Calif.: Parallax.

Titmuss, Christopher. 1988. "Interactivity: Sitting for Peace and Standing for Parliament." In *The Path of Compassion: Writings on Socially Engaged Buddhism,* 2d ed., edited by Fred Eppsteiner, 182–89. Berkeley, Calif.: Parallax.

Turner, Denys. 1995. *The Darkness of God: Negativity in Christian Mysticism.* Cambridge: Cambridge Univ. Press.

Ullman, Richard K. 1959. *Between God and History.* London: Allen and Unwin.

Vigil, Mariló. 1986. *La vida de las mujeres en los siglos XVI y XVII.* Madrid: Siglo Veintiuno.

Walzer, Michael. 1985. *Exodus and Revolution.* New York: Basic.

———. 1987. *Interpretation and Social Criticism.* Cambridge, Mass.: Harvard Univ. Press.

Washington, Margaret, ed. 1993. *Narrative of Sojourner Truth.* New York: Vintage Classics.

Watts, Jonathan, Alan Senauke, Bhikkhu Santikaro, eds. 1997. *Entering the Realm of Reality: Towards Dhammic Societies.* Bangkok: International Network of Engaged Buddhists.

Weber, Alison. 1990. *Teresa of Avila and the Rhetoric of Femininity.* Princeton: Princeton Univ. Press.

Weber, Max. 1958. *The Religion of India: The Sociology of Hinduism and Buddhism.* New York: Free Press.

West, Cornel. 1982. *Prophesy Deliverance! An Afro-American Revolutionary Christianity.* Philadelphia: Westminster.

Wilber, Ken. 1995. *Sex, Ecology, Spirituality: The Spirit of Evolution.* Boston: Shambhala.

Williams, Delores S. 1986. "The Color of Feminism: Or Speaking the Black Woman's Tongue." *The Journal of Religious Thought* 43, no. 1: 42–58.

Williams, Paul. 1989. *Mahayana Buddhism: The Doctrinal Foundations*. New York: Routledge.

Wilson, E. O. 1983. *Biophilia*. Cambridge, Mass.: Harvard Univ. Press.

Wittberg, Patricia. 1996. *Pathways to Re-Creating Religious Communities*. Mahwah, N.J.: Paulist.

Woods, Richard. 1996. "Mysticism and Social Action: The Mystic's Calling, Development, and Social Activity." *Journal of Consciousness Studies* 3, no. 2: 158–71.

Woolman, John. 1989. *The Journal and Major Essays of John Woolman*. Edited by Phillips P. Moulton. Richmond, Ind.: Friends United.

Zimmerman, Michael. 1995. *Contesting Earth's Future: Radical Ecology and Postmodernity*. Berkeley: Univ. of California Press.

Index

Abbey, Edward, 187
Abram, David, 187
action and contemplation: Eckhart on, 80–86; Ignatius of Loyola's dialectic of, 112–15, 127; Marguerite Porete on, 79, 80, 81, 83; Teresa of Avila on, 94–95; Western opposition of, 163
Adorno, Theodor, 7, 177
affective mysticism, 4
African American women, 143–58; Zilpha Elaw, 152–54; holy boldness in, 157–58; Rebecca Cox Jackson, 154–56; Jarena Lee, 145–49; in matrix of domination, 143; as Other, 143; spiritual autobiographies of, 144; subjectification process in, 144, 156–57; subjugation of, 143; Sojourner Truth, 149–52
African Methodist Episcopal (A.M.E.) Church, 147, 147n, 155
Agnes of Prague, 58, 66–67
agriculture, 139, 193
Aitken, Robert, 172
Allen, Richard, 147, 148
amazement, 46–48
Ana de San Bartolomé, 103
Ana de San José, 103
apocalypticism, 7
apophatic mysticism, 5
apophatic theology, 77–78
apostolic life, 2, 95
Aquinas, Thomas, 4, 85–86
arhat, 170
Aristotle, 163
Ariyaratne, A. T., 172, 174
Armstrong, Edward, 57
Arrupe, Pedro, 118–27; dialogue and

discernment in governance of, 124–27; governing the society in spirit of Ignatius, 120–21; Ignatian mysticism of service of, 104, 127; Ignatius of Loyola compared with, 127–28; liberation theology as influence on, 122–23; mystical experiences in Japan, 118–20; and Thirty-second General Congregation, 120, 124–25; at Vatican Council II, 121; "Witnessing to Justice in the World," 123
asceticism, 5, 47, 74
Asoka, 170
Autobiography (Ignatius of Loyola), 109, 111

Baldwin, James, 51
Bartoli, Marco, 58, 70
beatas, 102
Beatrice of Nazareth, 84
Beguines, 34–35, 38–39, 41, 43, 71, 79
Benefiel, Margaret, 24
Benjamin, Walter, 7
Berger, Peter, 8
Bernard of Clairvaux, 4, 79, 80
bias, unconscious, 19–21
Bible, the: God calling on people to do something in, 18; Israeli midwives in, 19; multiple readings of, 14; vocation and mission as characteristic of, 8
Black women. *See* African American women
Blake, William, 181
Bloch, Ernst, 7
Bloch, Maurice, 89
Bobin, Christian, 57
bodhisattva, 170
Boff, Leonardo, 56, 74